ESSAYS ON
ITALIAN POETRY AND MUSIC
IN THE RENAISSANCE,

1350–1600

ℰℬ

The Ernest Bloch Professorship
of Music and the Ernest Bloch Lectures
were established at the University of California
in 1962 in order to bring distinguished figures
in music to the Berkeley campus from time to time.
Made possible by the Jacob and Rosa Stern
Musical Fund, the professorship was founded
in memory of Ernest Bloch (1880–1959),
Professor of Music at Berkeley
from 1940 to 1959.

THE ERNEST BLOCH PROFESSORS

1964   Ralph Kirkpatrick
1965–66   Winton Dean
1966–67   Roger Sessions
1968–69   Gerald Abraham
1971   Leonard B. Meyer
1972   Edward T. Cone
1975–76   Donald Jay Grout
1976–77   Charles Rosen
1977–78   Alan Tyson
1979–80   William P. Malm
1980–81   Andrew Porter
1983   Ton de Leeuw
1983   James Haar

ESSAYS ON

Italian Poetry and Music

IN THE RENAISSANCE, 1350–1600

JAMES HAAR

———————————

University
of California Press
Berkeley, Los Angeles, London

University of California Press
Berkeley and Los Angeles, California

University of California Press, Ltd.
London, England

Printed in the United States of America
1 2 3 4 5 6 7 8 9

Grateful acknowledgment is given to the following publishers for permission to use music from which some of
the musical examples were drawn:

Editions de l'Oiseau-Lyre, Monaco:
Lucente stella che'l mio cor desfai and *Per tropo fede talor se
perigola. Polyphonic Music of the Fourteenth Century*, vol.
11, ed. W. Thomas Marrocco. © 1978.
Landini, *Non avrà ma' pietà questa mia donna. Polyphonic
Music of the Fourteenth Century*, vol. 4, ed. Leo Schrade.
© 1958.

University of Chicago Press:
Brumel, *Noé noé. Monuments of Renaissance Music II: Canti
B*, ed. Helen Hewitt. © 1967.
Verdelot, *Madonna, per voi ardo. A Gift of Madrigals and
Motets*, vol. 2, ed. H. Colin Slim. © 1972.

Hänssler-Verlag, D-7303 Neuhausen-Stuttgart:
Arcadelt, *Quando col dolce suono. Jacobi Arcadelt: Opera
Omnia*, CMM 31/II, No. 63.102, ed. Albert Seay.
© Copyright 1970 by Armen Carapetyan.
Wert, *Ah, dolente partita!* (Guarini). *Giaches de Wert: Opera
Omnia*, CMM 24/XII, No. 62,412, ed. Carol MacClin-
tock. © Copyright 1967 by Armen Carapetyan.

Library of Congress Cataloging in Publication Data

Haar, James.
   Essays on Italian poetry and music in the Renaissance,
1350–1600.

   (Ernest Bloch lectures)
   Includes bibliographical references.
   1. Vocal music—Italy—14th century—Addresses,
essays, lectures.   2. Vocal music—Italy—15th century—
Addresses, essays, lectures.   3. Vocal music—Italy—
16th century—Addresses, essays, lectures.   4. Italian
poetry—14th century—Addresses, essays, lectures.
5. Italian poetry—15th century—Addresses, essays,
lectures.   6. Italian poetry—16th century—Addresses,
essays, lectures.   I. Title.   II. Series.
ML1633.H2   1986   784'.0945   85-1009
ISBN 0-520-05397-4

For M.O.Z.E.

CONTENTS

ILLUSTRATIONS

(Following page 110)

1. Florence, Church of San Martino.
Seminario di Firenze, Cod. "Rustiche," fol. 25. Reproduced
as the frontispiece to G. B. Bronzini, *Tradizione di stile aedico
dai cantari al "Furioso"* (Florence, 1966).

2. A *cantastorie*.
Woodblock from *Varie Canzoni alla Villotta in lingua Pavana*,
undated early-sixteenth-century print
(Venice, Bibl. Marc. misc. 2213.9).

3. A *cantastorie*.
Woodblock from *Historia d'Apollonio di Tiro*, undated early-
sixteenth-century print (Venice, Bibl. Marc. misc. 1016–29).

4. A *cantastorie*.
Used as the frontispiece to an early edition of Pulci's *Morgante*;
reused in *La representatione di Dieci mila martiri*, undated early-
sixteenth-century print (Venice, Bibl. Marc. Rari 497). The singer-
player is perhaps Bartolomeo dell'Aveduto. See Walter Salmen,
Musikleben im 16. Jahrhundert, Musikgeschichte in Bildern, iii, 9
(Leipzig, 1976), no. 83.

5. *Ciarlatani* in the Piazza di San Marco, Venice,
late sixteenth century.
Woodcut by Giacomo Franco Forma. See Salmen,
Musikleben, no. 146.

6. *Canto de' Sartori: De sartor nui siam maestri.*
Perugia, Bibl. Com. Aug. MS 431, fol. 116ᵛ.

PREFACE

These lectures were given under the title "Italian Poetry and Music in the Renaissance." At the time the title did not strike me as pretentious. On reflection it seemed so much so that I have added the cautionary "Essays on . . . ," as indication of what should be obvious: these pages do not amount to anything like full coverage of the subject. They were of course not intended to be that. My goal was to show some of the changing relationships of word and tone that mark the development of Italian music from the mid fourteenth century to the end of the cinquecento. Even that is a big order; but I tried to meet the challenge as honestly and fairly as I could.

The reader should be warned that the footnotes in no way constitute a full bibliography of the subject. They do reveal my indebtedness to other scholars, above all to Nino Pirrotta, without whose masterful contributions on every important aspect of Italian music in the Renaissance I could never have undertaken these lectures at all. The rather large number of references to my own published articles is a simple reflection of the fact that my general views have been shaped by my own study of particular problems.

My thanks are due to my colleagues at Berkeley—faculty, staff, and graduate students in the Department of Music—for their hospitable welcome, steady cooperation, and stimulating company. I am especially grateful to Alan Curtis and the members of his collegium for their sensitive performance of music thrust into their hands at short notice.

James Haar
Chapel Hill, North Carolina

INTRODUCTION

In this book I shall deal with poetry in musical settings, with emphasis on declamatory and rhetorical aspects of those settings. For me the fundamental problem in the subject is this: Words have not only meaning but also a music of their own, and this verbal harmony is, down to almost the lowest level of sung jingle, self-sufficient. What then does music add, apart from serving as *aide-mémoire* or offering entertainment that may depend little on words for its success? Does the heightened declamation of musical performance add to the combination of sound and meaning in the words? It can as easily detract from it. And is genuine fusion of word and tone, the Greek ideal that musical humanists sought so earnestly and so inventively to recapture, a reachable goal or an attractive delusion? Italians for many centuries, and Germans of the Romantic and post-Romantic generations, thought this fusion not only possible but also relatively easy to achieve; for the French and especially the Anglo-Saxon world it has always seemed more difficult, at least in the realm of art music. There educated sentiment is very likely to get in the way of naive instinct, the result sometimes being a self-conscious one, words dressed up in musical clothes.

In the period that I propose to survey I shall assume that serious connection of word and tone was always intended, far from the goal though some of the results may at first appear to us. The nature of that connection was, however, not single but manifold. This period in Italian culture is a long one—some 250 years, from the age of Petrarch to the age of Marino. The poetry with which we will be concerned is, exclusively for the first 150 years and predominantly for the final century, *poesia per musica*. Literary theorists of the fourteenth century suggested a distinction between serious poetry and that intended for music, and Franco Sacchetti, in a sonnet addressed to a friend who wanted to see his "rime filosofiche e sottile" set to music, warns that music is best suited for love lyrics:

> Cosa sottile in canto poco muda
> agli amorosi versi par che sia
> musica di servir solo tegnuda.[1]

The dividing lines were not always drawn in the same places; in the sixteenth century the sonnet and canzone, untouched by earlier polyphonists, became favorites of madrigalists, and epic verse was set polyphonically while it continued to be sung in popular style by *cantimbanchi*. But only certain sonnets, certain canzoni, certain *ottava* stanzas were selected, and *cosa sottile* was on the whole avoided in favor of love poetry or vividly descriptive verse. One result of the long habit of such choice is that when Renaissance musicians did turn to poetry of real seriousness or subtlety they found their inherited compositional vocabulary faced with new challenges, a problem that became acute in the later sixteenth century.

Whether or not we give it the single label of Renaissance, this period in Italian history is marked by great and obvious diversity. Giotto and Caravaggio, the Florentine duomo and the new St. Peter's, at opposite ends of the time span, are extreme instances of that diversity. The unity that Jacob Burckhardt saw in the Renaissance is no longer so apparent to us, would not be so even were we to end this survey at the sack of Rome in 1527 or the opening deliberations of the Council of Trent a few years later. The great achievements of Dante, Petrarch, and Boccaccio, who received early canonization as the *tre corone* of Italian literature, were nevertheless permanent, despite some fifteenth-century falling away and despite the anti-Petrarchism of much later-sixteenth-century poetry; they gave a kind of unity to Italian culture that was notably lacking elsewhere in Europe. Music, and particularly secular music,

1. See Ettore Li Gotti and Nino Pirrotta, *Il Sacchetti e la tecnica musicale del trecento italiano* (Florence, 1935), p. 18n; Giosuè Carducci, "Musica e poesia nel mondo elegante del secolo xiv" (1870), in Carducci, *Edizione nazionale delle opere*, vol. 9 (Bologna, 1943), pp. 297–98.

was much less stable than poetry; in musical composition fashions changed quickly, novelty was prized. Even the oral tradition, from what we can guess about it, seemed to thrive on variety. Thus a setting of Petrarchan verse composed in the mid sixteenth century is so different in sound and concept from one written in the mid fourteenth century that they would seem to have almost no common ground. The "science" of music, or at least the basic laws for the writing of counterpoint, changed less; but that is a subject we will not be especially concerned with here. Only the continuing desire to make a piece of vocal music a genuine meeting of word and tone remained constant, and this would after all be true for the whole history of the art. Still, one has to start and stop somewhere, and the limits I have set include a repertory that I hope can be surveyed with profit even if some of the ground will have to be covered rather quickly. If we expect that change and diversity mark the development of vocal music in the Renaissance we will not be wrong; the discovery of some aspects of continuity will then be a kind of bonus.

A turning point in the history of Western music took place in the early decades of the sixteenth century, roughly the period 1510–40. Composers of this period, not only in Italy but in nearly all centers of high musical culture, began to give close attention to individual word accent and, increasingly, to the cadence of whole lines and groups of lines of text, which they set in as accurately declamatory a way as they could. The reasons for this preoccupation were in part humanistic concern, in part accommodation of popular currents in song; they will be dealt with in some detail, especially in the third chapter. The result was a style in which verbal rhetoric and musical rhetoric joined—*fused* is perhaps always too strong a word—in a musical "reading" of the text. To this was gradually added a vocabulary of rhetorical gesture suitable, at least in the opinion of composers and their adherents, for heightening the affective conceits of a poem and thus becoming "expressive" as well as correctly declamatory.

That a piece of vocal music should sound like a correctly and effectively rendered reading of the text may seem self-evident. That music should "express" the text is perhaps less inevitable as an assumption, but it has great and understandable appeal—students are forever looking for "expressive" spots in early music—because it is natural to want music to have meaning, preferably verbal meaning since we have words to describe that. Vocal music of the fourteenth and fifteenth centuries is not totally lacking in properties of just declamation or even of expressive gesture, but these qualities are not present in a way or to a degree that suggests any systematic effort to provide them. One could regard "pre-Raphaelite" music as archaic in these respects, not yet possessed of the technique required for achieving the representational, sometimes naturalistic results of the later Renaissance. Despite the unfashionable nature of such a view, I think there may be some truth in it, but it is not the whole truth; we have only to consider the deliberately antirepresentational quality of much twentieth-century art song to become aware that the sixteenth-century synthesis of word and tone, modified but not abandoned in the music of the next three centuries, was not so much the realization of an ideal as the adoption of a new set of conventions for matching verse and music.

What conventions governed the musical setting of text in earlier periods? It is not easy to give an answer with any degree of assurance. I hope to show some individual traits of interest in the music of the trecento and quattrocento; about its underlying aesthetic basis I am not so sure. Music could be and, I think, often was regarded as an ornamental over- or underlay to the text, appropriate to it but not intended to sound like a reading of it. In this sense Boccaccio's remark that Dante liked to give his lyric poems to musician friends to have them "dressed" in music is a telling one; other contemporary statements about musical settings make them sound rather like jewelers' settings.[2] An extreme form of this approach— one in which the relative importance of words and music is reversed—is to regard a piece of vocal music as an autonomous work of art to which words are appended, as in the case of directions given by a fourteenth-century theorist for cutting up and fitting a motet text to an already completed musical composition.[3] *Prima la*

2. Boccaccio speaks of Dante's youthful interest in seeing his lyric verse *rivestita* in music; see Nino Pirrotta, "Le tre corone e la musica," in *L'Ars Nova italiana del trecento* 4 (1975), ed. Agostino Ziino (Certaldo, 1976), p. 11. On the view of music as adornment of poetry see Dante, *Vita nuova*, xii (p. 32 in the edition of Fredi Chiappelli [Milan, 1965], where Amore counsels the poet that his ballatas should "falle adornare di soave armonia."

3. Aegidius de Murino, *Tractatus cantus mensurabilis*, in *Scriptorum de musica medii*

musica e poi le parole may seem a strange concept, yet a good deal of music seems to have been composed according to this aesthetic stance. A relationship of text and music that is not, does not even approximate, a "reading" of the text is something that will be useful to posit as we consider the earlier periods of our chosen time span.

---

aevi, ed. Edmond de Coussemaker, vol. 3 (Paris, 1864), p. 125: "Postquam cantus est factus et ordinatus, tunc accipe verba que debent esse in moteto et divide ea in quatuor partes; et sic divide cantum in quatuor partes; et prima pars verborum compone super primam partem cantus, sicut melias potest, et sic procede usque in finem; et aliquando est necesse extendere multas notas super pauca verba, super pauca tempore, quousque pervenienter ad complementum."

$\cdot 1 \cdot$

The Trecento

Tempting as it is to start this historical survey with the topic "Dante and Music," I shall not do so. There is of course a subject here since Dante's work is full of musical imagery and since he is known to have loved not only the speculative, "quadrivial" side of music but its practical application as well.[1] Some of Dante's poetry was given musical setting during his lifetime, but these settings have not survived; and he did not write *poesia per musica* of the sort used by musicians of the trecento. Both Boccaccio and Petrarch did; and though composers turned only rarely to their poetry during the fourteenth century, it is in their lifetime that a remarkable body of music, much of it surviving in large manuscript collections and a number of isolated fragments, was written and performed.

The repertory of madrigals and ballatas created in Italy during the century from the 1320s to the 1420s is one of the most remarkable phenomena in the history of music. It is larger, at least for the first part of this period, than the equivalent French output of secular mensural music; and although French influence is probably never absent and becomes more intrusive as the period draws to a close, this repertory is remarkably Italian in character, a celebration of the newly proud vernacular spirit in both poetry and music. Its origins remain shrouded in mystery, and its virtual disap-

---

1. For general discussions of Dante's musical interests see Arnoldo Bonaventura, *Dante e la musica* (Livorno, 1904); Rudolf Baehr, *Dante und die Musik* (Munich, 1966). See also Nino Pirrotta, "Ars Nova e Stil Novo," *Rivista italiana di musicologia* 1 (1966), 4–19; idem, "Dante Musicus: Gothicism, Scholasticism, and Music," *Speculum* 43 (1968), 245–57.

pearance in the "conciliar" age of the early fifteenth century is also something of a puzzle. Although we will be concerned primarily with the character of this music and its relationship to the poetry written for it, something should be said about both its beginnings and its end.

The poetic genres used by trecento musicians are described early—in the case of the madrigal earlier than any of the surviving verse. As for the music, its notational basis, in which lies much of its character, is given a full exposition in the *Pomerium* of Marchetto da Padova, written circa 1320, a date so early that for a long time it was thought that no music corresponding in time of composition to this theory had survived.[2] Even now we do not have any secular music known to be as old as Marchetto's work. Musical theory is usually judged to be a codification of practice, not an invention *ex ovo*; and indeed it must be so in this case. The madrigal as mentioned by Francesco da Barberino at the beginning of the fourteenth century must already have been sung, and by 1332 Antonio da Tempo could describe a performance practice suggesting that the genre was no longer anything new. The madrigals and ballatas collected in the oldest surviving musical source, the Rossi-Ostiglia manuscript, are thought to have been composed in the 1330s and 1340s, and they are clearly not first attempts. But we do not know just what preceded them, or where the impetus and skill to compose them came from.

Not, it would seem, from the art of the troubadours. The poetry set does not resemble troubadour or trouvère verse, though there is some overlap of subject in madrigals hinting at the *pastourelle* or, less often, the *sirventese* and *alba*. The music of the trecento is far more melismatic than that of the troubadours and, more important, makes full use, even in the monophonic ballata, of the principles of mensural notation, which troubadour and trouvère art tended to resist.[3] Neither the poets nor the composers of the tre-

---

2. Some Italian sacred polyphony of the early fourteenth century, including a motet by Marchetto, is included in Kurt von Fischer and F. Alberto Gallo, eds., *Polyphonic Music of the Fourteenth Century*, vol. 12 (Monaco, 1976). For a review of what is known about musical theory and practice in northern Italy in the early fourteenth century see F. Alberto Gallo, "Marchetus in Padua und die 'franco-venetische' Musik des frühen Trecento," *Archiv für Musikwissenschaft* 31 (1974), 42–56.

3. On this point see John Stevens, "The Manuscript Presentation and Notation

cento belonged to the classes from which the troubadours came. The composers were sometimes—perhaps often—their own poets, but this is being a "troubadour" only in a superficial modern sense. They were not *giullari* either, even though many of them were singers and instrumentalists of great skill. Most were clerics, some functioned in an administrative, perhaps also a musical, capacity in the *cappellae* of ecclesiastical and secular magnates. In general they belonged to the lower ranks of a class described as containing "jurists, judges, notaries, functionaries," a group already observable at the court of Frederick II and in strong contrast to the older "chivalric circle" that identified itself with the art of the troubadours.[4] In Florence some of the minor composers were craftsmen—a painter of *cassoni*, a copyist, a slipper maker.[5] The patrons of this art were, in Florence, the new merchant aristocracy; in the North they were the recently established lords of Lombardy and the Veneto. In almost every respect there would appear to be a break between the older troubadour art and that of the trecento. A few resemblances of practice do exist. Poetic-musical contests were held during the fourteenth century, one of them featuring three of the most important of the early madrigalists; the use of the *senhal* or hidden name was carried over from troubadour poetry; and several of the manuscripts containing trecento song, particularly those of Florentine origin, were organized by composer and genre, a feature typical of troubadour-trouvère sources.[6] These are not trivial things; but they suggest a sentimental rather than a meaningful connection.

of Adam de la Halle's Courtly Chansons," in *Source Materials and the Interpretation of Music: A Memorial Volume to Thurston Dart*, ed. Ian Bent (London, 1981), pp. 32, 52.

4. Antonino da Stefano, *La cultura alla corte di Federico II imperatore* (Palermo, 1935), p. 226.

5. On these figures see Nino Pirrotta, ed., *The Music of Fourteenth-Century Italy*, vol. 5 (American Institute of Musicology, 1954), p. iii.

6. For a contest between Giovanni da Cascia and Jacopo da Bologna at the court of Mastino II della Scala, mentioned by Filippo Villani, see W. Thomas Marrocco, *The Music of Jacopo da Bologna* (Berkeley, 1954), p. 3. The *senhal* was common in the poetry of the early madrigalists. On the use of one such name see Ettore Li Gotti, "Anna, o l'amor segreto," *Accademia* (Palermo) 1, no. 1 (1945), 9–11; cf. Nino Pirrotta, "Note ad 'Anna,' o dei dispetti amorosi," ibid. 1, no. 2 (1945), 7; see also Pirrotta, "Marchettus de Padua and the Italian Ars Nova," *Musica Disciplina* 9 (1955), 69–70; Mario Fabbri and John Nádas, "A Newly Discovered Trecento Fragment: Scribal Concordances in Late-Medieval Florentine Manuscripts," *Early Music History* 3 (1983), 79–80. Manuscripts organized by composer and genre include the Squarcialupi Codex (Florence, Bibl. Med.-Laur. MS Pal. 87), Florence, Bibl. Naz.

Since a number of trecento composers were clerics one might suppose that secular song was derived from Latin polyphony, from the motet or the conductus.[7] If this is so, the evidence has been remarkably well hidden; there is now known to be a little more sacred polyphony of Italian origin from this period than was once thought, but it is still small in amount by comparison with secular music, and if one influenced the other it looks very much as if motets and especially Mass movements were influenced by madrigals and ballatas, not the other way around. It is much more likely that the *lauda*, a genre of Italian devotional poetry and music that rose to prominence in the climate of religious revival in the thirteenth century, might be related to secular Italian art. Unfortunately we know more about the lauda in the thirteenth century, when it was monophonic in texture and quite plainly syllabic in text setting, than in the fourteenth century, when it appears to have become more elaborate and when *contrafacta* of ballatas were used by the *laudesi*.[8] The substratum of trecento polyphony, a two-voice discant structure with emphasis on the perfect consonances of unison, fifth, and octave, is of course indebted to the contrapuntal art of the thirteenth century, which was at first centered in the Île-de-France but by the end of the century had spread through Europe. This was the technical foundation of trecento musical art; whether French music exerted a stylistic influence beyond this remains, for the early trecento, an open question. Finally, several of the most prominent trecento composers were not only church musicians but also organists: Landini, known as Francesco degli Organi; Giovanni degli Organi, Landini's successor at San Lorenzo in Florence; and Andrea degli

---

Cent. MS Panciatichi 26, and the newly discovered MS Florence, San Lorenzo, Arch. cap. 2211.

7. The hypothesis that the conductus was an important source for trecento secular music, presented by Leonard Ellinwood, "Origins of the Italian Ars Nova," *Papers Read by Members of the American Musicological Society*, 1937:29–37, is no longer widely accepted, but there is still no general agreement on the origins of trecento music. For some contrasting views of the subject see Nino Pirrotta, "Per l'origine e la storia della 'caccia' e del 'madrigale' trecentesca," *Rivista musicale italiana* 48 (1946), 305–23; 49 (1947), 121–42; Kurt von Fischer, "On the Technique, Origin, and Evolution of Italian Trecento Music," *The Musical Quarterly* 47 (1961), 41–57; Marie Louise Martinez, *Die Musik des frühen Trecento* (Tutzing, 1963).

8. On the lauda in the fourteenth century see Frank A. D'Accone, "La compagnia dei laudesi in Firenze durante l'Ars Nova," in *L'Ars Nova italiana del trecento* 2 (Certaldo, 1970), pp. 253–80.

Organi, a Florentine Servite monk who played the newly installed organ at the Santissima Annunziata in 1379.[9] What they played may have been mostly improvised, but a collection of sacred and secular keyboard music from the period, the Faenza Codex, does survive, music suitable for any keyboard instrument but especially apt for the organs of the time. The style of this keyboard music suggests close kinship with the vocal art of trecento composers. The Faenza Codex comes from late in the period, but organists may have been playing something of the sort much earlier, and their practice could have affected the art of composers and performers of vocal music.

The end of trecento art comes gradually; in the early fifteenth century Italian music is already international in character, its most distinguished composer the transplanted Liègeois Johannes Ciconia. About the time of the great Councils aimed at ending the longest and deepest schism the Church had to this point known, polyphonic music to Italian words becomes increasingly rare, and the surviving Italian manuscripts of the period are full of French-texted music. Thus begins what has become known as the *segreto del quattrocento*, the paucity of Italian music in the flush of the early Renaissance.[10] Just why this happened is indeed something of a mystery, one for which an explanation will be attempted in the next chapter.

The song literature of the trecento was probably never popular or in general cultivation, at least not at the artistic level seen in the surviving sources. Nor was it in vogue throughout Italy. Its beginnings would seem to be in the Veneto, particularly at the courts of the Scaligeri in Verona and the Carraresi in Padua—the latter the home of the theorist-composer Marchetto. The Visconti in Milan, particularly Luchino (in power in the 1340s), were other early patrons. But the three earliest composers known to us by name were

9. For information on individual trecento composers see the relevant entries in Stanley Sadie, ed., *The New Grove Dictionary of Music and Musicians* (London, 1980). On Giovanni degli Organi see Frank A. D'Accone, "Giovanni Mazzuoli: A Late Representative of the Italian Ars Nova," in *L'Ars Nova italiana del trecento: Convegni di studi, 1961–1967* (Certaldo, 1968), pp. 23–38.

10. The term comes from Fausto Torrefranca's controversial but informative study *Il segreto del quattrocento* (Milan, 1939). Torrefranca was concerned mainly with the late fifteenth century, but his book has a great deal of material on popular Italian *poesia per musica* of the whole of the quattrocento.

Jacopo, from Bologna, Piero, possibly from Perugia, and Giovanni, from Cascia near Florence;[11] this suggests that the art was being practiced in Tuscany and Emilia as well as in the North, where it was first patronized. Giovanni was eulogized by Filippo Villani, who gives us an account of a troubadour-like contest held in Verona about 1350:

> Giovanni da Cascia, when he frequented the court of the Veronese despot Mastino della Scala, and contended in artistic skill with magister Jacopo da Bologna, a most expert musician—the two of them spurred on by the tyrant's gifts—sounded [*intonuit*] many madrigals and much other music [*sonosque multos*] and ballatas of wonderfully sweet and most artful melody, showing by these things how great and how extensive was his learning [*doctrina*] in the art.[12]

Giovanni was then composer, singer, and probably instrumentalist as well. He may have been a poet too; of the twenty or so poems surviving in musical settings attributed to him, only one has a textual ascription, a rather shaky one (to Sacchetti) in a peripheral source.[13] He seems to have written, despite Villani's statement, no ballatas, only madrigals and a few caccias.[14] Giovanni's madrigals are of high quality; a discussion of them will serve both to characterize the music of the first generation of trecento composers and to illustrate the madrigal as a genre.

What was the madrigal as Giovanni da Cascia came to it? For Francesco da Barberino, writing at the turn of the century, it was a rather new species of *voluntarium*, a "rudium inordinatum con-

---

11. See Giuseppe Corsi, *Poesie musicali del trecento* (Bologna, 1970), p. xxxiv, on the possible identity of Piero with a Magister Petrus Andreutii mentioned as "doctor . . . in arte cantus" in Perugia in 1335.

12. Filippo Villani, *De origine civitatis Florentie et eiusdem famosis civibus* (ca. 1381); the passage is cited by Corsi, *Poesie musicali*, p. 23, from the second redaction (ca. 1395) of Villani's work. In the first version of this passage Jacopo's name is not given, nor are ballatas mentioned. There is a fourteenth-century depiction of three musicians, identified as Giovanni, Jacopo, and Piero, standing together as if in contest. See Kurt von Fischer, "'Portraits' von Piero, Giovanni da Firenze, und Jacopo da Bologna in einer Bolognese Handschrift des 14. Jahrhunderts?," *Musica Disciplina* 27 (1973), 61–64.

13. See Corsi, *Poesie musicali*, p. xcix.

14. No ballatas ascribed to Giovanni have survived, but it is possible that he wrote some of the monophonic ballatas in the Rossi Codex (Rome, Bibl. Ap. Vat. MS Rossi 215); in this case he might have improvised an instrumental accompaniment, or had a *tenorista* to accompany him.

cinium," that is, a poem of unfixed form and lowly status, designed for music.[15] To the anonymous author of a treatise written a few years later madrigals were "words applied to several melodies," one of them a slow-moving tenor, the other a voice that not only makes counterpoint against the tenor but also is ornate in character ("ire melodiando"). The music should be in Italian melodic style ("aere italico"), though some admixture of French style ("aere gallico") is permissible. The verse can be a free mix of seven- and eleven-syllable lines, but the pattern in the first stanza must be adhered to in subsequent ones. In subject matter there is much use of trees, flowers, rustic surroundings, and rustic girls ("villanellis"), though conversations and proverbs ("bonae sententiae") may also be seen.[16] By 1332 Antonio da Tempo could say of the madrigal that its rustic beginnings, still evident in its subject matter and vocabulary—which he thought different from those of all other types of poetry—were now altered by subtler modes of versifying and composing. Madrigals for Antonio were composed of *terzine* in a variety of line lengths and rhyme schemes, some with a *ritornello* of one or two lines at the end, some without. Their music should remain rustic or madrigalistic ("rusticales sive mandriales") so that the sound befits the words. Though it can be sung by one person a madrigal is more beautiful sung by two or more; and Antonio ends by saying that he has heard madrigals that to his musically untutored ear sounded very good indeed.[17]

Antonio da Tempo's definition of the word *madrigal* as coming from *mandria*, or "herd of sheep," was probably sheer invention; it

15. Francesco da Barberino, *Documenti d'Amore* (ca. 1300–1310); see Oreste Antognoni, "Le glosse ai Documenti d'Amore di M. Francesco da Barberino e un breve trattato di ritmica italiana," *Giornale di filologia romanza* 4 (1882), 96. The passage is cited in F. Alberto Gallo, "Madrigale," in *Handwörterbuch der musikalischen Terminologie*, ed. Hans-Heinrich Eggebrecht (Wiesbaden, 1972–), p. 2 (articles are separately paginated).

16. These remarks are from a brief treatise attached to a copy of Antonio da Tempo's *Summa*; see Santorre Debenedetti, "Un trattatello del secolo xiv sopra la poesia musicale," *Studi medievali* 2 (1906–7), 59–77. Passages relevant to the madrigal from this anonymous work (called by Debenedetti *Capitulum de vocibus applicatis verbis*) are cited by Gallo, "Madrigale," p. 2. Gallo gives a date of ca. 1315–20 for the *Capitulum*.

17. Antonio da Tempo, *Summa artis rithmici vulgaris dictaminis* (1332), ed. Giusto Grion (under the title *Delle rime volgari*) (Bologna, 1869); cited by Gallo, "Madrigale," pp. 2–3.

took root, however, and even today the etymology of the word remains uncertain. It is probably derived from *matricalis*, "something homely," and refers to poetry on the popular side of vernacular language.[18] Though the connection with shepherdesses and scenes of nature is a natural one, it is unlikely that genuine rustics ever sang madrigals; as Giosuè Carducci observed, the poets and composers were, from the first, probably city folk, who wrote idyllic daydreams about an Arcadian life.[19] The verse may be unpretentious when compared to a canzone or sonnet, but it is hardly folk poetry.[20] What is perhaps most interesting in Antonio da Tempo's description is his statement that the madrigal sounds best if two or more singers perform it. In contradistinction to the older ballata, which remained monophonic until after mid-century, the madrigal was evidently a polyphonic genre from the beginning.[21] The music might be lowly in comparison to a French motet of the time, yet it conformed to basic rules for making counterpoint and was written in clearly mensural musical language and thus could not possibly have been the work of a musically untrained person.

Antonio says that he had heard madrigals performed that pleased him greatly. Whether this means that one or more generations of composers preceded Giovanni da Cascia is unclear; but Giovanni was surely continuing, not initiating, a practice. The texts he chose, or was given to set, or perhaps wrote himself, conform to Antonio's description of the madrigal in being composed of varying numbers of *terzine* followed by a two-line ritornello. Their rhyme schemes vary; this aspect of the madrigal remained *inordinatum* to

18. Gallo, "Madrigale," p. 1. In the bibliography of his article Gallo cites the most important works dealing with the vexed question of the origin of the term.

19. Giosuè Carducci, "Musica e poesia nel mondo elegante del secolo xiv" (1870), in Carducci, *Edizione nazionale delle opere*, vol. 9 (Bologna, 1943), p. 328: "Nel *madrigale* il cittadino de' Comuni italiani esce un poco a sollazzo alla campagna, e sollazzandosi gitta alla natura uno sguardo senza troppa passione: egli ha fretto di tornarsene al suo negozio o al palazzo della Ragione e agli studi, e si spiccia con pochi versi."

20. The four madrigals in Petrarch's *Canzoniere*, refined in style and each slightly different from the others in rhyme scheme, are evidence of this; see Ulrich Schulz-Buschhaus, *Das Madrigal: Zur Stilgeschichte der italienischen Lyrik zwischen Renaissance und Barock* (Bad Homburg, 1969), p. 21ff. But in only one of these four poems does Petrarch use the word *pastorella*.

21. See the description in the anonymous *Capitulum* cited above and in n. 16. Gallo, "Madrigale," p. 2, reads Barberino's term *concinium* as referring to polyphony.

the end.[22] In theme the poems include both the "rustic" pastoral
and the sententiously moralizing, the two types mentioned in the
early-fourteenth-century description of the madrigal cited above.
Here is a pastoral example. This madrigal, accompanied by a portrait of Giovanni, is the opening piece in the Squarcialupi Codex,
the great retrospective collection of the trecento repertory copied
sometime in the first half of the fifteenth century and later presented as a gift to Giuliano de' Medici.[23]

> Agnel son bianco e vo belando *be*
>   e per ingiuria di capra superba
> belar convegno e perdo un boccon' d'erba.
>
> El danno è di colui io dico in fé,
>   che grasso mi de' aver con lana bionda
> se capra turba che non m'abbi tonda.
>
> Or non so bene che di mi sarà
>   ma pur giusto signor men mal vorrà.

The language is simple and the theme rustic, but the message,
from the innocent lamb of a poet complaining of injuries received
from a proud she-goat, is a lover's plaint not without artifice.

A number of Giovanni's poems are allegories of love, cast in the
language of the hunt (*Nel bosco senza foglie*), a dream vision (*Nel mezo
a sei paon ne vidi un bianco, Sedendo a l'ombra d'una bella mandorla, La
bella stella che sua fiamma tene*), or a fable (*Donna già fui leggiadra in-
namorata*, about a woman turned into a serpent to torment her
lover). A madrigal addressed with some bitterness to the faithless
Amor, *Più non mi cura de la tua rampogna*, ends with a ritornello that
seems to hint at a proverb, given a flip tone by the *versi sdruccioli*:

> Così ti fida in Amor come in monico;
>   credilo a me che tutto dì ne romico.

22. Although the rhyme scheme *a b c a b c d d* is often given as the norm for
the trecento madrigal, it was never used to the exclusion of other patterns and was in
fact not even especially common until the sixteenth-century revival of trecento madrigal forms. See Schulz-Buschhaus, *Das Madrigal*, p. 32.

23. For the most recent hypothesis on the date of copying of this manuscript,
placing it at about 1415–19, see Kurt von Fischer, "Paolo da Firenze und die
Squarcialupi-Kodex (I–Fl 87)," *Biblioteca di Quadrivium, Serie musicologica* 9 (1969).

There is also a text, surviving only in part, that is a satirical fable about other artists who, though crows, try to deck themselves out in the plumage of other birds.[24]

On the whole the texts are direct, personal in tone, and full of pastoral imagery. The spelling and precise wording differ from source to source; the language is often "Tuscanized" in manuscripts of Florentine provenance, or "northernized" in sources from the Veneto.[25] The music also differs in detail from one manuscript to another, so that neither the poetic nor the musical "original" can be determined. For the music this has often been taken to be a reflection of improvisatory practice; perhaps even Giovanni himself did not sing his madrigals the same way every time, and for both text and music the sources may reflect regional performance practice.

If the music had not survived one could imagine a song style of simple charm, drawing on a repository of folk tune and aimed at direct projection of the text. But the music does survive, and it is not at all simple or direct, at least in modern terms. An example will show what I mean. The madrigal *O tu, cara scienzia mia, musica* is an apostrophe by the poet-singer to his art, an art to which his whole being responds in sympathetic vibration and which he serves as advocate since from it springs all knowledge of love.

> O tu, cara scienzia mia, musica,
> > o dolce melodia con vaghi canti
> che fa' rinovellar tuttor gli amanti,
>
> Et io son corda di tua consonanzia,
> > che imaginar solea tuo bel trovato,
> or son procuratore ed avocato.
>
> Però ritorno a te, musica cara,
> > ch'ogni atto bel d'amor da te s'impara.[26]

The musical setting of this poem features an elaborately florid melody in the upper part, accompanied by a quieter lower voice

---

24. *Fra mille corvi una cornachia bianca,* a text related to a paraphrase of an Aesop fable set by Jacopo da Bologna. For this and the other texts set by Giovanni referred to above see Corsi, *Poesie musicali,* pp. 11–28.

25. Corsi, *Poesie musicali,* pp. xcviii–xcix and passim.

26. On the meaning of this poem see Corsi, *Poesie musicali,* p. 19. He disagrees with the earlier interpretation of Carducci.

(Ex. 1).[27] This is not in any special way a response to the musical theme of the text but is typical of all of the music of Giovanni, his contemporaries, and his immediate successors; it illustrates the *ire melodiando* of the early-fourteenth-century description of the genre as clearly as one could wish.

In bare outline the form of the piece is simple enough. Each line of the *terzine* receives separate setting, so distinct in shape and content that the result is three submovements (the whole of course to be repeated for the second stanza); the ritornello, not as markedly different in character from the rest of the piece as is sometimes the case, serves as a kind of coda, but it is also to be repeated since there is music for only one line. Each line of text begins and ends with a long melisma, with syllabic declamation sandwiched in between. The syllables to which the melismas are sung might be repeated; indeed there is evidence that they were.[28] Each line of text is sung only once, except for the third verse of the *terzine*, which in several sources for this piece is repeated.

If we look a bit more closely at the music we see that there is little repetition, hence little interest on the composer's part in overt gestures toward musical unity. There is some small-scale melodic sequence, and perhaps some degree of consistency in the kind of melodic ornament employed—though this is hard to determine since the manuscript sources differ so much in that element.[29] The third line of the *terzine* and the ritornello end on the same note, approached the same way; however, the cadence is so abrupt that this passes almost unnoticed. A more marked cadential articulation, a slowing down as the note D is approached, can be seen in the opening of the piece, where it occurs twice (in the middle of the

27. I have transcribed this piece from the Squarcialupi Codex. For a modern edition from this source see Johannes Wolf, *Der Squarcialupi Codex* (Lipstadt, 1955), p. 12. For other scholarly editions, based on concordant sources, see Nino Pirrotta, ed., *The Music of Fourteenth-Century Italy*, vol. 1 (American Institute of Musicology, 1954), no. 12; W. Thomas Marrocco, ed., *Polyphonic Music of the Fourteenth Century*, vol. 6 (Monaco, 1967), p. 56.

28. *O tu, cara scienzia* begins in one source (the Reina Codex) with several repeated notes in place of one long note; see Pirrotta, *Music of Fourteenth-Century Italy*, vol. 1, no. 12. There are other examples of repeated syllables or vowels; see fols. 6^v–7 of London, Brit. Lib. Add. MS 29987 (a facsimile of this manuscript exists, edited by Gilbert Reaney [American Institute of Musicology, 1965]).

29. In some madrigals there seems to be consistent, thematic use of single ornamental figures. An example is Giovanni da Cascia's *Nel mezo a sei paon*; see Pirrotta, *Music of Fourteenth-Century Italy*, vol. 1, no. 10.

first line of text and at the end of the second); but its somewhat arbitrary placement would seem to deny it formal significance. In fact we see here one element of Giovanni's style. There are really no cadential formulas to punctuate the music; it simply runs on until it stops, either by gradual degree or by a joltingly quick drawing together of upper and lower voice, the latter usually producing a unison finish. The notes chosen to end the subsections and the piece as a whole, G, D, and A, are not unrelated tonally, but if tonal planning were an important element in the work one might expect it to end on D, not A.

The melodic lines in *O tu, cara scienzia* follow on the whole a descending curve, a feature that has been found characteristic of earlier trecento polyphony in general.[30] Not all of Giovanni's melodies are bound to a pattern of constant descent; what is more important, they nearly all cadence low and leap to a high position for the beginning of a new poetic line. This seems to me a deliberate choice of declamatory style, a technique designed to call the listener's attention to the beginning of each verse whether or not the sense of the text suggests separation from the preceding line.[31] Such a technique stresses the musician's role as orator, or cantor, rather than as reader of the text; it is deliberately artificial in character.

Giovanni's melodic line is marked by artifice rather than naturalness in almost every respect. The florid melismas, though bound to a kind of metrical regularity by the nature of Italian notation, which did not permit large-scale syncopation, are irregular in phrase structure; the syllabic patter tends to begin at an unexpected point. When it does begin, one might say that the music becomes more natural since one can hear the words, and their accentual patterns are on the whole correctly handled; but in this piece Giovanni tends to give each syllable the same short note value, and when a word or syllable is lengthened or given a short decorative flourish one cannot count on its being an important bit of text. (See the melisma on "con" in the phrase "con vaghi canti.") In other madrigals Giovanni does allow himself an occasional bit of realism,

30. On this see Martinez, *Die Musik des frühen Trecento*, p. 18 and passim.
31. This musical separation is less marked in the transition from line 2 to line 3, where "Che fa rinovellar" continues the thought of the preceding line, but it is hard to tell whether such continuity is deliberate on Giovanni's part since in the second stanza lines 2 and 3 are not closely related.

as in the onomatopoeia of "bè, bè" in *Agnel son bianco*, represented by single-note exchange between the two voices; but this is rare, and it of course makes little sense when, as in *Agnel son bianco*, the second stanza provides no textual excuse for such naturalism.

The fact that the lower voice synchronizes its text delivery with that of the upper one (there are some exceptions to this in Giovanni's music, more in that of the following generation of composers) is another constructivist, artificial feature of this music, reminiscent of organal practice. The whole relationship of words to music is formal, almost ritualistic, and this is a deliberate feature; the text underlay for a piece occasionally differs from one source to another, but within a single source the words are carefully aligned with the notes, with lines sometimes drawn to connect the two where the alignment might otherwise be unclear.[32]

What did the listener of the time hear of the text? The piece was sung "O . . . o . . . o . . . o tu cara scienzia mia mu . . . . . . sica, O . . . o . . . o dolce melodi . . . a con . . . vaghi can . . . . . . ti, Che . . . che . . . chefarinovellartuttorgliaman . . . . . . ti," and so on. The cadence of the verse does not come through very well. (Trecento composers sometimes use elisions, sometimes not; and instances of hypermeter, implicit in the first and fourth lines of *O tu, cara scienzia*, tend to be emphasized rather than regularized in the musical settings.) The sense of this madrigal could be grasped on first hearing if it were sung with very clear diction at a rather slow speed; for many other madrigals such immediate grasp would be difficult. One wonders if the audience saw or knew the poems before hearing them sung. The fact that the poetry had some circulation apart from its musical settings encourages the supposition that it was read for its own sake.[33] Sacchetti released his poems to be set as soon as they were written, or says he did; but not all of his poetry is accompanied by extant musical settings, and perhaps it was not all set to music.[34] Texts honoring a ruler, or verse designed

---

32. These cautionary lines are particularly evident in the somewhat carelessly written London MS (see above, n. 28).

33. For an account of the purely literary sources of the trecento madrigal see Corsi, *Poesie musicali*, pp. lxxix–lxxx.

34. On Sacchetti's attitudes toward music and his relationship with contemporary musicians see Ettori Li Gotti and Nino Pirrotta, *Il Sacchetti e la tecnica musicale del trecento italiano* (Florence, 1935), p. 25ff.

for a musical-poetic contest, would surely have been more effective if known in advance; for example, the text of Jacopo da Bologna's *Lo lume vostro dolce mio signore*, in which the opening letters of each line spell the name Luchinus, must have been read in advance since neither Luchino Visconti nor anyone else could have been expected to "hear" an acrostic. Poems mixing Latin and French with Italian in interlinear design would surely have been more effective in performance if known in advance. Though there is no evidence that listeners of the time prepared themselves in advance, both the style of the music and the nature of some of the texts make one at least hope that they did.

How was the music performed? By two solo singers—the composer and another man, initially. Since *donzelle* are often described as singing, madrigals were also sung by women, at least on occasion. To what extent various kinds of instruments, depicted in the illuminations of the Squarcialupi manuscript and in many paintings of the period, were used to accompany singers is uncertain, but it clearly did happen, and pieces were also played rather than sung, as the testimony of Simone Prudenzani's sonnets describing performance of this music in the early fifteenth century bears out.[35] Since all contemporary references to music talk about its "sweetness" one would assume that madrigals were sung rather gently. This is what a madrigal by Jacopo da Bologna advises:

> Oselleto salvazo per stazone
> dolci versiti canta cum bel modo:
> tal e tal grida forte, ch'i no l'odo.
>
> Per gridar forte non se canta bene,
> ma con suave, dolce melodia
> se fa bel canto e zò vol maistria.[36]

The music for madrigals suggests, on the other hand, that each line should begin with rather forceful sound, perhaps tapering off after

35. Santorre Benedetti, ed., "Il 'Solazzo' e il 'Saporeto' con altre rimi di Simone Prudenzani d'Orvieto," *Giornale storico della letteratura italiana*, suppl. 15 (Turin, 1913), 104, 108–10.

36. Corsi, *Poesie musicali*, p. 42, there given in "northern" linguistic form as found in the Reina Codex; in other sources the poem is more "Tuscan" in detail. This text was set both as a madrigal and as a canonic caccia; "sweetness" would be especially hard to achieve in the latter.

the opening melisma. The tempo could be adjusted, within the limits suggested by theorists describing trecento notation, to permit clear enunciation of the syllabic passages. Was the elaborate *fioritura* sung precisely as notated? Probably not; it seems likely that singers learned the basic piece and then sang it freely, or as they remembered it; hence the large number of variants in madrigals that enjoyed wide circulation. The melismatic passages are notated in precise rhythmic values in all their variant forms, and they are usually sung with near-metronomic accuracy when this music is performed today. I doubt that this is what originally took place. The singer-composers were famed for their skill in performance as well as for their artifice in writing; they must therefore have had not only a highly developed technique but also an individual and effective manner of projecting their music, a fully developed rhetoric of song. Theorists, composers, and scribes were proud of being able to notate rather complex rhythms, and any musician who could read from the notated page was looked at with respect.[37] But the written page was probably not much closer a guide to truly effective performance than is the published version of a twentieth-century popular ballad.

Carducci was shown, as he was writing a monograph on its poetry, a piece of trecento polyphony by a musician friend who said he found it "hard to believe that our ancestors sang such music, which could satisfy no taste or seem good to any one of any period."[38] The piece was a ballata by Landini, to us far easier to grasp than a madrigal by Giovanni da Cascia; what would these nineteenth-century scholars have thought of the latter? We have learned much about the music of the trecento since Carducci's time, yet its style is hard for modern performers to make their own. Dance music of the period is now played with vivid accent, and the more animated caccias, with their cries of victory and shouts at errant dogs, are sometimes projected well; but the madrigal remains

37. See, for example, Benedetti, "Il 'Solazzo,'" p. 116, a poem in which Solazzo with two other singers (one on the tenor, one on the contra) sang music by Landini ("il Cieco"), fra Bartolino, "Çacchera," and frate Biaggio, then some "Strambotti de Cicilia a la reale," all presumably from memory. Then, it is especially noted, he took out some written music "correctly" (=mensurally?) notated and sang from it: "un ruotol trasse puoi, che non solo una, / Scritte et solfate de tucta raggione, / Ch'eran ben cento a 'vançarne ongniuna."

38. "Musica e poesia," p. 333.

elusively alien, is far too often sung with monotonous and ineffective "straightness" of style. Perhaps someday it will come into its own with performers.

The madrigal was much admired at the time, doubtless. But a remark by Sacchetti indicates something of value about its performance as contemporaries heard it. In one of his novelle he tells of a notary sent with a message to Bernabò Visconti. The notary, small and unathletic, arrived just as Bernabò was setting out on horseback. For a joke Visconti gave the poor ambassador a large horse on which the stirrups were hopelessly beyond his reach and forced him to ride out and give his message as he rode. This the unfortunate notary did as best he could, bouncing uncontrollably as he rode, and "whatever he said, he said with many notes, as if he were singing a madrigal, according to the jolts he received, which were not few."[39] This passage is usually cited simply as a reference to the term *madrigal* in literature; it tells us, however, something we would otherwise not know, namely that listeners of the time were struck not only by the long melismas in the music but also by the singers' habit of repeating vowels or syllables on these melismas, as if they were stuttering.

The nature of the musical sources for this florid melodic style has been a subject of debate. It is thought to have come out of improvisatory vocal practice, a professional singer's way of showing off his craft, yet in many ways its style is curiously unvocal. If the ornamental lines were improvised, one might expect to find a basic melody underneath them. Some pieces are so much more heavily ornamented in one source than in another that something akin to what happened with the keyboard transcriptions of madrigals seems to have taken place.[40] But older sources do not show consistently less ornamentation than more recent ones do. I have tried to "reduce" madrigals to basic melodic lines, without much success. The madrigal would seem to have been full of melismatic decoration from the first, just as it was polyphonic from the first.

39. Novella lxxiv; cited, for example, in Carducci, "Musica e poesia," p. 334. For the whole tale see Franco Sacchetti, *Il trecentonovelle*, ed. Vincenzo Pernicone (Florence, 1946), pp. 163–64.

40. See, for example, the madrigal *Sedendo al'ombra d'una bella mandorla* of Giovanni (Pirrotta, *Music of Fourteenth-Century Italy*, vol. 1, no. 16), where the comparatively simple version in one source (Squarcialupi) may be compared with the more heavily ornamental version in another (Panciatichi 26).

The melismatic vocal style of the madrigal may, on the other hand, be derived from instrumental, not vocal, practice. A number of pieces of trecento polyphony, sacred and secular (the latter partly French, partly Italian), survive in keyboard intabulation in a manuscript dating from the early fifteenth century.[41] Included in the Faenza Codex are five pieces by Giovanni da Cascia's contemporary and presumably friendly rival Jacopo da Bologna. They are much more highly ornamented than the vocal models, at least in the right hand; the vocal tenor is, curiously, left almost untouched, even in passages where it is heard alone. The keyboard ornament is different not so much in kind as in degree from that of the voice, as an example will show. The opening line of the setting by Jacopo of Petrarch's *Non al suo amante più Diana piacque* is given in Example 2, both in its vocal version and in keyboard intabulation. Note in particular the turn figure, common to voice and keyboard.

As an experiment I copied out the various ornaments used to decorate melodic steps and small skips in a single madrigal, Maestro Piero's *Quando l'aere comenza a farse bruna*.[42] These ornaments, characteristic of all Italian music of the middle fourteenth century though of course not a complete vocabulary, certainly look, when taken out of context, like keyboard figures—they include runs, turns, even incipient trills (Ex. 3). While it is of course possible that all this ornament was invented by singers and then transferred to the keyboard, it is equally possible and, for me, more likely that things happened the other way around. Nino Pirrotta has conjectured that the style of the madrigal rose out of two-part organ pieces improvised by keyboard players.[43] This hypothesis is in-

41. Faenza, Bibl. Com. MS 117. There is a modern edition of the manuscript, edited by Dragan Plamenac: *Keyboard Music of the Late Middle Ages in Codex Faenza 117* (American Institute of Musicology, 1972); there is also a facsimile: *An Early-Fifteenth-Century Italian Source of Keyboard Music: The Codex Faenza, Bibl. Com., 117* (American Institute of Musicology, 1961). For literature on the manuscript see "Sources of Keyboard Music to 1660," in *The New Grove Dictionary* 12:718.

42. Rome, Bibl. Ap. Vat. MS Rossi 215, fol. 7ᵛ; modern editions in Nino Pirrotta, ed., *The Music of Fourteenth-Century Italy*, vol. 2 (American Institute of Musicology, 1960), no. 2; Marrocco, *Polyphonic Music of the Fourteenth Century* 6:14.

43. Nino Pirrotta, "Una arcaica descrizione trecentesca del madrigale," in *Festschrift Heinrich Besseler*, ed. Institut für Musikwissenschaft der Karl-Marx Universität (Leipzig, 1961), pp. 155–61. Pirrotta's article is a study of the *Capitulum* edited by Debenedetti, for which see n. 16 above. His speculation (p. 159) that the madrigal may be derived from two-voice clausulae played by organists is made almost in passing; whether he would approve my seizing on it and blowing it up into a major hypothesis I do not know, but I am grateful to him all the same for the suggestion.

triguing on a number of counts. It would help to explain not only the ornaments but also the character of the tenor lines, which are mostly stepwise (as if lying easily under the fingers) but not real melodies in their own right, and not taken from any precomposed source as tenors customarily were in this period. It would also help to account for the "set" nature of the contrapuntal points of rest on consonances reached rather abruptly by vocal standards, sometimes even by an augmented interval. Finally, it would help us to understand the madrigal's being born, as it were, with a two-voice polyphonic structure and style different from that of any other music, French or Italian, of the time. We know that a number of trecento composers were organists. Except for the Faenza manuscript and a few scattered fragments there is no surviving organ music from this period, but we may assume that the art of improvised counterpoint on the organ was an old one and that a century before the Faenza repertory was collected the style might have been a simpler one.[44]

This hypothesis has the merit of offering an explanation for the character of the trecento madrigal. Its acceptance leads, however, to another problem. We have been used to thinking that early instrumental music was, except for dance music insofar as we can judge from the little that survives, dependent on and derived from vocal music. If we reverse things in the case of the madrigal we must look upon this song form as the work of trained—usually church-trained—musicians who owed nothing to the popular song of their time and whose approach to *poesia per musica* was to set the text into a preconceived musical pattern rather than to let the words speak and form musical utterance as they did so.[45] If the madrigal is looked at from this angle it is the apparently decorative

44. See, for example, the comparatively simple instrumental intabulations in the Robertsbridge Codex (London, Brit. Lib. Add. MS 28550), possibly of Italian origin; they are edited in Willi Apel, ed., *Keyboard Music of the Fourteenth and Fifteenth Centuries* (American Institute of Musicology, 1963), pp. 1–9. In the *Purgatorio* (ix, 139–45) Dante speaks of singing accompanied by the organ: "Io mi rivolsi attento al primo tuono / e *Te Deum laudamus* mi parea / udir in voce mista al dolce suono. / Tale imagine appunto mi rendea / ciò ch'io udiva, qual prender si suole / quando a cantar con organi si stea: / che con sì or no s'intendon le parole."

45. It is possible to see the influence of instrumental music not only in the trecento madrigal but also in late-cinquecento vocal music. This is discussed in chap. 6 (pp. 137–40).

opening and closing melismas that are fundamental to the style; the syllabic middle parts are the fillers, rarely memorable in themselves and often appearing to be gotten through as quickly as possible—even though they carry the sense of the text. There are exceptional passages, but almost no complete pieces, where a naturalistic textual expression breaks through this mould of artifice. And later in the century things begin to change, though much more in the ballata than in the madrigal. Giuseppe Corsi's remark that the words were "simply pretexts for the music, which was not yet subservient to poetry," is one that I at first dismissed as the view of a literary historian not really immersed in the music.[46] Now I think he is right. This does not lessen the beauty of the madrigal; for me it does change how one should approach its study.

In the work of the next generation after Giovanni da Cascia the madrigal becomes even more elaborately melismatic and also somewhat freer in structure, particularly in the relationship of the upper line or lines to the tenor; but nothing essential is changed in the madrigals of Gherardello and Lorenzo, and even in the work of Landini and his end-of-the-century contemporaries the madrigal, now a waning genre, keeps its basic stylistic character. After 1400 the madrigal is virtually extinct as a musical form. It will not be revived until early in the sixteenth century, when it is reborn as a much different poetic form and in totally changed musical dress.

The caccia, often treated as a separate form, will not be considered in detail here since I think it is a subgenre of the madrigal. Its canonic musical style was derived from the *fuga* practiced in various ways, and in several countries, from the thirteenth century on; in fact the term *caccia* would seem to refer primarily to the technique of musical chase, not the hunter's chase.[47] Images of the hunt are found in the early madrigal; Giovanni's *Nel bosco senza foglie* is an example. The poetic form of the madrigal was expanded beyond the limits of *terzine* to accommodate the spun-out canonic structure of the music; but stanzas followed by ritornello mark the caccia as a madrigal in fundamental concept. Texts dealing with the hunt were a natural choice for the music of the caccia, not its origi-

---

46. *Poesie musicali*, p. xcvn. Corsi does exaggerate the casualness of text underlay in the musical sources.

47. On this see Pirrotta, "Per l'origine," esp. pp. 308ff.

nal reason for existence. The naturalism of some of the text setting is different in degree but not in kind from that of the madrigal.

Most of what I have to say about the ballata, the other great genre of trecento music, will be contained in the next chapter since in its mature form the polyphonic ballata seems to me to point toward the future as much as it exemplifies trecento art. There are ballatas in the earliest surviving layer of fourteenth-century music, however, and so they deserve some attention here. The ballata as a poetic form has a longer history than the madrigal. Whether or not it is derived from the provençal *balada*,[48] it was current as a round-dance song long before Boccaccio gave it literary fame in the *Decameron*. Closely linked with the devotional lauda in its own country, the ballata is part of an international family of dance-song poetry with a structure of alternating choral refrain and solo stanzas. Its formal subcategories, as defined by theorists according to the length of the *ripresa* or refrain, need not concern us here. In content the trecento ballata is usually a love poem, often in direct address to the loved one; *bonae sententiae* are also to be found, especially later in the century.

Proof of the ballata's greater age is the fact that in the early-trecento repertory it is found as a monophonic song; not until 1360 or so did it begin to receive polyphonic dress. The earliest ballatas are all anonymous, and there are none surviving under the names of the first generation of composers, who evidently made their reputation as madrigalists in the strict sense of the word. The ballatas found in the Rossi manuscript differ from madrigals not only in being single-line music (to which some sort of accompaniment may have been improvised) but also in having an elusively individual melodic line, which sometimes suggests in outline a rather simple tune. They have, however, been "madrigalized" through the use of abundant melodic *fioritura* and so do not differ as much from the madrigal as one might expect. Two examples will illustrate this. The first, *Lucente stella che'l mio cor desfai*, has a three-line *ripresa* followed by two-line *piedi* sung to a second musical section; then a three-line *volta* is performed to the music of the *ripresa*,

48. For this hypothesis see B. R. Suchla, *Studien zur Provenienz der Trecento-Ballata* (Göttingen, 1976). On the ballata in general see Kurt von Fischer, "Ballata," in *The New Grove Dictionary* 2:87–88, and the bibliography given there.

which is repeated to end the piece (Ex. 4). The second, *Per tropo fede talor se perigola*, is a *ballata minima* with a one-line *ripresa* (Ex. 5). Its *versi sdruccioli* are notable in a reading, but the musical setting in true madrigalian fashion lays no stress on this bit of *musica verbalis*. Notice in this piece the simple but effective device of setting the *ripresa* one tone lower than the *stanza*.[49]

Toward the end of the century the ballata rises in favor as the madrigal declines. In the hands of Landini, set for two or more often three polyphonic voices (only one or two of them texted), it reaches great heights of artistic perfection, and at the same time shows evidence of a profound stylistic change. The vocal music of the end of the trecento becomes much more French—or, better, international—in style, and remains so through most of the fifteenth century. The madrigal with its profoundly Italian, perhaps Mediterranean, sound, disappears just as, or even before, trecento visual art gives way to the new classicizing tendencies of quattrocento Florentine painting and sculpture.

49. Exx. 4 and 5 are given after the edition of W. Thomas Marrocco, *Polyphonic Music of the Fourteenth Century*, vol. 11 (Monaco, 1978), nos. 45, 62; see also Pirrotta, *Music of Fourteenth-Century Italy*, vol. 2, nos. 31, 27.

·*II*·

The Puzzle of the Quattrocento

T<small>HE</small> <small>WRITING OF</small> *poesia per musica* did not come to an end as the fourteenth century gave way to the fifteenth; the composition of *musica per poesia* very nearly did. The later sources of trecento polyphony contain music by Italians active in the years 1400–1420, men such as Matteo da Perugia, a cantor at the Milanese cathedral; Antonello da Caserta, a southerner who seems to have spent some time in central and northern Italy; and several people all confusingly named "Zacar"—one of them a papal singer. Transalpine names also appear, among them that of Johannes Ciconia, who worked in Padua in the first decade of the century. But the number of pieces is not very great, and the composers are better known for music written to Latin or French texts. The enormously prolific Francesco Landini (d. 1397) seems to have had no real successors. Although there are manuscripts of Italian provenance containing secular music of the early, middle, and later fifteenth century, these sources are devoted largely to music set to French texts and written by northern composers.[1] There is only a trickle of Italian song

1. Italian music in early-fifteenth-century sources has been collected by Gilbert Reaney, ed., *Early-Fifteenth-Century Music*, vols. 5, 6 (American Institute of Musicology, 1975–77). A full and conveniently organized account of the many manuscripts containing secular music from 1460 to the end of the century is that of Allan W. Atlas, *The Cappella Giulia Chansonnier (Rome, Bibl. Ap. Vat. C. G. XIII, 27)*, 2 vols. (Brooklyn, 1975–76), 1:233–58; see also Leeman L. Perkins and Howard Garey, eds., *The Mellon Chansonnier*, 2 vols. (New Haven, 1979), 2:149–83, an account that includes a few manuscripts not described by Atlas. Mid-century sources not mentioned in either of the two works just listed are briefly described in Heinrich Besseler, ed., *Guillelmi Dufay: Opera Omnia*, vol. 6 (American Institute of Musicology, 1964), pp. xv–xxiii.

mixed in this flood of French music: no madrigals; a few ballatas; some very odd forms such as rondeaux with Italian texts, making one suspect that some of the music may originally have been written for French verse. The amount of Italian-texted music in what are usually considered the central sources increases a little in the third quarter of the century but remains small right up to and beyond the turn of the century. The repertory of the *frottola*, which rises to prominence about 1490, is to be found in a different group of manuscript and, later, printed sources.

One of the ironies of fifteenth-century secular music as it has come down to us is that though the chanson is its dominant genre and most of the composers are of French or Flemish origin, a great deal of it survives in Italian manuscript sources; if there were no Italian collections of this music we would know much less about it than we do.[2] This has been explained by the known popularity of French music in Italian courtly centers, notably Florence, Naples, and Ferrara. The explanation will not quite do, at least if it is limited to postulating an acceptance by Italians of music created and circulated in France and Burgundy, then exported across the Alps. It seems more likely that French musicians resident in Italian cities wrote a good deal of this music, and perhaps some of the poetry as well, for their Italian patrons.[3] In other words, the dominant forms of secular music cultivated in aristocratic Italian centers were French. This may also be considered an irony of a sort, but not quite the same sort. The most famous documented example is a letter from Guillaume Dufay to Piero and Giovanni de' Medici, written from Geneva in 1456, enclosing four new compositions on French and Latin texts (Dufay was later asked by Antonio Squarcialupi to set an Italian text written by Lorenzo de' Medici; we do not know if he complied with this request).[4]

2. Most of the secular music of Guillaume Dufay, for example, survives in Italian sources, and the same is true of many later-fifteenth-century chanson composers.

3. For a composer such as Josquin des Prez, who lived in Italy for forty years or more, this must be true, at least as regards the music of his earlier chansons.

4. See Craig M. Wright, "Dufay at Cambrai: Discoveries and Revisions," *Journal of the American Musicological Society* 28 (1975), 90. Dufay lived in Italy from 1420 at the latest until the mid-1430s, and retained close connections with several Italian courts; see Lewis Lockwood, "Dufay and Ferrara," in *Papers Read at the Dufay Quincentenary Conference* (1974), ed. Allan W. Atlas (Brooklyn, 1976), pp. 1–25.

How can one account for the disappearance of the trecento tradition and the near-monopoly enjoyed by French musicians during a period of great artistic activity in Italy? In architecture and sculpture Italians were creating marvels, little touched by what was going on in the North. Though Flemish painting was much admired in Italy, it can hardly be said to have played a dominant role in the work of Italian painters. If the fifteenth century is perhaps not one of the greatest periods in Italian vernacular literature, still plenty of *poesia per musica*, in the form of ballatas, strambotti, and new genres like the Venetian *giustiniana*, was written. This poetry was doubtless sung; but very little of it seems to have been written down, and it was certainly not regarded as worth saving and collecting in the way the trecento repertory had been.

For Italians and Italophiles this seeming interruption in the progress of vernacular art has generated searches for lost musical treasure—so far not very successful—as well as explanations of various kinds. These explanations are centered on a few general hypotheses: (1) French influence on Italian musical culture became so dominant by the end of the fourteenth century that it ended by stifling the native tradition; (2) after the small school of local composers died out, there was no place in Italy to get the kind of musical training provided by the *maîtrises* of some of the great churches and cathedrals of northern France (roughly from a bit south of the modern Belgian border up to Antwerp), hence musicians had to be imported into Italy; (3) the kind of *poesia per musica* that delighted aristocratic audiences in the trecento went out of fashion and was replaced by French verse chiefly cast in the old but newly popular form of the rondeau; (4) Italian men of letters, preoccupied with humanistic concerns, viewed the poetic and musical art of the trecento with disdain, preferring simple performances of Latin verse sung "to the lyre" in what they imagined to be the fashion of the ancients. Though none of these hypotheses is completely satisfying, each deserves some attention here.

1. Scholars dealing with the musical repertory of the trecento have long been concerned with the infusion of French elements into its notation; pieces appearing in different sources have been closely examined in an effort to determine the relative degree of

gallicization imposed on a presumed Italianate original.[5] The written language of music is important, of course, and French notational ideas did affect Italian practice and even, as Alberto Gallo has shown, Italian theory.[6] The amount of rewriting of old music in newer style is actually not very great, and in any event old versus new, as in *tempus* versus *modus* notation, is not precisely the same thing as Italian versus French. Of greater importance, it seems to me, is whether music was originally conceived in Italian or in French style (the *aere italico* and *gallico* of the early-trecento commentator).[7] In broad terms it seems safe to say that the madrigal, from its beginnings up to its final days in the early years of the fifteenth century, remained fundamentally Italian in concept; the ballata, as polyphonic music a newer genre, was much more affected by French musical rhetoric, something that can be seen clearly in the work of Landini. From the earliest period in the trecento, certain metric schemes in the music, notably *novenaria* and, even more, *senaria imperfecta* (in modern terms 9/8 and 6/8, respectively), were associated with French song; and these meters carried with them associations of rhythmic, perhaps even melodic, patterns.[8] This can be observed in pieces in the Rossi Codex, music dating from as early as the 1330s.[9] As we have seen, a mix of French and Italian elements was observable to the earliest trecento commentators;

5. On this see Kurt von Fischer, "Zur Entwicklung der italienischen Trecento-Notation," *Archiv für Musikwissenschaft* 16 (1959), 87–99.
6. Prosdocimus de Beldemandis, a self-avowed champion of Italian notation in the early fifteenth century, unwittingly (?) included basic French concepts in his discussion of the *ars ytalica*. See F. Alberto Gallo, *La teoria della notazione in Italia dalla fine del xiii all'inizio del xv secolo* (Bologna, 1966), chaps. 12–13.
7. See chap. 1, n. 16.
8. *Novenaria*, corresponding to *tempus perfectum cum prolatione perfecta*, and *senaria imperfecta* (also called *gallica*), corresponding to *tempus imperfectum cum prolatione perfecta*, are measures in common use in French music of the Ars Nova; the Italian *octonaria* and *duodenaria* have no precise French equivalents, though music written in them can be "rewritten" in French notation.
9. Examples include *Amor mi fa cantar a la francesca*, a ballata; *Du' ochi ladri, sot'una girlanda*, a madrigal with a "French" ritornello; and *L'antico dio Biber fra sette stelle*, which has alternating lines of French and Italian texts and shows French stylistic elements in its first section, followed by a sturdily Italian ritornello. The pieces are printed in Nino Pirrotta, ed., *The Music of Fourteenth-Century Italy*, vol. 2 (American Institute of Musicology, 1960), nos. 16, 26, 32; they may also be found in W. Thomas Marrocco, ed., *Polyphonic Music of the Fourteenth Century*, vol. 8 (Monaco, 1972), nos. 11, 23; vol. 11 (1978), no. 5.

pure *italianità* was not yet an ideological necessity to anyone. There is no doubt that the music of Landini is far closer to that of Machaut than is the work of Giovanni da Cascia or that of Gherardello and Lorenzo, Florentine composers who were contemporaries of the French poet-musician. What I see as some of the most important French elements in Landini's art, his use of rhythmically unified phrase structures and especially his adaptation of French cadential formulas, will be dealt with later; these are matters affecting not just musical style but the whole verbal-musical amalgam.

The matter of French influence on Italian culture in the later Middle Ages is a complex one, far beyond my capacity to treat here. As one of Dante's three great divisions of the Latin tongue, French enjoyed high status and was widely known in literary circles from the dugento on. Curiosity about and imitation of French customs and fashions were widespread. Folgore di San Gimignano writes of "gente costumata, a la francesca / cantar, danzar a la provenzalesca."[10] This trend continued in the fourteenth century. Among the poems in the Rossi manuscript are madrigals with French as well as Latin lines interwoven.[11] The earlier trecento composers did not set all-French texts, but in Landini's time they began to do so, and in the next generation French came to replace Italian as the main language of polyphonic song. How well Machaut's music was known in Italy I am not sure, though the music of Landini certainly shows awareness of it; some fourteenth-century French polyphony survives in manuscript fragments of Italian origin, but large amounts of French music did not begin to appear in Italian sources until the generation of composers after Machaut, among them musicians active at the papal court in Avignon. The temporary return of the papacy to Rome in 1377, and the existence of rival papal courts during the years of the Great Schism that followed, gave great impetus to the process of infusion by which French literary and musical culture became dominant in Italy. Nowhere was pro-French sentiment stronger than in Florence, home of the later stages of trecento music. A remark by the sixteenth-century Venetian statesman Marco Foscari might be taken as apply-

10. See Gallo, *La teoria della notazione*, p. 33.
11. See n. 9 above. On the use of French in northeastern Italy in the fourteenth century see Giuseppe Corsi, *Rimatori del trecento* (Turin, 1969), pp. 13–14.

ing to Florence throughout this period: "In the heart of every Florentine, if it could be cut open, there would be found in the very center a lily of gold" (the heraldic sign of the French monarchy).[12] If Italian composers were themselves writing *alla francesca* by 1400, even to the point of setting French texts, it is not surprising that as a whole group of northern musicians arrived in Italy they continued to practice the art they knew, and chiefly in the language they knew best.

2. The theory that the local school or schools of trecento composers died out, that the movement simply ran its course, is tempting in its simplicity and in its somewhat romantic coloration; it is also convenient if one wishes to prolong the Middle Ages through the fourteenth century, then turn over a new, Renaissance leaf in 1400. It is, I fear, too simple to be true. Before dismissing it, however, we should look for any help it might give us. First of all, for the whole period 1325–1400 the number of active composers, or at least of men who left more than one or two pieces behind them, was small, about sixteen in all.[13] Adding the more shadowy figures, including some who were probably not full-time or professional musicians, would bring the number up to only about two dozen. The figure is not surprising, for it is a greater number of polyphonists than any other culture, even that of France, produced during the period. Of course there must have been more musicians than this capable of performing the music, perhaps even of composing a little; but we do not know anything about them. The circles of dilettantes and music lovers who enjoyed this art were also small, limited to a few northern-Italian courts and the slightly precious groups, chiefly Florentine, described to us in the verse of Sacchetti, Giovanni Gherardi da Prato's *Paradiso degli Alberti*, and the sonnets of Prudenzani.[14] This was never the whole musical culture of the

---

12. Cited by Hans Baron, *The Crisis of the Early Italian Renaissance*, rev. ed. (Princeton, 1966), p. 97.

13. See the tables of composers in Kurt von Fischer, *Studien zur italienischen Musik des Trecento und frühen Quattrocento* (Bern, 1956), pp. 85–88.

14. Giovanni Gherardi da Prato, *Il paradiso degli Alberti*, ed. Antonio Lanza (Rome, 1975) (see also the informative introduction in the edition of Alessandro Wesselofsky, 3 vols. [Bologna, 1867]); Santorre Benedetti, ed., "Il 'Solazzo' e il 'Saporeto' con altre rimi di Simone Prudenzani d'Orvieto," *Giornale storico della letteratura italiana*, suppl. 15 (Turin, 1913). Both works were written in the 1420s, but while Prudenzani was speaking of his own time, in a provincial milieu where tre-

Italian peninsula, most of which was orally transmitted and is un-known to us except for scattered fragments and descriptive hints. This music was a high art, and in this period great art reached masses of people only in cathedrals and their decoration. So the death of Italian music is not in question, only the disappearance of a somewhat rarified phenomenon. The song of the troubadours came to an end; why should not trecento polyphony have followed the same course?

In France polyphony was born in churches and monasteries. Its practice, at least at a high artistic level, may have been a special and infrequent thing; nevertheless its appeal, as a form of embellishing the Divine Service, was lasting, not to be wiped out by changes of fashion or even by ecclesiastical stricture. The composers of the tre-cento were for the most part church musicians as well; but they tended to be organists first and singers second. The small amount of sacred polyphony extant tells us that its practice was, in com-parison with French practice, very special indeed. Italian church-goers heard mostly chant, interspersed with organ music played in an *alternatim* fashion; the introduction of a polyphonic Credo was something of an event.[15] By the time this began to change the French had already arrived in full force.

Secular song as handled by Giovanni da Cascia and his contem-poraries may first have been heard as entertainment for the clergy; but it soon began to be patronized, and commissioned, by secu-lar rulers and aristocratic circles. As was pointed out earlier, the northern-Italian centers for this patronage were Visconti Milan, Verona under the della Scala family, and Padua under the rule of the Carraresi. By 1400 or shortly thereafter conditions were much altered in these cities. Milan was in turmoil after the death of Giangaleazzo Visconti, the Scaligeri were gone from Verona, and

---

cento music was still performed along with newer works, Gherardi wrote of an ear-lier period. (The work describes cultured diversions at a villa outside Florence in the year 1389, with Landini and other trecento musicians present.)

15. A *Patrem* by Bartolo da Firenze survives, and is thought to date from 1350 or earlier; see Nino Pirrotta, ed., *The Music of Fourteenth-Century Italy*, vol. 1 (Ameri-can Institute of Musicology, 1954), no. 1. For a passage in Filippo Villani's *De origine civitatis* describing the effect on a congregation of a polyphonic Credo, perhaps that of Bartolo, see Pirrotta, "Per l'origine e la storia della 'caccia' e del 'madrigale' tre-centesca," *Rivista musicale italiana* 49 (1947), 142.

Venice had ended the rule of the Carrara family and taken Padua into its territorial domain. The old patrons were, in other words, gone. Florence, though preoccupied in a struggle with the Visconti at the end of the fourteenth century, did not undergo any such drastic change; in Florence there was, on the other hand, no single dominant source of patronage before the rise of Cosimo de' Medici, and the circles that gave encouragement to Landini and other local musicians passed out of existence, replaced by other groups with other things on their minds.[16] Landini's successor as organist at San Lorenzo, his pupil Francesco da Bartolomeo, is not known to have been a composer. Giovanni (Mazzuoli) degli Organi (d. 1426), a friend of Landini who may have been organist at the duomo in the early fifteenth century, apparently carried on the tradition, as did his son Piero (d. 1430); but this we shall never know much about since his surviving music is illegible in the source containing it and the pages set aside for his music in the Squarcialupi Codex are blank.[17] And Squarcialupi himself, though he won fame during his long tenure (1432–80) as organist at the cathedral, has left us no music. Thus the Florentine tradition of organist-composers seems to have declined; even though it was to be revived in the early years of the sixteenth century it never again became dominant in Florentine musical life. Some indication that the Florentines themselves felt the native art had run its course may be derived from the manuscript collections that preserve it. Most of them were written in the early fifteenth century; one, the Squarcialupi Codex, was almost certainly planned as a monument, lovingly and elabo-

16. The *Paradiso* of Gherardi was considered old-fashioned in subject matter and language by the Florentines of the 1420s, and the humanistic circles now dominating Florentine culture were not much interested in polyphonic music. See the introduction to Lanza's edition of the *Paradiso* (n. 14 above); cf. Nino Pirrotta, "Music and Cultural Tendencies in Fifteenth-Century Italy," *Journal of the American Musicological Society* 19 (1966), 127–61, esp. 135ff.

17. See Frank A. D'Accone, "Giovanni Mazzuoli: A Late Representative of the Italian Ars Nova," in *L'Ars Nova italiana del trecento: Convegni di studi, 1961–1967* (Certaldo, 1968), pp. 23–38. Professor D'Accone has recently discovered a manuscript in the Biblioteca Laurenziana in Florence that may be of slightly later date than the Squarcialupi Codex and that contains music by both Paolo da Firenze and Giovanni degli Organi, the two composers whose music is missing in the Squarcialupi MS. Unfortunately the Laurenziana MS is a palimpsest, scraped down and reused for nonmusical purposes; at the moment little of the music has been found legible. See D'Accone, "Una nuova fonte dell'Ars Nova italiana: Il codice di San Lorenzo, 2211," *Studi musicali* 13 (1984), 3–31.

rately executed, to past glories; others such as Florence, Bibl. Naz. Cent. MS Panciatichi 26 and the recently discovered San Lorenzo MS 2211, may be, in their less expensive and less careful way, aimed at the same thing.

Florence was not full of northern singers, at least not until the period of papal residence there in the mid-1430s and the subsequent transfer of the Council of Ferrara to Florence in 1439.[18] Until the late 1430s there were never more than a couple of polyphonic *cantori di San Giovanni*; when the Medici wished to bring Florentine music up to date—in the great churches and also for their own entertainment—they, like everybody else in Italy, imported northern singer-composers. And, poorly as musicians seem to have been paid in fifteenth-century Florence, a surprising number of distinguished musicians spent some time there; indeed, one of the greatest of the *oltremontani*, Heinrich Isaac, made it his home for a good deal of his adult life.[19]

The new patrons of music at the turn of the century were chiefly ecclesiastical magnates, cardinals, and bishops in attendance at Church councils, or the numerous antipopes of the early fifteenth century. In their retinues were musicians of distinction, mostly French or Flemish and trained in the thorough methods employed at wealthy and highly organized chapels in France, Burgundy, and Flanders. Among them are such figures as Ciconia, from Liège, the young Dufay, from Cambrai, and Arnold and Hugo de Lantins, all of whom went to Italy for varying periods of time.[20] Composers

18. On some northern musicians in Florence in the early fifteenth century, see Frank A. D'Accone, "A Documentary History of Music in the Florentine Cathedral and Baptistry during the Fifteenth Century" (Ph.D. diss., Harvard University, 1960), p. 71ff.; Gino Corti, "Un musicista fiammengo a Firenze agli inizi del quattrocento," in *L'Ars Nova italiana del trecento* 4 (1975), ed. Agostino Ziino (Certaldo, 1976), pp. 177–81.

19. See Frank A. D'Accone, "The Singers of San Giovanni in Florence during the Fifteenth Century," *Journal of the American Musicological Society* 14 (1961), 307–58, esp. 332–33, 338ff. It is only fair to add that there were also many native Florentines in the cathedral-baptistry chapel throughout the middle and later fifteenth century; but they are not known as composers.

20. One reason so many northern composers went to Italy in the fifteenth century was that their chances of receiving benefices to augment their salaries was much better there, through the papal court and ecclesiastical and secular princes who had direct access to it. On this question see Christopher Reynolds, "Musical Careers, Ecclesiastical Benefices, and the Example of Johannes Brunet," *Journal of the American Musicological Society* 37 (1984), 49–97.

such as these, masters of both the rhythmically complex style of the *ars subtilior* and the solo-song style with textless subordinate voices as practiced in French circles, occasionally set Italian texts, ballatas or hybrid forms such as Italian-texted rondeaux; but the form most favored by their patrons was the ceremonial Latin motet with its floridly encomiastic texts and imposing sonorities. In this style Italian composers could only imitate their northern colleagues; and the kind of training given to the choirboys and *petits vicaires* in such a place as the cathedral of Cambrai was simply not available in Italy. Although we do not know how trecento musicians were trained, it would seem to have been a process of individual discipleship rather than any sort of systematic work.[21] Thus whichever Italian musicians did serve in princely or ecclesiastical chapels—and there were in fact a certain number of them at all times—did so for the most part in subordinate roles.

3. Ciconia appears to be one of the few northern composers of the early fifteenth century who made a genuine attempt at carrying on Italian traditions. He even wrote a few madrigals in what looks like a deliberately retrospective trecento style.[22] This he may have done because of his position in the Padua of the last days of the Carraresi. (He also of course wrote motets celebrating Venetian dignitaries.) Whether Dufay was much affected by Italian musical tradition is harder to say, and indeed the question might have struck contemporaries as irrelevant; what was expected of composers was new music to new poetry (Dufay's setting of the opening stanza of Petrarch's *Vergine* cycle is an interesting exception), not adherence to a now outmoded fashion.

Poetry in the older forms was still being written, and the ballata—now heavily influenced by the French virelai—was still occasionally set by musicians. At this time the ballata as designed for

21. Some Italian musicians, such as Antonello da Caserta, did cultivate the *ars subtilior*, which they appear to have learned in French centers such as Avignon. The best-known Italian cathedral school, the Scuola degli accoliti in Verona, founded in 1440, seems not to have been a real center for the teaching of *canto figurato* until the late fifteenth century; see Antonio Spagnolo, *Le scuoli accolitali in Verona* (Verona, 1904); Enrico Paganuzzi, "La scuola degli accoliti e la questione dei chiericati," in *La musica a Verona*, ed. G. B. Pichi (Verona, 1976), pp. 71–77.

22. See Suzanne Clercx, *Johannes Ciconia: Un musicien liégeois et son temps (vers 1335–1411)*, 2 vols. (Brussels, 1964), vol. 2, nos. 1–4.

music seems to have been undergoing a change. Mixed in with love lyrics and moralizing themes was verse of a more popular kind, such as the following text, set by Anthonius Zachara da Teramo:[23]

> Ciaramella, me dolçe Ciaramella!
>   O tu che porti Fra Maçante sotto,
> polito e bello con la chiercha rasa;
>   poy che'l martello to' dà sì gran botto,
> tosto m'abrazza, strengi e pur me basa,
>   chè'n questa terra da me n'è più bella.
> Ciaramella, ...

Other texts, such as *Morir desio po' che Fortuna omay*, set by Bartholomaeus de Bononia, show a Petrarchism enfeebled in tone and language.[24] It is almost as if the ballata were "going underground," losing its favored status as aristocratic *poesia per musica*.[25] It never quite disappeared, and in fact experienced a revival toward the end of the fifteenth century when texts by Angelo Poliziano and others were set in serious if not particularly Italianate style. Its most conspicuous appearance in the later quattrocento is, however, in the form of the octosyllabic *barzelletta*, antiliterary in tone and popularesque in the jingly sound of its verse.

A special case in the category of *poesia per musica* in the quattrocento is the work of Leonardo Giustinian (d. 1446) and his imitators. Giustinian's poetry, which has been described as deriving its style and content from the "immaginatione amorosa popolare" of his time,[26] is written in a variety of forms and meters, including the ballata. His poems were intended chiefly for music and became

23. Reaney, *Early-Fifteenth-Century Music* 6:20. On this piece, and Zachara's use of the popular idiom, see Nino Pirrotta, "'Zacharias musicus,'" *Quadrivium* 12, no. 1 (1971), 153–75, esp. 156–57. Pirrotta gives a transcription of *Ciaramella* on pp. 172–74. Zachara's background was that of the Neapolitan *Regno*, which at this time included central Italy as well as Naples. On Zachara see John Nádas, "New Light on Magister Antonius dictus Zacharias de Teramo," *Studi musicali* (forthcoming).

24. Reaney, *Early-Fifteenth-Century Music* 5:44.

25. The generation of Burchiello (d. 1449) seems to have had a special predilection for down-to-earth poetic theme and language. See Antonio Lanza, *Polemiche e berte letterarie nella Firenze del primo '400* (Rome, 1971).

26. Domenico de Robertis, "L'esperienza poetica del quattrocento," in *Storia della letteratura italiana*, ed. Emilio Cecchi and Natalino Sapegno, vol. 2, *Il quattrocento e l'Ariosto* (Milan, 1966), p. 446f.

known in their musical form as *giustiniane* or, since they were sung in a Venetian style—*l'aere venetiano*—as *venetiane*. These are said to have been sung everywhere: at weddings and banquets, on street corners.[27] One of the perils of popular fame was that much more poetry than Giustinian actually wrote was attributed to him; or perhaps his name simply became synonymous with the whole genre. What precisely the *aere venetiano* was we do not know since this music must have been largely improvised. A few pieces setting texts attributed to Giustinian have survived; they will be discussed below. Here is an example of Giustinian's *poesia per musica*, a text in *terza rima* for which a partial musical setting is extant.[28]

> Io vedo ben che'l ben servire e vanno
> e pazzi son quellor, che se afaticha
> per perdere nela fin ogni suo affano.
>
> Moro di doglia, e pur convien, che dica
> i pianti, che me struze e'l gran dolore,
> dove el mio cor si pasca e se nutrica.
>
> Ben posso sempre biastemare amore
> e starme sempre lacrimoso e afflicto
> poy che ho perduto un si lizadro fiore.

Another musical-poetic genre absent from the trecento repertory but rising to prominence in the fifteenth century is the *strambotto*, long practiced in Sicily but acclimatized in Tuscany and northern Italy. As one of the principal forms used in the frottola repertory of the late fifteenth century, it attains its chief period of glory later. It is worth noting, however, that Sicilian song had achieved some popularity in the rest of Italy quite early in the fifteenth century. A piece described as "from Sicily" is mentioned as being sung in one of Prudenzani's sonnets, circa 1420.[29] A description by Gianozzo Manetti of an evening's musical entertainment

27. Walter H. Rubsamen, "The Justiniane or Viniziane of the Fifteenth Century," *Acta Musicologica* 29 (1957), 172–84, citing a letter (p. 172) by Giustinian's contemporary Piero Parleone.

28. Bertold Wiese, ed., *Poesie edite ed inedite di Leonardo Giustiniani* (Bologna, 1863; repr. Bologna, 1968), p. 385.

29. Benedetti, "Il 'Solazzo,'" p. 116. There is also a description of a Venetian youth singing *siciliane* in Gherardi's *Paradiso degli Alberti*, 52 (p. 75 in Lanza).

after a banquet in Venice in 1448 tells us that the guests, Florentine exiles, performed Sicilian "symphonias et cantilenas," amused themselves further with "venetis cantinunculis et symphonis," and also sang "gallicas cantilenas et melodias."[30] The humanistic terminology is not very helpful, nor does Manetti say whether or what instruments were used (in the *symphonias?*), still less whether the music was sung from memory or read from written versions.

Improvised musical performance, by respected *improvvisatori* or the humbler but very popular *cantimbanchi* and *canterini*, who sang strambotti, *terze rime*, sonnets, and especially *ottave rime* on chivalric themes, played a large role in fifteenth-century musical culture. This will be the subject of another chapter, but these forms should be mentioned here as part of the body of *poesia per musica* that replaced the trecento repertory.

Manetti's comment about young Florentines singing Sicilian, Venetian, and French music leads us to what was the center of attention during most of the quattrocento, the French chanson: the ballade, the virelai, and above all the rondeau. How much of this poetry, which is largely anonymous, may have been written in Italy we do not know; at least some of it probably was. It was certainly in vogue there. The situation may seem anomalous, but it is not unique in the history of vocal music. One need only think of the enormous craze for Italian opera and secular cantata in eighteenth-century Germany—which was then full of Italian musicians. And the social position of eighteenth-century German-texted music in relation to that of court-sponsored Italian art may also suggest a parallel: French music was fashionable as well as popular in the fifteenth century, yet its vogue did not preclude enjoyment by Italians of an unpretentious, semipopular local music.

4. The view that humanistic currents in quattrocento culture were indifferent if not antagonistic to polyphonic music is one made current by Nino Pirrotta in a typically stimulating article.[31] Trecento musicians were mostly clerics; if they were well educated it was within a scholastic tradition of little relevance to the neo-Ciceronian and neo-Platonic interests of fifteenth-century scholars.

30. Cited in Rubsamen, "Justiniane," p. 173.
31. "Music and Cultural Tendencies in Fifteenth-Century Italy" (see n. 16 above).

Pirrotta's argument is not of course this simple; and in any event the humanists' power in this area should not be exaggerated, for it did not check the popularity of French polyphony, no less "medieval" in concept and style than that of Italian musicians. Still, it is hard to imagine a humanistic scholar such as Giorgio Valla, who was interested in music but only that of antiquity, reading the *Pomerium* of Marchetto da Padova with pleasure or for profit. And when Marsilio Ficino took up his lyre (a lute, or perhaps a viol of some sort) to sing the Orphic hymns he would not have concerned himself with mensural rhythms and contrapuntal rules, whether he knew anything about them or not, because the ancients knew nothing of all this; the one thing the Greeks had insisted on—close accentual and metrical coordination between word and tone—was obviously lacking in mid-fifteenth-century polyphonic music. An interest in making contemporary music conform to ancient practice in this and other respects was indeed to come, but did not really begin until nearly the end of the century.

In some areas relevant to our subject humanistic tastes may have exerted an influence. The trecento novella, framework for much *poesia per musica*, faded from popularity in favor of dialogues, epistles, and orations.[32] Gherardi's *Paradiso degli Alberti*, a chain of novelle that includes numerous references to music making by Landini and others, was set in the Florence of 1389 but was probably written toward the end of Gherardi's life in the 1420s; it was considered hopelessly out of date in subject and language when it appeared.[33] A literary *certame coronario* was held in Florence in 1441; in this contest entrants read vernacular poems in various forms, including sonnets and *terze rime*, on the stated classicistic theme of *amicizia*. No music is mentioned. If this is compared to the troubadour-like contest of madrigalists at the Scaligeri court a century earlier, the changes in taste and in the role of vernacular music seem clear. Vernacular poetry had its defenders, such as Cino Rinuccini, in the early fifteenth century, and the *tre corone* of the preceding century were regarded with respect if not always with admiration. On the other hand, the madrigal was nearly dead, the ballata undergoing

32. De Robertis, "L'esperienza poetica del quattrocento," p. 361.
33. See above, n. 16.

change. The newly popular forms of Italian sung poetry were untainted by scholastic learning; they laid no claim to be regarded as *musica* in any exalted sense, and therefore could be enjoyed in improvisatory music making by humanists as well as anybody else.

We should thus not overemphasize the negative role played by fifteenth-century humanists with regard to Italian music. The schools run by Vittorino da Feltre and other fifteenth-century scholars included music in the curriculum; just what they taught is not clear, though there was probably some practical instruction in singing and possibly the more genteel instruments, and some Boethian theory. Medieval theory was always a useful adjunct to instruction in mathematics, and could be used for this purpose without intention of forming polyphonists out of students; so perhaps the work of Jean de Muris, the most widely read theorist of the later Middle Ages, found a place in these curricula.[34] Then, in the same courts that patronized humanistic scholars were musicians of scholastic stamp (Dufay, so much admired by the Medici, was a doctor in canon law) as well as *improvvisatori* and lute singers. But, by common agreement, one expected the polyphonists to be *oltremontani*, the improvisatory music makers to be Italian.

Consideration of what quattrocento Italian music does survive is not easy since it is difficult to disentangle it from the predominantly French musical tradition of the time. The place to begin, it seems to me, is the later part of Francesco Landini's career, when the Italian ballata was already showing considerable French influence. It has often been pointed out that Landini's later music has recognizably French traits. While the two-voice ballatas have text in both parts the three-voice works have one or even two textless voices accompanying the chief line; the ballatas are often written with first and second endings (the French *ouvert* and *clos*) for their stanzas; and French rhythms, especially the *senaria gallica* or *imperfecta* (6/8), are common. What strikes me as equally important is the nature of Landini's melodic lines and their relationship to the text. First of all, the amount of melodic *fioritura* is considerably less than

34. The theorist Johannes Legrense (Gallicus), a strong Boethian who opposed some of the ideas of Marchetto, was an avowed pupil of Vittorino da Feltre. See Cecil Adkins, "Legrense," in *The New Grove Dictionary* 10:614–15.

that seen in earlier trecento music. This is perhaps a consequence of the choice of rhythmic scheme; one could put it another way by saying that these meters, inclining toward a slightly singsong regularity (though subject to variation through use of hemiola or syncopation) and not really affording room for the elaborate and often irregular melismas of the Italianate madrigal, were chosen because a simpler kind of declamation was desired. Then, regarding this declamation, although Landini does not give up opening and closing melismas (which were, for that matter, common in French song as well), they are not only less elaborate than in the madrigal but also less different from what is in between. Though there is some completely syllabic setting, the text is not spit out rapidly as in the earlier madrigal; rather it is delivered at a gentle pace, hardly uniform but perhaps making it easier to follow the text than in most madrigals. The poetry is still set line by line, yet the melody as a whole is more unified, with gracefully arched shapes and with a good deal of internal repetition and often a recognizable tonal scheme. In particular Landini's mature music is without the abrupt, attention-calling leaps to a high tessitura for the opening of a new line, something we have seen to be a trademark of the madrigal. Finally, and perhaps most important, the melodic line is defined by cadential figures, which serve both to mark the ends of lines of text and to prepare the listener for them. They can also be used for internal musical punctuation within a phrase; in fact the musical line is so clearly defined by these cadential figures that in some pieces one tends to hear the music as a series of deliberately articulated phrases with audible punctuation. These cadences are not all identical in melodic detail, but many of them resemble the figure that has long been called the "Landini cadence," a syncopated melodic suspension (not necessarily dissonant in Landini's music) moving downward by step and then leaping up a third. Landini surely did not invent this sign of cadential articulation; he did use it enough that it is a recognizable feature of his style. Whether clearly audible cadential forms are meant to underscore verbal cadences is a question of some importance to us. At the ends of the *ripresa* and the stanza, yes; at the ends of lines of verse, yes. It is less clear that cadences within lines are designed to support poetic caesuras; these do not necessarily come at the same place in the line in successive stanzas, or even in *volta* and *ripresa*, of the ballatas set by Landini.[35] Still, the possibility exists in Landini's style, as it did not in earlier Italian polyphony, of giving something like a cadenced and punctuated reading of the text through musical means.

The ballata *Non avrà ma' pietà questa mia donna* will illustrate these points (Ex. 6).[36] The text is by Bindo d'Alesso Donati:

> Non avrà ma' pietà questa mia donna,
> se tu non fai, Amore,
> ch'ella sia certa del mio grande ardore.
>
> S'ella sapesse quanta pena i' porto
> per onestà celata nella mente
> Sol per la sua belleçça chè conforto
> d'altro non prende l'anima dolente,
>
> Forse da lei sarebbono in me spente
> le fiamme che la pare
> di giorno in giorno acrescono 'l dolore.

In this piece the cadences are clearly audible; one can hear each line of text coming to an end, and the tonal levels of C and A are clearly subordinate to that of G, on which both halves of the piece finish. The only strong melodic cadences inside the poetic line are those of the opening four bars, "Non avrà" (the *volta* opening should probably set "Forse da lei" to this music), and the middle of the second line of the stanza, which, I think, should set the phrase "Per onestà" (and, less satisfactorily, "D'altro non prende" in the second *piede*). The opening line of the poem (mm. 1–11) makes especially subtle use of the language of melodic cadence: the first gesture cadences strongly on G, ending "Non avrà"; this is followed by a kind of echo of the cadence pattern on C, but without a real stop (mm. 5–6, "ma' pietà"); and there is a suggestion of cadence on D

---

35. The text underlay need not be the same for all stanzas, of course. The sources give only the *ripresa* and half the stanza with the music; the remainder of the text (not always present in every source) is given at the end of the piece.

36. The piece is given in Ex. 6 as printed in Leo Schrade, ed., *Polyphonic Music of the Fourteenth Century*, vol. 4 (Monaco, 1958), p. 144. For its manuscript sources see Schrade's commentary to vol. 4, p. 117. It was this piece, known from a transcription by Raphael Kiesewetter, that gave rise in the late nineteenth century to the notion that the "Landini cadence" was a special feature of the composer's personal style; see David Fallows, "Landini Cadence," in *The New Grove Dictionary* 10:434.

three bars later ("questa mia don-"), which is a kind of advance echo of the real cadence on A ("-na"). The second and third lines of the *ripresa* are composed without internal cadential break, and so is the first line of the stanza, although there is an interesting melodic parallelism toward its end (mm. 39–40, 41–42, all on "por-"). The second line has three cadential feints (mm. 46–47, 50–51, 52–53)—on G, A, and D, the tonal centers of the piece—before reaching its *verto* or *chiuso* ending. The *verto* cadence is, by the way, the same as that used to end the first line of the *ripresa*; the *chiuso* cadence duplicates that of the *ripresa*'s conclusion. These symmetrical uses of melodic formulas give Landini's music a kind of fin-de-siècle grace; they are also prophetic of much that is to come in fifteenth-century music.[37] Finally, it should be pointed out that, as a result of Landini's emphasis on cadential articulation, one's attention is drawn to the ends of poetic lines, not their beginnings as in the madrigal. This seems to reflect a different approach to setting poetry, one closer to reading the text aloud than to the deliberately artificial declamation of the earlier madrigalists.

Italian-texted music of the first two decades of the fifteenth century shows a disconcerting variety of style, ranging from the rhythmic intricacy of the *ars subtilior*[38] to compositions full of syllabic text setting and naturalistic motifs. Among the latter is Zachara's *Ciaramella, me dolçe Ciaramella!*, a three-voice ballata in which a pun on the lady's name, which also means a kind of bagpipe, is underscored by the music (Ex. 7).[39] Note here the splitting of the word *Ciaramella*, a feature of text repetition seen in several works of the period, sometimes involving the musical and textual repetition of a phrase, as in Prepositus Brixiensis's *O spirito gentil, tu m'ay percosso* (Ex. 8).[40] These pieces, to me, illustrate the course toward popular

37. The music of Machaut makes much use of melodic rhyme. See Gilbert Reaney, "The Ballades, Rondeaux, and Virelais of Guillaume de Machaut: Melody, Rhythm, and Form," *Acta Musicologica* 27 (1955), 40–58, esp. 50.

38. An example of this is Antonio da Cividale's *Io veggio per stasone*. See Reaney, *Early-Fifteenth-Century Music* 5:1.

39. The piece is printed in Ex. 7 after the edition of Reaney, *Early-Fifteenth-Century Music* 6:20; here and in Exx. 8 and 9 I have given modern time signatures and altered some of Reaney's editorial accidentals. On Anthonius Zachara see above, n. 23.

40. Given after Reaney, *Early-Fifteenth-Century Music* 5:85. See also Anthonius Zachara's *Nudo non era preso altro vestito* (Reaney, 6:20).

style the ballata was beginning to take. Particularly telling in this regard is a ballata by Nicolaus Zacharie, *Già per gran nobiltà triumpho et fama* (Ex. 9),[41] an unusual text for the time in that it celebrates Pope Martin V (Colonna), performing a function that the older madrigal had occasionally fulfilled but was now more likely to be seen in the form of a Latin motet. The internal musical repetitions in this piece give it immediacy of effect; still more striking is its square-cut phrase structure, in which the *settenari* are given just about half the space of the *endecasillabi*, resulting in something close, by the standards of the time, to a ditty. Although Landini's cadential formulations are present, the piece as a whole is far from the Florentine composer's aristocratic level of composition. From here it is not a long step to the late-fifteenth-century octosyllabic barzelletta and its simple, often very symmetrical musical dress.

In the Italian pieces of Ciconia one sees a stylistic division between the madrigals, which seem deliberately retrospective in style (though their ornamental lines are full of repetition and rather four-square in rhythmic design), and the ballatas, which are close to what other early-fifteenth-century composers were doing with this form. Two of the ballatas, *Lizadra donna ch'el mio cor contenti* and *O rosa bella, o dolce anima mia*, stand out from the others in their use of repeated phrases of text, with the music of the texted voice rising or falling in sequential steps and with occasional imitative correspondences heard in the textless tenor. *O rosa bella* is particularly striking in this respect; and the repeated phrases are so closely integrated, text to music, that a whiff of timelessly natural song, as opposed to the elegant artifice of the trecento, comes to us (Ex. 10).[42] *O rosa bella* has been called a *giustiniana*. There is no reason to think that the poem was written by Giustinian, whose ballatas are long and more complex in structure and language than this little poem; still, Giustinian's verse is full of *rose*, and the poem could be the contemporary work of someone familiar with Giustinian's approach to the love lyric.[43] *O rosa bella* was sung, along with other works of

41. Given after Reaney, *Early-Fifteenth-Century Music* 6 : 137. Nicolaus Zacharie may have been the son of Anthonius; see Pirrotta, "'Zacharias musicus,'" p. 163n.

42. Ex. 10 is given after Rome, Bibl. Ap. Vat. Cod. Urb. lat. 1411, fol. 7ᵛ, with a few corrections of detail from Paris, Bibl. nat. MS n. acq. fr. 4379, fol. 46ᵛ. A modern edition, not entirely accurate, may be found in Clercx, *Ciconia* 2 : 75.

43. See Nino Pirrotta, "Ricercare e variazioni su 'O rosa bella,'" *Studi musicali* 1

Ciconia and pieces by some contemporaries, such as Anthonius Zachara, by Prudenzani's Solazzo.[44]

Far better known than Ciconia's setting is a later one attributed to two English composers, Dunstable and Bedyngham (Ex. 11).[45] It is probably not by Dunstable, who is not known to have any Italian connection; it may or may not be the work of Bedyngham. But it is by a foreigner, judging from the fact that the piece was composed by someone who did not understand the ballata at all (the piece ends musically at the end of the stanza, without allowing for repetition of the first part) but instead treated the poem as if it were a French ballade.[46] If it is the work of an English composer it is an example of the *contenance angloise* admired in France and Italy during the first half of the fifteenth century.[47] English musicians did in fact live and work in Italy in this period; the court of Ferrara seems to have been a particular haven for them, as was the nearby city of Bologna.[48] This later setting of *O rosa bella*, which enjoyed great popularity, does not use Ciconia's repeated tune sequences; but it does have clearly audible fragments of tunes, one of which ("in curtesia") seems to acknowledge Ciconia's setting—or could they both come from a source of popularesque song, something close to the repertory of the improvised *giustiniana*? Snatches of such tunes, to become common in the quodlibets of the end of the fifteenth century, turn up from time to time in earlier music. An example is a melody found with its Italian text under a Latin trope in the Amen of a Credo by Dufay (Ex. 12); it is the kind of tune that might also have been used in the lauda repertory.[49]

(1972), 59–77, esp. 63–64. The text is found in *Il fiore delle elegantissime canzoniete del nobile messere Leonardo Giustiniani* (Venice, 1472[?]); this appearance in print is guarantee not of its authenticity but of its popularity in the later fifteenth century.

44. Benedetti, "Il 'Solazzo,'" p. 110, a poem giving several pieces by Ciconia and mentioning the composer by name. The "O rosa bella" mentioned there continues "che m'alegri il core"; thus it may not be the piece in question.

45. The first part of *O rosa bella* is given in Ex. 11 as transcribed by Pirrotta, "Ricercare e variazioni," p. 75.

46. See Pirrotta, "Ricercare e variazioni," pp. 64–67.

47. In the opinion of David Fallows the vogue for English music on the Continent lasted from about 1420 to the 1440s; see his "Robertus de Anglia and the Oporto Song Collection," in *Source Materials and the Interpretation of Music: A Memorial Volume to Thurston Dart*, ed. Ian Bent (London, 1981), pp. 99–128, esp. p. 99. The special character of English music was noted as early as the Council of Constance in 1416; see Pirrotta, "'Zacharias musicus,'" p. 165n.

48. Fallows, "Robertus de Anglia," passim.

49. See Gustave Reese, *Music in the Renaissance* (New York, 1954), p. 61. The

We would of course like to know more about the popular tradition in Italian music in the fifteenth century; it would be particularly valuable to have some *giustiniane* and early strambotti, since a
line of descent to the frottola repertory of the last decades of the
century could then be drawn. When Ottaviano de' Petrucci began
to publish what he had of this repertory at his disposal, he usually
called his collections simply "frottole." In two books he was more
specific: *Libro quarto* (1505) is entitled *Strambotti, ode, frottole, sonetti,
Et modo de cantar versi latini e capituli,* and book six (1506) has at the
head of its index "Frottole Sonetti Stramboti Ode. Iustiniane numero sesante sie [*sic*]." Though Giustinian's musical (rather than literary) abilities were mentioned by as late a figure as Pietro Bembo,[50]
we have no reason to think that the *giustiniana* of the early fifteenth
century was still current in Petrucci's time; but the publisher may
well have wanted to inject a Venetian note into his publications of
frottolas, the bulk of which came from Mantua and the Venetian
terraferma rather than from Venice itself.

Walter Rubsamen made a special study of four pieces in Petrucci's sixth book, pieces that he convincingly identified as the
giustiniane in that collection.[51] He went further, finding that two of
the texts are lines from poems with firm attribution to Giustinian
himself. The *giustiniane* in Petrucci's volume are three-voice compositions (text in the top line only) with a floridly melismatic vocal
line. For the most elaborate of these pieces, *Aime sospir non trovo
pace,* Rubsamen found in a manuscript source dating from the
1460s (not, as it turns out, of northern-Italian provenance) a simpler
setting, syllabic except for a bit of cadential ornament, of the same
music for the same text.[52] This led Rubsamen to postulate that what

work, published in Heinrich Besseler, ed., *Guillelmi Dufay: Opera Omnia,* vol. 4
(American Institute of Musicology, 1962), p. 25, after Bologna, Civ. Mus. Bibl. Mus.
MS Q 15, fol. 34, uses the melody by turns in all four voices, with both the Italian
text and a Latin trope underlaid to it. The same Italian text, with a similar melody,
appears as the *ripresa* of Antonio Capriolo's *Chi propitio ha la sua stella* (Petrucci, *Frot-
tole libro nono* [1508 (=1509)], fol. 21ᵛ); this was pointed out by William F. Prizer in
"The Frottola and the Unwritten Tradition: Improvisors and Frottolists at North
Italian Courts" (paper read at the annual meeting of the American Musicological
Society, 1980).

50. Rubsamen, "Justiniane," p. 174.
51. See above, n. 27.
52. Escorial MS IV.a.24, fol. 85ᵛ. The poem is a quatrain of awkward *novenari*
that does not suggest Giustinian as author but that does show northern-dialect

Petrucci printed were samples of *giustiniane* as they were ornamented in performance, so that a bit of mid-fifteenth-century song style was caught and preserved for posterity. This conclusion has not been universally accepted; and I do not myself find Rubsamen's argument altogether convincing.[53] Yet the evidence is there, and Rubsamen's perhaps overenthusiastic interpretation of it is certainly understandable. I think that *Aime sospir non trovo pace* as found in the Escorial chansonnier may indeed be a simple *giustiniana*, though lacking whatever touches of individuality the *aere venetiano* may have had; what Petrucci got hold of would seem to be a kind of intabulation, perhaps for stringed instrument with accompanying parts to be played by a *tenorista*. Written-out improvisation, always a paradox, seems very unlikely indeed here, and I doubt that what Petrucci printed is a convincing sample of the *aere venetiano*.

Having tried to take away some of Rubsamen's conclusions, I should in compensation try to add something of my own. *Moro de doglia e pur convien che dica*, the third of Petrucci's *giustiniane*, is, as Rubsamen says, part of a long *sirventese* in *terza rima* with secure attribution to Giustinian.[54] Its upper line is ornamented, though not so heavily as that of *Aime sospir*; no simple version of the piece is known to exist, but I think it could be boiled down to almost the same basic tune (see Ex. 13).[55] This seems to me additional evidence that a stock melody, something Giustinian and his peers may have used as a basis for improvisation, does in this case exist: a bit of the buried treasure of quattrocento music.

Italian pieces become more frequent in some of the manuscripts of the second half of the fifteenth century; they are found

traces; the manuscript is, however, in all likelihood of Neapolitan provenance. See Martha K. Hanen, "The Chansonnier El Escorial Ms. IV.a.24" (Ph.D. diss., University of Chicago, 1973), pp. 44–45.

53. In the view of Nino Pirrotta, "Ricercare e variazioni," pp. 60–63, the fifteenth-century *giustiniana* must have been a combination of poetic, musical, and mimetic improvisation that could never have been written down; thus the pieces printed in Petrucci's sixth frottola book could at best be no more than indirect reflection of the real *giustiniana*. Despite its brevity, Pirrotta's article is one of the best things one can read on the music of the quattrocento.

54. See above, and n. 28.

55. (a) and (b) in Ex. 13 are given after Rubsamen, "Justiniane," p. 180, with a slight change in barring; (c) is my hypothetical reduction of the melody in (d), transcribed from Petrucci, *Frottole libro sexto* (1506), fol. 3ᵛ.

chiefly in manuscripts of Neapolitan provenance from the 1460s through the 1480s.[56] Florentine sources are, on the other hand, devoted chiefly to French music; Florence, so proud of its trecento tradition, had moved—except for the lauda and the incipient carnival song—almost entirely into dependence on French music in the period of Piero and Lorenzo de' Medici. The Neapolitan sources are particularly rich in strambotti, and from these it is—given the limited extent of our knowledge—only a step to the repertory of the frottola, which becomes evident as a genre in the 1480s.

There is in fact a case to be made for the South as place of origin for the new trends in Italian secular song that are evident in the last two decades of the century. The roots of the frottola are in the poetry and song of *improvvisatori*. These musicians could be found everywhere in Italy; a generation of particularly talented and active ones flourished in Naples in the later fifteenth century. Among them were Benedetto Gareth (il Chariteo) and the young Serafino Aquilano. These were men famed for their style—*aria*—of singing poetry, their own and that of others. They were in part continuing an old tradition, in part doing new things—such as declaiming Petrarchan sonnets in addition to the strambotti, *terze rime*, and barzellette that were the *poesia per musica* of the moment. Music on texts associated with the *improvvisatori* was beginning to be recorded in manuscript collections; it could thus become known in areas outside its place of origin, though written music did not satisfy the felt need to hear singers versed in its style.

Musicians from the realm of Naples did try their fortunes in the north of Italy, appearing at the Sforza court in Milan and elsewhere. The retinue of the Neapolitan princess Eleanora d'Aragona, who married Ercole d'Este in 1473, certainly included musicians, and at Ferrara the newly fashionable vernacular song mingled with northern polyphony, represented by the Estense chapel under Johannes Martini, and the local *improvvisatori*, of whom the celebrated Pietrobono was chief.[57] It was in this atmosphere that Isa-

56. These include Escorial MS IV.a.24, the Mellon Chansonnier, Montecassino MS 871, and Perugia MS 431. See Allan W. Atlas, "On the Provenance of the Manuscript Perugia, Biblioteca Comunale Augusta, 431 (G 20)," *Musica Disciplina* 31 (1977), 45–105.
57. Pietrobono, for many years the most important lute singer at the Ferrarese court, made several trips to Naples in the 1470s and 1480s. See Lewis Lockwood,

bella d'Este grew up, and when she left Ferrara for Mantua as the bride of Francesco Gonzaga she began her long career as patroness of poets and musicians.

Amid the flow of strambotti (now mostly written in a formal scheme identical to that of the *ottava* stanza) by well-known poets such as Luigi Pulci, as well as by countless amateur rhymesters, a new repertory of *poesia per musica* was developing, some of it Petrarchistic in language but much of it deliberately anti-Petrarchan, written in popular octosyllabic verse of a jesting, sometimes mockamorous cast; the barzelletta, humble descendant of the trecento ballata, was its commonest form. *Capitoli* in *terza rima*, long a staple of the improvisers' art, also appeared from the pens of a new generation of poets, as did *ode*, four-line stanzas of unpretentious language, often of a moralizing cast. The more Petrarchistically inclined poets were writing sonnets as well; the printing of Petrarch's *Canzoniere* in 1470 made its contents more easily available, and the compilation of personal *canzonieri* by poets such as Sannazzaro began at this time. With the advice of the poet Galeotto del Carretto, Isabella d'Este collected poems and if possible their authors, men such as Niccolò da Correggio, Antonio Tebaldeo, and Vincenzo Calmeta.[58] Poems were circulated by letter, and musicians employed specially for the purpose were asked to set them.

The most famous musicians associated with the frottola are not Neapolitan but Veronese: Marchetto Cara and Bartolomeo Tromboncino, both in the employ of the Gonzaga court. Neither of these men was active as a poet;[59] and although they were well known as performers they do not fit into the category of *improvvisatori*. In

"Pietrobono and the Instrumental Tradition at Ferrara in the Fifteenth Century," *Rivista italiana di musicologia* 10 (1975), 115–33.

58. Walter H. Rubsamen, *Literary Sources of Secular Music in Italy (ca. 1500)* (Berkeley, 1943). For a Mantuan collection of frottolistic verse see Claudio Gallico, *Un libro di poesia per musica dell'epoca d'Isabella d'Este* (Mantua, 1961).

59. According to William F. Prizer, *Courtly Pastimes: The Frottole of Marchetto Cara* (Ann Arbor, 1980), p. 41, Cara did write both words and music for one barzelletta in Petrucci's fifth book; and Prizer cites a letter of Cara to Federico Gonzaga discussing poetry. The indication "M. C. C. V." given by Petrucci for the barzelletta *A lo absentia* could mean something like "Marchetto Cara Cantor Veronensis"; Petrucci usually says "C. & V." when abbreviating "Cantus et Verba." But it took no great skill to write a barzelletta, after all; and though musicians like Cara were ordinarily given texts to set, enough to keep them busy, they may well have written one on occasion themselves.

fact the frottolists as a whole seem to be a group of musicians who wrote settings of fashionable verse on commission; only rarely in Petrucci's prints does one find the statement "Cantus et Verba" after a composer's name, indicating that the musician wrote his own poetry.[60] They did supply musical models for the use of others to declaim poetry; there are twelve of these in Petrucci's ten surviving books of frottolas, called "modo" or "aer" and giving music for sonnets and *capitoli* and, unspecifically, for Latin verses. There are none for barzellette, possibly because this verse form was less regular than the others; and, curiously, none for that favorite of the improviser's art, the strambotto. A sample of these *arie* is given in Example 14, an anonymous and textless "modo di cantar sonetti," providing a simple means for dilettantes of the frottola to sing their own verse or that of a friend.[61] Note that the top voice alone seems designed for singing, over a supporting bass and two filler parts that may or may not have been performed exactly as written. The quatrains of a sonnet would be sung using repetition of the middle phrase for the two interior lines; the terzets would use the three phrases sung straight through. The many repeated notes in the melody would allow for varied word accents and thus give the performer a good deal of flexibility.

Composers of frottolas were sometimes Church musicians as well, and some of them, like Cara, had received sound technical training.[62] They were not composers of Masses and motets, any more than the French musicians in various Italian chapels were—except for a few stray pieces—composers of frottolas. The simple texture and vivid declamation of the lauda, the frottola, and the Florentine carnival song may have influenced the polyphonic style of northern composers, but that is another subject. Still, the frot-

60. Michele Pesenti and Paolo Scotto are two frottolists who seem occasionally to have written their own texts, if the phrase "Cantus et Verba" after their names in the frottola volumes can be taken at face value. See the inventories of Petrucci's books in Knud Jeppesen, *La Frottola*, vol. 1 (Copenhagen, 1968). One amusing text proclaiming the composer as poet is Pesenti's "Questa e mia l'ho fatta mi / Non sia alcun ch'ardisca dire / Che non l'habbia fatta mi" (*Frottole libro primo* [1504], fol. 10).

61. Ex. 14 is transcribed from Petrucci, *Frottole libro quarto* (1505), fol. 14. The piece is printed in Rudolf Schwartz, ed., *Ottaviano dei Petrucci: Frottole, Buch I und IV* (Leipzig, 1935), p. 58.

62. Cara probably attended the Scuola degli accoliti in Verona (see Prizer, *Courtly Pastimes*, p. 49, and the sources cited there); and he was for a time *maestro di cappella* of the Gonzaga court chapel.

tolists were regarded as composers, not improvisers. A letter from Isabella d'Este explains that the musical setting of a text sent her by Cardinal Luigi d'Aragona could not yet be delivered because musicians "need time to compose, correct, and write down their compositions" (the musician in question was Cara).[63] The frottola thus occupies an intermediate position between the French chanson and the popular art of the improvisers—a position reflected in its style as well as its function.

The origins of the frottola are not entirely clear, but among them must be the vocal and instrumental traditions of improvised music in northern Italy, the strambotti of the South, and possibly some Spanish music by way of the Neapolitan court, where the contemporary *villancico* was well known.[64] The octosyllables of the barzelletta were sung to a lilting dance rhythm that matches and gives great verve to the singsong text rhythms, suggesting the popular appeal of the improviser's art but giving it in composed, "corrected" form, with inner voices written in contrapuntal style, as in Example 15, the *ripresa* of a barzelletta by Galeotto del Carretto set to music by Tromboncino. Carretto asked in a letter of 1497 to have this and other barzellette as set by Tromboncino sent to him, along with a new "aerea de capitulo."[65]

The literary level of the poetry of the frottola repertory has often been described in disparaging terms. This seems to me beside the point; it is clear that the poets were writing at the level, and in language, currently fashionable, ranging from Petrarchan borrowings to local dialect and snatches of popular verse. The *questione della lingua* could wait; for the moment it was entertainment that

63. Prizer, *Courtly Pastimes*, p. 40.

64. The *villancico* seems a strong candidate as a genre influencing the frottola, especially those barzellette of fairly simple chordal texture. (The influence could of course have been reciprocal.) Bass patterns characteristic of the *villancico*, often close to later-sixteenth-century patterned basses such as the *Romanesca* and *folia*, can be found in the frottola as well. See Edward E. Lowinsky, *Tonality and Atonality in Sixteenth-Century Music* (Berkeley, 1962), chap. 1, and the literature cited there. Lowinsky inclines to think that the direction of influence was from Italy to Spain; but Italian music earlier than the frottola repertory shows these characteristics only in pieces emanating from the South, where Spanish musical culture was strong.

65. See Alfred Einstein, *The Italian Madrigal* (Princeton, 1949), pp. 45–46. On the use of fifteenth-century *ballo* tunes in the frottola see the unpublished paper of William F. Prizer referred to above, n. 49. Ex. 15 is transcribed from Petrucci, *Frottola libro quinto* (1505), fol. 38ᵛ.

was wanted. And the music, which to me has great charm and more variety than it is often given credit for, suits the text extremely well, is indeed its servant in a way that trecento music never was. The aristocratic musical amateur as depicted in Castiglione's *Cortegiano* knew something of the art and had been taught to sing, to play a lute or viol, to read music. These people could not compete with virtuoso improvisers or with northern polyphonic singers, but they were more than just listeners; they wanted music they could perform themselves. And since many of them were amateur poets or had friends who were, they wanted not just French chansons but settings of the fashionable verse of the moment. The social milieu in which Italian song flourished at the end of the quattrocento was profoundly different from that of a century earlier. It is true that as Sacchetti wrote poems he sent them off to be set by local composers; but the results were rarely suitable for amateur performance. A kind of musical *embourgeoisement* had taken place in Italy; the seemingly infertile native musical culture of the quattrocento had in fact brought about a revolution in taste and a new relationship between word and tone.

·*III*·

The Early Madrigal:
Humanistic Theory in Practical Guise

THE WORD *madrigal* has entered ordinary English speech. It is listed in every dictionary, defined as a love poem set to part music, sometimes employing "madrigalisms (q.v.)"; note that its presumed rustic origins have been forgotten.[1] This is the sixteenth-century madrigal, which like the contemporary chanson enjoyed a tremendous and lasting national and international popularity. Madrigals were written and performed everywhere on the Italian peninsula, in Germany, Poland, and Scandinavia, and even—in transalpine linguistic dress—in England. Like its fourteenth-century predecessor, the cinquecento madrigal started life without benefit of very accurate definition; but before long the term became synonymous with the art of Italian secular song. In the seventeenth century the progressive madrigal transformed itself into the continuo song and the cantata; the more conservative side of the genre also lasted, if in somewhat attenuated condition, well into the Baroque age. Madrigal singing was revived earlier than almost any other species of "old" music;[2] and even today the singing of madrigals is central to

1. See C. T. Onions, ed., *The Shorter Oxford English Dictionary on Historical Principles*, 3d ed. (Oxford, 1973), p. 1256: "1. A short lyrical poem of amatory character. 2. *Mus.* An old style of contrapuntal unaccompanied part-song for several voices." Wordier, and of questionable accuracy, is the entry in *Webster's Third New International Dictionary of the English Language, Unabridged* (Springfield, Mass., 1976), p. 1357: "1. A medieval short lyrical poem esp. of love. 2a: A polyphonic part-song originating in the 14th century that has parts for three or more voices and is marked by the use of a secular text and a freely imitative style and counterpoint and that in its later development esp. in the 16th and 17th centuries is often marked by a distinctive melody in the upper voice and by being designed for accompaniment by strings that either double or replace one or more of the voice parts."
2. See Joseph Kerman, "Madrigal, iv," in *The New Grove Dictionary* 11:481.

the activity of early-music performing troups. To the perhaps prejudiced ear of the musician the fame of the Renaissance madrigal owes more to the beauty of the web of sound created by a long succession of composers—from Arcadelt through Rore, Lasso, and Wert to Marenzio and Monteverdi—than it does to the quality of the verse set. Demanding poetry like much of that of Tasso was difficult for musicians to come to terms with; and the *poesia per musica* of the sixteenth century is not on the whole distinguished or even very memorable. Only occasionally, as in happily achieved settings of Petrarch, or in the rare matching of poetry both good in itself and well suited for music, as with Sannazaro's or Guarini's pastoral verse, the pathos-laden stanzas of Tasso, or the lyric *ottave* of Ariosto, is there a really even blend of poetic and musical interest. Yet the great achievement of the madrigal is its success in making words sing; in this genre the fabled ideal of the antique concept of music as words in tone came to life as it never did in avowedly humanistic exercises, for even the noble experiment of *dramma in musica* that was the early opera owed its vitality to the expressive vocabulary developed by generations of madrigalian composers.

So familiar is this madrigal to us that we have to learn to be surprised at the choice of name. We should recall, however, that the trecento madrigal really did die, and that for a long time the term was out of use. Why it should have been revived in the sixteenth century is not altogether easy to explain. *Frottola* lasted surprisingly long as a generic name, considering its slightly pejorative associations (though its use in Petrucci's prints may mislead us into thinking that it was more generally used than it really was);[3] but it could not suit the taste of the vernacular humanists of the sixteenth century. Terms such as *ballata* still had formal connotations, however often the form might be violated in practice. *Canto* and *canzone* as terms for song in general were possible candidates, and they were used a good deal in the sixteenth century;[4] it looked for a time as if

3. Petrucci used the word in a generic sense, perhaps also as a synonym for *barzelletta*. The word is probably derived from the medieval Latin *frocta*, meaning a motley group, and always had a slightly pejorative connotation; in modern Italian it means a fib or minor lie. On *frocta* meaning poetry of slight consequence, as defined by Antonio da Tempo in the fourteenth century, see the citation in William F. Prizer, *Courtly Pastimes: The Frottole of Marchetto Cara* (Ann Arbor, 1980), p. 7.

4. Some representative titles from the first part of the sixteenth century are

canzone might well become the term in common use for poetry in musical setting in the cinquecento. The proud associations of the canzone with the *stil nuovo*, and the revival of the Petrarchan canzone as a verse form, surely stood in the way of its general adoption.

In 1507 Antonio da Tempo's *Summa artis rithmici vulgaris dictaminis*, one of the chief fourteenth-century treatises to describe the madrigal, appeared in print, doubtless published in the belief that there were readers with a nostalgic appreciation for trecento poetic art. One of these readers must have been Pietro Bembo, whose view of the madrigal as among the *rime libere*, with no fixed rhyme pattern and permitting free choice of seven- and eleven-syllable lines, can just about be reconciled with Antonio's allowance of various rhyme schemes and the presence or absence of a ritornello. (In any event the sixteenth-century madrigal often ends with a rhymed couplet serving as a kind of ritornello.) True, Bembo ignores the division of the madrigal into terzets and indeed its whole strophic nature, so he cannot be said to follow fourteenth-century precepts very closely. Strophic poems, apart from the canzone and cycles of *stanze*, were going out of fashion; the ballata certainly shows evidence of this, at least in the examples set by musicians.[5] Poets of Bembo's time knew what the fourteenth-century madrigal was like; they even imitated its formal schemes from time to time.[6] Perhaps the old reputation of the madrigal as *inordinatum* had somehow persisted and thus made the term attractive to sixteenth-century writers. There was a definite liking among poets of the early sixteenth century for a genre without fixed rules or repetition schemes. (We should recall that the *formes fixes* of French poetry were passing out of fashion at about this time.) Writing a canzone or even a sonnet took some work; a madrigal could be dashed off fairly easily, especially if one made use of the pocket Petrarch edition every amateur

---

Canzoni nove con alcuni scelte de varii libri (Rome, 1510), *Motetti e canzone libro primo* (Rome, ca. 1521), and *Canzoni, Frottole et Capitoli . . . Libro Primo de la Croce* (Rome, 1526). In the late sixteenth century the term *canzone* was also used in a quite different sense, as an abbreviation for *canzone alla napolitana*.

5. See Don Harrán, "Verse Types in the Early Madrigal," *Journal of the American Musicological Society* 22 (1969), 27–53, esp. 30–36.

6. Sannazaro's *Quando vostri begli occhi un caro velo*, for example, uses the rhyme scheme of Petrarch's *Nova angioletta*. On this and other imitations of the trecento madrigal see Ulrich Schulz-Buschhaus, *Das Madrigal: Zur Stilgeschichte der italienischen Lyrik zwischen Renaissance und Barock* (Bad Homburg, 1969), pp. 27–41.

poet carried with him. From the early sixteenth century on, many people must have felt as Antonfrancesco Grazzini (il Lasca) later put it: "Non tengo conto già di un madrigale, ch'io ne fo cento il giorno."[7] To bestow on this new genre of poetry—the rather fragile content of which was given a decorative dress of Petrarchistic language—a time-honored name was surely a nostalgic gesture toward a past age of greatness in vernacular literature. (Presumably no one in the sixteenth century cared or indeed knew anything about the music of the trecento madrigal; there was alas no Vasari in the field of music.)

I do not mean to imply that any one person named the new madrigal; the poetry was too chameleon-like, now resembling a ballata, now appearing to be a canzone stanza, sometimes so short and slight that one would be hard put to give it any name at all. The word itself appeared from time to time in the late fifteenth century; for example, Boiardo called a poem of his a madrigal because of its rustic subject material, a late reference to the madrigal's presumed origin.[8] By the time Bembo started work on the *Prose della vulgar lingua* during the reign of Leo X, the madrigal had achieved a kind of loose definition as a poetic genre; but the term was still used for any unpretentious kind of poem—apparently it had a better sound than the undignified *frottola*—just as the word *oda* dignified poetry that hardly justified such an honored name. As early as 1504 Vincenzo Calmeta referred to an otherwise unspecified body of poetry as *madrigali*; Cesare Gonzaga wrote to Isabella d'Este in 1510, enclosing what he called a *madrigaletto* for Marchetto Cara to set to music.[9] In 1521 Tromboncino informed the Venetian Senate that he had written music for many "Canzoni, madrigali, soneti, Capitoli et stramboti, Versi latine, et ode latine, et vulgar barzelete frotole et dialogi."[10] Note the high rank of the madrigal, now clearly achieving distinct status, in this list. By 1520 madrigalistic settings

7. Cited by Schulz-Buschhaus, *Das Madrigal*, p. 7n.
8. The poem is *Cantati meco inammorati augelli*. See F. Alberto Gallo, "Madrigale," in *Handwörterbuch der musikologische Terminologie*, ed. Hans-Heinrich Eggebrecht (Wiesbaden, 1972–), p. 6.
9. Vincenzo Calmeta, *Prose e lettere edite e inedite*, ed. Cecil Grayson (Bologna, 1959), p. 54, a letter to Isabella d'Este, dated from Urbino 5 November 1504, in which Calmeta speaks of the elegy "a ciò che dal sonetto e de le madrigali quanto al numero sia distinto." For Gonzaga's letter see Prizer, *Courtly Pastimes*, p. 39, doc. 50.
10. Cited in Knud Jeppesen, *La Frottola*, vol. 1 (Copenhagen, 1968), p. 147.

of madrigalistic verse were indeed being written, though not by Tromboncino and not in Mantua or the Veneto. The home of the new kind of song that was soon to conquer all of Italy was Florence.

In the first decade of the sixteenth century the Italian peninsula was undergoing turmoil not unlike that seen at the turn of the preceding century: the Neapolitan and Milanese states had collapsed; Florence had cast out the Medici, then Savonarola, and was uneasily trying to return to old republican ways; Venice seemed to prosper despite the animosity of Pope Julius II and the hostile envy of most Italian rulers, but the Venetians were heading toward the debacle of Agnadello; and nearly all of Italy still reeled from the effect of the French invasion of 1494–95, which should have disillusioned the most ardent Francophiles. There is no evidence that French music went out of style or that northern musicians were sent packing for ideological reasons, though of course the breakup of a court such as the Sforza establishment in Milan was followed by the departure of many who had served that court; nonetheless one should not discount a feeling of national, or at any rate Tuscan, patriotism as an ingredient in the rise of the madrigal.

No disasters from the outside overtook the small city-states of Mantua and Ferrara at this time, and there the poets and composers of the frottola continued to practice their art. This was, at least with regard to music, very much a local art; the barzellette of Cara, Tromboncino, and their fellow musicians seem to me in particular to be written in a local musical dialect, with occasional resemblance to the Spanish *villancico* but quite unlike the Italian pieces emanating from Neapolitan and Florentine circles. The strambotto as composed in the North and printed by Petrucci shows, on the other hand, much closer affinities with music of the 1470s and 1480s found in such sources as the Montecassino manuscript, which comes from Naples.[11] And the frottola remained rather localized in its sphere of influence. Judging from the provenance of its manuscript sources the Florentines hardly knew it; and though a few

11. A few pieces in Neapolitan sources do suggest the northern barzelletta style of the next generation; an example is *Alle stamenge donne*, in Montecassino, Arch. della Badia MS 871, no. 133. See Isabel Pope and Masakata Kanazawa, eds., *The Musical Manuscript Montecassino 871* (Oxford, 1978), p. 508; Federico Ghisi, "Canzoni profane italiane del secondo quattrocento in un codice musicale di Montecassino," *Revue belge de musicologie* 2 (1948), 8–20, esp. 15.

frottola collections were printed in Rome, Naples, and Siena, the frottola seems to have enjoyed only limited popularity outside the Veneto and the Po valley. This repertory remained essentially one of solo song. Very few of the frottolas printed by Petrucci look as if they were intended for four singers; the middle parts, even when they do not jump about nervously, remain fillers, and the bass lines often resemble dance-tune formulas that must have been in common use among instrumentalists. Frottolas as Petrucci prints them do not have text provided for the lower voices; those that do seem fully vocal in character may have been intended for special purposes, such as choral interludes in spectacles.[12] A few frottolists, among them the aging Cara, tried their hand at the new madrigal style, but the results are not very convincing.[13] Of course there is some stylistic overlap between frottola and madrigal. For the most part, however, the melodic and rhythmic imagination of the frottolists seems dominated by the trochaic octosyllables of the barzellette they knew so well; when it sets other kinds of verse their music seems much less self-assured, lacking crispness and definition.

French music remained dominant in Italy in the early years of the sixteenth century; but along with the classical chanson of Josquin des Prez and his contemporaries there were within the repertory of the chanson new currents that were to be of decisive importance for Italian music. The long dominance of the solo song with accompaniment had gradually given way in the later fifteenth century to a polyphonic texture in which the inner parts, or at any rate the tenor, approached the upper voice in character and importance. When four-voice writing came to replace compositions for three voices as the norm, this movement toward equality of the voices gathered momentum. Music written just around the turn of the sixteenth century shows in addition a greater emphasis on syllabic declamation of text and a decidedly increased use of melodic motives each conceived for a particular phrase of text and each shared in imitative exchange among all the voices. These stylistic

12. On this see Nino Pirrotta and Elena Povoledo, *Li due Orfei da Poliziano a Monteverdi* (Turin, 1969), pp. 57–106; pp. 37–75 in the English version, *Music and Theatre from Poliziano to Monteverdi*, trans. Karen Eales (Cambridge, 1981).

13. For a discussion of Cara's "madrigalistic" style see Prizer, *Courtly Pastimes*, pp. 129ff., 147–51.

changes are not of course unique to the chanson; they are seen in the motet, perhaps the most experimental genre of the day, and even in the more conservative Mass cycle. The chanson may indeed be the most conservative genre of French music near the end of the fifteenth century; but this statement would hold true only for the "classical" style of the successors of Dufay, not for chansons using currently popular tunes or those influenced by Italian modes of singing.

Once again the question of Italian influence arises. The style of Italian music at the close of the fourteenth century, itself affected by French musical thought, is said to have exerted an influence on the chanson writing of the young Dufay and his contemporaries.[14] Does this story repeat itself? Were musicians like Isaac and Agricola affected by the Florentine carnival song? Were Josquin and the many other French composers who lived in or passed through Milan, Ferrara, and the cities of the Veneto struck by the art of the frottolists? Were all visitors to Italy influenced by the singing of laude, so different from the liturgical and devotional polyphony of the princely chapels? The answer to these questions could hardly be no; but the nature and extent of Italian influence on French music are very uncertain and hard to pinpoint. Far easier to demonstrate is the effect the new French style, whatever may have been its origins, had on Italian music after about 1515.

An example of the new French chanson style will be helpful here. The piece given in Example 16 is from Petrucci's *Canti B* (1502), there ascribed to Antoine Brumel, a composer who joined the chapel of Alfonso I d'Este around 1505. There is no text other than the incipit "Noé, noé, noé."[15] This work might seem a poor choice for a discussion of words and music; yet the piece is so obviously conceived for words and so typical of the equal-voiced texture of the new chanson that it actually serves my purpose well (I

14. See Heinrich Besseler, "Dufay in Rom," *Archiv für Musikwissenschaft* 15 (1958), 1–19; Kurt von Fischer, "On the Technique, Origin, and Evolution of Italian Trecento Music," *The Musical Quarterly* 47 (1961), 56–57.

15. Petrucci, *Canti B* (1502), fol. 28ᵛ. See Helen Hewitt, ed., *Canti B numero cinquanta, Venice, 1502* (Chicago, 1967), pp. 161–63. Ex. 16 is given after Professor Hewitt's transcription, but I have omitted the Latin text given by her as found in a later German concordance; it is clearly not the original text and fits the music quite clumsily.

have added repetitions of "noé, noé" everywhere to give the singers something to say; they fit very easily).[16] Note that after the sparingly decorated chordal writing of the first section (mm. 1–20) a series of imitative exchanges begins among all the voices; the top part does not necessarily lead, temporally or in any other way. (For instance, the obvious anacrusis of the phrase beginning in measure 21 is given to the superius on the downbeat.) The prolonged melodic and harmonic sequence beginning in measure 33 has been the subject of debate with regard to its tonal character, not a pertinent issue here.[17]

Of relevance to this discussion is the fact that in a piece conceived, as this one is, for four voices of equal importance, delivering their words and melody in staggered imitation, one does not automatically think of the text as being presented by a single person—that is, by four singers acting as one. It can also be construed as four separate though harmonious readings of one text. If "noé, noé" is part of a prayer the piece could be thought of as an act of communal worship, welling up from all sides; but if one imagines a descriptive or frankly secular text for this music that interpretation would not serve. This point is to me an important one, its very obviousness adding to its significance. In the solo-song tradition that had hitherto prevailed, a song could be equated with a single reading of a poem. This would not hold completely for the trecento madrigal, where the lower voice, whether completely or only partially subordinate to the upper line, was considered an integral part of the piece; but in trecento music this lower voice was, I think, a vocal stylization of an instrumental accompaniment, not a vocal *persona*; besides, trecento madrigals are not readings of their poems in the sense I mean here. For the music of the quattrocento and most of the frottola literature the solo concept does prevail. If we look upon the new style of the early sixteenth century as the adoption of a convention whereby several voices are meant to represent one person, my point loses much of its force. Even in music

16. There are a number of "noé" pieces in the sixteenth-century chanson and motet repertory, some with Latin, others with French, texts following. Barton Hudson, "Brumel," in *The New Grove Dictionary* 2:380, considers Ex. 16 a sacred piece, but it is certainly not a liturgical one.

17. See the remarks of Edward Lowinsky on this piece, in his introduction to Hewitt, *Canti B*, pp. xi–xiv.

that uses the same material for all voice parts, however, the difference in timbre among the voices will always be noticeable. Singers now think, and perhaps always thought, of the part they sing as their version of the song; and in both chanson and madrigal contrasting melodic material is used for the same texts. In the madrigal this diversity of material is at first limited; it grows as the genre matures, and in the later madrigal, as we shall see, textual as well as musical contrast is employed in the presentation of the poetry. The existence of verbal as well as musical counterpoint is thus made possible, and a song may come to represent not just a straightforward declamation of text but a ruminative, many-layered reading of it. Although discussions of the musical innovations of the early sixteenth century have stressed the text-oriented quality of the melodic writing and the contrapuntal equality of the voices, the meaning of this combination for the profound change in relationship between words and music has, I think, been taken for granted or overlooked.

The solo song did not of course disappear in the sixteenth century. The improvisatory tradition was necessarily a solo one; lute singers and viol singers continued to be sought after; writers of humanistic bent placed solo song above all other categories of music; and polyphonic madrigals could be sung as solos with accompaniment. More than a few traces of solo-song writing can be found in the early madrigal and in occasional pieces later on; and the revival of the written solo song in the later sixteenth century is an important phenomenon. Nevertheless it seems to me that the nearly equal-voiced polyphony of the early sixteenth century represents a fundamental change in the character of song literature.

Some of the newer kinds of chansons dating from the turn of the century must have been known to the frottolists. Certainly the use of popular tunes as tenors, practiced in the *chanson rustique* popular at the court of Louis XII, seems to have had some influence; pieces with tenors and refrains drawn from popular tunes, probably later in date than most of the repertory of the *chanson rustique*, turn up in the frottola prints.[18] It also seems likely that the

18. For the popular tunes contained in the frottola repertory see Fausto Torrefranca, *Il segreto del quattrocento* (Milan, 1939); Knud Jeppesen, *La Frottola*, vol. 3, *Frottola und Volkslied: Zur musikalischen Überlieferung des folkloristischen Guts in der Frottola* (Copenhagen, 1970).

vogue of the quodlibet, a combination of textual and musical scraps drawn from various sources, including popular tunes, spread from France to Italy at this time.[19] The quodlibet is a marked feature of the *villota*, a genre of secular song that flourished in the Veneto in the first decades of the sixteenth century, more or less independently of the frottola. *Villote* are four-voice pieces using a combination of imitative polyphony and chordal declamation, very much after the fashion of the new chanson. The texts, which tend, as the name suggests, to refer to peasant life, are lively, and so is the music; some of these pieces were evidently popular successes, finding their way into printed collections of the 1520s and even turning up in some of the early manuscript sources of the madrigal.[20] Though many of these pieces are anonymous, from the few composers' names that we do have it appears that they are the work of Italian musicians. Curiously the declamatory patterns chosen to set the texts of the *villote* seem more French than Italian; the lilt of the frottola is absent, and so is the graceful rhythmic flow of the early madrigal. *Vrai dieu d'amor chi mi conforterà* (an Italian piece despite its half-French incipit) shows this French declamatory style (Ex. 17). The *villota* thus gives evidence of the adoption—at no very exalted level of technique or expression, to be sure—of the modern French chanson by Italian musicians, but not yet its total assimilation. It is possible that the so-called "madrigals" sung by Ruzzante and other entertainers at Ferrara and in Venetian circles in the 1520s were *villote* or something very like them.[21]

19. On popular tunes in French music at the turn of the sixteenth century see Howard Mayer Brown, "The *Chanson Rustique*: Popular Elements in the Fifteenth- and Sixteenth-Century Chanson," *Journal of the American Musicological Society* 12 (1958), 16–26; on the quodlibet (or *incatenatura* or *zibaldone*) in Italian music see Torrefranca, *Il segreto*, passim; Claudio Gallico, *Un canzoniere musicale italiano del cinquecento* (Florence, 1961), pp. 40–42.

20. The central focus of Torrefranca's *Il segreto del quattrocento* is the *villota*, and his book remains the most thorough study of the genre. Among the sources for the *villota* is a manuscript set of partbooks of the 1520s (Venice, Bibl. Marc. MS cl. ital. 1795–98), which also contains some early madrigals. See Francesco Luisi, ed., *Apografo miscellaneo marciano: Frottole Canzoni e Madrigali con alcuni alla pavana in villanesco* (Venice, 1979).

21. *Vrai dieu d'amor* is transcribed from Bologna, Civ. Mus. Bibl. Mus. MS Q 21, no. 46, where it is attributed to "F. P." See Torrefranca, *Il segreto*, p. 529, and Gallico, *Un canzoniere*, p. 100, on the composer and his putative identification as fra Piero da Hostia. Jeppesen, *La Frottola* 1:66, identifies the composer as Francesco Patavino. On the "madrigals" of Ruzzante sung at a banquet in Ferrara, see Howard Mayer Brown, "A Cook's Tour of Ferrara in 1529," *Rivista italiana di musicologia* 10 (1975), 216–41, esp. 224–25.

During the second decade of the century the *villota* and later additions to the frottola repertory in the North (and also in Naples, the work of the youthful Giovan Tomaso di Maio), as well as the carnival song and a noticeable revival of the ballata in Florence, help to fill a gap, once termed an "artistic pause," between Petrucci's frottola prints and the first appearance of madrigals in manuscripts dating from the late 1520s.[22] Apparently there was not a great deal of new Italian music in wide circulation during this period, for the printed collections of the 1520s, most of which come from Rome, have a strange blend of old and new music and an odd mixture of genres, including motets and chansons as well as frottolas, *villote*, and a few madrigals. This does not mean no music was being written, merely that it was circulating in manuscript among small groups of enthusiasts, some of whom may have commissioned and paid for musical settings that they then regarded as theirs. In this kind of society it is more remarkable that printers such as Petrucci, Andrea Antico, and Valerio Dorico got the music they did than that much music remained for a while—in some cases permanently—unpublished.

The traditional view of the early madrigal is that it evolved from the frottola as the result of two important developments: the turn toward verse of higher literary quality, observable in the later frottola, and the change from accompanied-solo texture to a style in which all four voices, now fully texted, take nearly equally important roles in presenting the poetry. I have argued elsewhere that this view has serious flaws, on grounds that will be restated in the following paragraphs.[23]

A basic weakness in the theory that the madrigal evolved from the frottola is that very few composers wrote in both genres. The frottola was popular in the cities of the Veneto and the Po valley, where its composers were employed; it seems not to have been in

22. "Artistic pause" is Alfred Einstein's expression (*The Italian Madrigal* [Princeton, 1949], p. 139). On this transitional period in Italian secular music see Walter H. Rubsamen, "From Frottola to Madrigal: The Changing Pattern of Secular Italian Vocal Music," in *Chanson and Madrigal, 1480–1530*, ed. James Haar (Cambridge, Mass., 1964), pp. 51–87; Frank D'Accone, "Transitional Text Forms and Settings in an Early-Sixteenth-Century Florentine Manuscript," in *Words and Music: The Scholar's View*, ed. Laurence Berman (Cambridge, Mass., 1972), pp. 29–58.

23. James Haar, "The Early Madrigal: A Re-appraisal of Its Sources and Its Character," in *Music in Medieval and Early Modern Europe*, ed. Iain Fenlon (Cambridge, 1981), pp. 163–92.

vogue in Florence, where nearly all the early madrigalists were active. There may have been more than one kind of madrigal at the beginning; the native Florentines setting Italian texts before the arrival of Philippe Verdelot (presumably in 1521) were working in a somewhat different vein, deriving from the Franco-Flemish tradition of Isaac, than that of Verdelot's chansonesque style.[24] I shall return to this Florentine protomadrigal. Once the new madrigal as represented by Verdelot began to circulate, it spread to Medici circles in Rome, where Verdelot is known to have visited in 1523. Costanzo Festa, a musician in papal service, is one of the small number of composers outside Florence to cultivate the madrigal at this time; Sebastiano Festa, about whose life and career we know little but who may have been in Rome in the 1520s, is another.[25] Madrigals were soon being written in Ferrara, though not by the older frottolists; Maître Jhan, Alfonso della Viola, and perhaps Adrian Willaert, before his departure for Venice in 1527, are the composers involved; Ferrarese-Roman contacts, through Cardinal Ippolito d'Este, seem the likeliest channel.[26] Notice that only three of the composers so far named are Italians: Costanzo and Sebastiano Festa and Alfonso della Viola. Some native Florentines could be added to the list; but, unlike the frottola, whose music is nearly all the work of Italians, the early madrigal is basically the achievement of northerners. If we accept the view that the madrigal is more closely related to the chanson than to any Italian genre this is not so

24. See Frank D'Accone, "Alessandro Coppini and Bartolomeo degli Organi, Two Florentine Composers of the Renaissance," *Analecta Musicologica* 4 (1967), 38–77; idem, "Bernardo Pisano: An Introduction to His Life and Works," *Musica Disciplina* 17 (1963), 115–35. Professor D'Accone has edited the works of these three composers and other Florentine madrigalists in vols. 1 and 2 of *Music of the Florentine Renaissance* (American Institute of Musicology, 1966–67). On Verdelot's background and career see H. Colin Slim, "Verdelot," in *The New Grove Dictionary* 19:631–35; on the date of his arrival in Florence see Richard Sherr, "Verdelot in Florence, Coppini in Rome, and the Singer 'La Fiore,'" *Journal of the American Musicological Society* 37 (1984), 402–4.

25. On Sebastiano Festa see Walter H. Rubsamen, "Sebastian Festa and the Early Madrigal," in *Gesellschaft für Musikforschung: Bericht über den internationalen musikwissenschaftlichen Kongress, Kassel, 1962*, ed. Georg Reichert and Martin Just (Kassel, 1963), pp. 112–26.

26. Ippolito I d'Este (d. 1520), Ariosto's patron, maintained a chapel and took musicians with him on his trips to Rome and elsewhere. See Lewis Lockwood, "Este," in *The New Grove Dictionary* 6:258–59; idem, "Jean Mouton and Jean Michel: French Music and Musicians in Italy, 1505–1520," *Journal of the American Musicological Society* 32 (1979), 197, 211, 214, 218ff.

surprising; and yet something has changed, for the older generations of northern composers working in Italy had only rarely set Italian texts. Now the *oltremontani* were being asked regularly, perhaps almost exclusively, to provide music for Italian poetry. Verdelot, who knew the style of the new chanson so well, has left us practically no chanson settings at all, and Arcadelt apparently wrote the bulk of his chansons after his return to the North in the 1550s.[27]

The argument that the frottola changed into the madrigal as the result of a rise in the literary standards of *poesia per musica* seems to me fundamentally unconvincing. It is true that sonnets appear more frequently in the later books of Petrucci's frottola prints, that a number of Petrarchan texts are included there, and that poets were busily imitating Petrarch, sometimes modeling their sonnets on individual poems from the *Canzoniere*, in the years around 1510.[28] But I think Petrarch's sonnets found their way into the repertory of the frottolists—where they mingle with strambotti and barzellette—not as the result of an urge toward self-improvement but in response to the demands of current fashion. The Petrarchism of poets writing in the early years of the sixteenth century was a kind of innocent preamble to the neo-Petrarchan movement of the 1520s; Bembo's early verse, some of it appearing in frottolistic settings, shows this clearly.[29] And the desire for musical settings of Petrarchan sonnets was, I believe, a response to the great vogue of Petrarch as declaimed by *improvvisatori*, men like Serafino and the Unico Aretino, at the turn of the century. The music supplied by composers such as Tromboncino for Petrarchan verse is not much different from that used for humbler poems; and when on occasion the frottolists attempted a more elaborate style the result strikes me as self-conscious and stylistically insecure.[30]

27. On Arcadelt's career and the approximate chronology of his work see Albert Seay, "Arcadelt," in *The New Grove Dictionary* 1:546–50.

28. See Walter H. Rubsamen, *Literary Sources of Secular Music in Italy (ca. 1500)* (Berkeley, 1943), p. 24.

29. See Pietro Floriani, "La giovinezza umanistica di Pietro Bembo fino al periodo ferrarese," *Giornale storico della letteratura italiana* 143 (1967), 25–71. About the Petrarchism of the frottolistic period Floriani says that it was based on "uno schema, ormai meccanico, della psicologia amorosa"; even the vocabulary was "piuttosto libero, o almeno non sottoposto ad un canone rigoroso di 'linguaggio poetico'" (p. 59).

30. See Einstein, *Italian Madrigal*, p. 104ff., on the tentative character of the Petrarchan settings of Tromboncino and Cara.

The sonnet is usually handled by the frottolists as if it were a sub-species of the ballata, with repeated musical phrases; through-composed settings of such a long scheme do not work well in this style (the sonnet was, for that matter, to prove difficult for the first generation of madrigalists as well).[31]

As for the poetry of the early madrigal, I do not see why it should be thought so much better than that of the frottolists. The style of the lover's complaint changes from the "Io son l'uccello che non pò volare" of the strambotto to the "Madonna, io v'amo et taccio" of the madrigal; that is, however, only a change in the fashion of poetic dress. The octosyllabic verse of the barzelletta disappears from the scene, though it will turn up again later; but if we compare the opening of a barzelletta we have already seen (Ex. 15) with that of a madrigal we will presently look at, is there such a difference in quality of poetic thought?

Se gran festa me mostrasti
  a la ritornata mia
per che già te cognoscia
  Donna mia non me gabasti.
  (Carretto, in Petrucci, *Frottole*,
  bk. V, fol. 38ᵛ)

Madonna, per voi ardo
  et voi non le credete;
perchè non pia quanto bella sete?
  (anon.; set by Verdelot
  [Slim, *A Gift* 2 : 353])

Neither text seems to me very distinguished; if the madrigal is more flexible in rhythm, the barzelletta has a kind of sturdy forthrightness compared to which the madrigal droops like a Pre-Raphaelite lily.

The "Madonna" text is typical of the poetry set by the first generation of madrigalists.[32] They chose Petrarch much less often than has been supposed, and when they did they selected stanzas from canzoni and sestine, as well as Petrarch's four madrigals, much more often than they did sonnets.[33] The sonnet is of course not the sole, or even the best, indicator of elevated literary tone; yet its comparatively infrequent use when placed against the large amount of ca-

31. The difficulties arose when composers turned from schematic, two-section form to through-composed settings of sonnets. See, for example, *Candida rose nata in dure spine* (a compilation from two Petrarchan sonnets) as set by Eustachio Romano in Petrucci, *Frottole libro undecimo* (1514), fol. 14ᵛ; the piece is discussed in Howard Mayer Brown and Edward Lowinsky, eds., *Eustachio Romano: Musica Duorum, Rome, 1521* (Chicago, 1975), pp. 16–17. Verdelot shows a similar hesitancy in dealing with the sonnet; see Haar, "The Early Madrigal," pp. 84–89.

32. On the vogue of "Madonna" texts see Einstein, *Italian Madrigal*, p. 174ff.

33. Haar, "The Early Madrigal," pp. 172–73.

sual madrigalistic verse set in the early years of the madrigal tells us that this new repertory, while different in poetic and musical character from that of the frottolists, was not necessarily more ambitious in artistic aim. Members of the Florentine educated classes such as Lorenzo Strozzi, Niccolò Machiavelli, and Lodovico Martelli wrote poems or circulated verse written by poets they knew, men like Claudio Tolomei and Luigi Cassola, many of them with Roman connections that led easily to Florence in the period of the Medici papacies.[34] They commissioned musicians to set this poetry much as the Gonzaga and Estense and their courtiers had commissioned frottolas; and as the madrigal began to spread, the same patterns of exchange and commission were used in Rome, Ferrara, and eventually nearly every city, large or small, in Italy.[35] The madrigals were sung by a mix of amateur and professional musicians gathered in *accademie*; they were collected into manuscript partbooks, of which a fair number survive.[36] A few stray pieces found their way into print at an early date; but the history of the published madrigal really begins with two collected editions, one of the works of Verdelot beginning in 1533, the other of Arcadelt's madrigals starting probably in 1538. By the time these collections were made the first period in the history of the madrigal was drawing to a close.

The other half of the frottola-into-madrigal hypothesis is the argument that by a process of gradual change composers began to underlay text to all parts of their music and thus to conceive the music as vocal polyphony rather than as solo song.[37] I said earlier that I believe this process took place in the French chanson at the end of the fifteenth century, and that the new chanson influenced the frottola to some degree and the madrigal to a very large one. Some clarification is in order here. First of all, by "process of gradual change" I do not mean that text seeped like molasses from one

34. For Strozzi, see D'Accone, "Transitional Text Forms," p. 32f.; for Machiavelli and Martelli see H. Colin Slim, *A Gift of Madrigals and Motets*, 2 vols. (Chicago, 1972), 1:85–87.

35. For a reference to Willaert's being asked (in 1534) to set individual poems, see Richard J. Agee, "Ruberto Strozzi and the Early Madrigal," *Journal of the American Musicological Society* 36 (1983), 1. See also below, chap. 5, n. 4.

36. On the sources of the early madrigal see Haar, "The Early Madrigal," p. 166ff.

37. This view is held by Alfred Einstein and Walter Rubsamen; see the latter's "From Frottola to Madrigal," p. 58ff.

voice to another, first to the tenor and then to the bass and alto, even if texted duos with instrumental accompaniment are one of the possible ways to perform late-fifteenth-century chansons; I mean rather that the transfer of techniques and concepts from sacred polyphony, which had a long tradition of fully vocal performance, to secular song took a long time gaining full acceptance.[38] Composers of secular music were usually trained and active in the making of sacred polyphony, and the transfer of techniques that worked and that clearly gave aesthetic satisfaction was an easy one. The tradition of solo song was nonetheless deeply rooted, both historically and by the very nature of the texts it set. Indeed there is something artificial about the use of vocal polyphony, based in concepts of communal worship, for music accompanying texts that stress individual thought and feeling. Perhaps this is why early secular polyphony often took the form of the round canon, a genre emphasizing the individuality of each participant; and surely choral refrains in dance songs, common in several European countries, must originally have stressed communal sentiment in contrast to the text of the solo sections.[39] Two of the most perceptive scholars to deal with the music of the Italian Renaissance, Alfred Einstein and Nino Pirrotta, have each in his own way seen secular polyphony as a kind of aberration, in Pirrotta's view a *maniera* imposed on the essentially soloistic tradition of song.[40]

It is tempting to speculate on how such a change took place. One aspect of the process is purely graphic: the use of choirbook format, in which all parts of a composition are on a single page or a single opening of one book, and the text residuum is entered on whatever empty space remains, gives way to employment of part-

38. Not all sacred polyphony of the mid and late fifteenth century has full text throughout, although this does not mean that the parts were not sung; in some places, such as the Sistine Chapel and Cambrai Cathedral, no instruments—not even the organ—were used in polyphonic music. See Craig M. Wright, "Dufay at Cambrai: Discoveries and Revisions," *Journal of the American Musicological Society* 28 (1975), 199–202.

39. In the early-sixteenth-century MS Florence, Bibl. del Conserv. B 2440, there are ballatas with text for all voices in the *ripresa* but for the top voice only in the stanza. See Rubsamen, "From Frottola to Madrigal," and the remarks of Nino Pirrotta in the discussion following the paper (pp. 59–60, 74–75).

40. Nino Pirrotta, "Novelty and Renewal in Italy, 1300–1600," in *Studien zur Tradition in der Musik: Kurt von Fischer zum 60. Geburtstag*, ed. H. H. Eggebrecht and Max Lütolf (Munich, 1973), p. 60.

books in which each vocal part, whether sung or played by a single person or a group, is notated in a separate book. This happened first in sacred music, and even there it was resisted in conservative places such as the Sistine Chapel. When Petrucci began to print part music he used partbooks for sacred music, single volumes (of surprisingly small size and thus not choirbooks in one sense of the word) for secular music; the appearance in 1520 of Bernardo Pisano's music to texts by Petrarch and others marked the beginning of the use of partbooks for secular song.[41] This graphic innovation was surely made for the sake of convenience, and was at first not fully grasped by the scribes who copied the music; in this period there are partbooks not fully texted and single-volume books with text in all voices.[42] It has had its share of inconvenience for modern students; sets of partbooks have not always been fully preserved, for one thing. And generations of musicologists have labored to score music transmitted in partbook form. Only recently have scholars, following the lead of enterprising performers of old music, come to see the real advantages of partbooks.

The fact that partbooks are convenient for performers, including modern ones who have learned how to sing from them, does not in itself mean that the music in each book need be sung to a full text. The clear priority of sacred music, for which fully vocal performance was the norm, in use of partbooks does suggest that more consideration of each voice as a partner in a full vocal *concentus* was now in the minds of composers of songs. Sacred and secular music were not yet regarded as identical in their approach to text setting; theorists who gave rules for how text and music should be accommodated to each other stressed, at least until the middle of the sixteenth century, the fact that their rules were meant primarily for Masses and motets, not for secular genres.[43] The distinction was never completely done away with; but by 1530 it had in practice be-

41. The change took place in manuscripts at about the same time; the manuscript sources of the 1520s are mostly partbooks.
42. This may in some cases be deliberate; see above, n. 39.
43. See, for example, the remarks of Giovanni Lanfranco (*Scintille di musica* [1533]): "Et cio sia detto inquanto alle Messe: & Motetti: Perche ne delle Canzoni Franzese: ne di Madrigali io non ne parlo"; cited by Don Harrán, "New Light on the Question of Text Underlay prior to Zarlino," *Acta Musicologica* 45 (1973), 24–50, esp. 44.

come so slight that modern scholars looking at the music of this period could refer to the madrigal as a kind of secular motet.[44]

All of this does not explain completely how the change from solo song to secular polyphony took place, and perhaps it says little about why such a transformation should have occurred. The whole phenomenon was probably not the result of conscious plan; in collections of early madrigals there are some pieces in which the upper part, or a soprano-tenor duo, is clearly of greater importance than the remaining voices, while other works show a fully equal distribution of melodic material. And I realize that the distinction I am drawing would not have been in the minds of sixteenth-century musicians in the way I am presenting it here. The real reason I am reluctant to see the madrigal as little more than a fully texted frottola is that I think the madrigal drew heavily for its conceptual and technical basis on a truly polyphonic genre, the chanson, whereas the frottola, remaining essentially soloistic, was affected by the new chanson style in a much more superficial way; in the madrigal as represented by the work of Verdelot and Costanzo Festa I see a clear break with the frottola, not an evolutionary change.

No one has seriously doubted that Florence was the birthplace of the madrigal. The circles of poets and patrons responsible for its early cultivation are less clearly defined. A Florentine brand of *petrarchismo*, proudly local and not much interested in Bembo's theories, did flourish in the first quarter of the century, according to the views of local writers of the next generation.[45] Literary questions were debated in the Orti Oricellari, and members of the Rucellai family were certainly active as patrons; Cosimo Rucellai wrote poetry himself.[46] Other well-known Florentines who wrote madrigal texts in this period are Lorenzo Strozzi, Lodovico Martelli, Luigi Alamanni, Francesco Guidetti, Benedetto Varchi, and Niccolò Machiavelli. It is clear that Verdelot was associated with these Floren-

44. The comparison goes back at least to mid-nineteenth-century historians of music. See August Wilhelm Ambros, *Geschichte der Musik*, vol. 3 (1868), 3d ed. (Leipzig, 1893), p. 495.

45. On this see Haar, "The Early Madrigal," p. 177.

46. On Cosimo Rucellai (d. 1519) see Niccolò Machiavelli, *Arte della Guerra*, I, i, in *Opere*, ed. Ezio Raimondi (Milan, 1966), p. 401. Machiavelli was evidently a close friend of Rucellai as well as of Lorenzo Strozzi, to whom the *Arte della Guerra* is dedicated. The Orti Oricellari were closed in 1522 when an anti-Medicean plot was discovered, but literary discussions of the kind held there surely continued to take place in Florence during the following decade.

tine *littérateurs* in the 1520s, just as Arcadelt was to be ready at hand to set texts given him in the Medicean Florence of the mid-1530s.[47] One literary discussion in the Rucellai gardens centered on a single Petrarchan canzone, according to Antonfrancesco Doni. A setting of this text, *Una donna più bella assai che'l sole*, may be found in a manuscript of Florentine provenance dating from the 1520s, and this certainly suggests close collaboration between literary figures and resident musicians.[48]

According to standard musicological accounts the founders of the madrigal are the Frenchman Philippe Verdelot, the gallicized Fleming Jacques Arcadelt, and the Italian Costanzo Festa.[49] This is certainly an oversimplification. First of all, Verdelot was much older than Arcadelt, and may even have died before the latter's arrival in Florence; Arcadelt's musical style seems to me clearly representative of the 1530s, Verdelot's of the 1520s. Festa is more difficult to categorize; he was older than Arcadelt, but lived long and was active as a composer for nearly thirty years.[50] Most of his madrigals seem from their style to be relatively early, though some pieces appear to show knowledge of what Arcadelt was doing. He is not known ever to have lived in Florence, but he certainly understood the Florentine madrigal. The whole question is complicated by conflicting attributions in the sources, and made difficult both by the relative homogeneity of style in the early madrigal and by the bluntness of our stylistic perceptions of this music.

Other musicians have been proposed as cofounders of the madrigal. Sebastiano Festa, whose small output was published in Rome in the later 1520s, did set Petrarchan verse in chansonesque style.[51] Another Roman contender is Elzéar Genet (named Carpentras

47. Verdelot and Machiavelli must, for example, have worked together closely on the canzoni set by the composer for performances of *La Clizia* and *La Mandragola*. See Slim, *A Gift* 1:92ff.; Pirrotta, *Music and Theatre*, pp. 130–41.

48. See Antonfrancesco Doni, *I Marmi* (1552), ed. Ezio Chiorboli (Bari, 1929), 1:202ff. The piece in question is in Bologna, Civ. Mus. Bibl. Mus. MS Q 21; see Gallico, *Un canzoniere*, p. 88.

49. Einstein, *Italian Madrigal*, chap. 3: "The Early Madrigal."

50. On Festa's career as a composer of madrigals see Iain Fenlon and James Haar, "Fonti e cronologia dei madrigali di Costanzo Festa," *Rivista italiana di musicologia* 13 (1978), 212–42. On an early visit (1514) by Festa to Ferrara (and thus the earliest documented notice of his activity) see Lewis Lockwood, "Jean Mouton and Jean Michel," p. 230.

51. See, for example, the pieces by Sebastiano Festa in William F. Prizer, ed., *Libro Primo de la Croce (Rome: Pasoti and Dorico, 1526)* (Madison, 1978).

after his native city), a papal singer whose Italian secular output is clearly influenced by the early-sixteenth-century chanson.[52] Frank D'Accone has suggested that the madrigal rises in part out of the activity of a group of Florentine composers including Bartolomeo degli Organi and Alessandro Coppini, in the generation born about 1470, Francesco Layolle and Bernardo Pisano, both born about 1490, and Francesco Corteccia and Matteo Rampollini, born around the turn of the century.[53] Although I agree that one can see in at least some of the music of the older composers in this list an effort to write Italian song in the new manner, in my view no stylistic synthesis is reached. Pisano's mature secular music, probably written partly in the Rome of Leo X, is contrapuntally elaborate, even somewhat fussy by comparison with that of Verdelot; again I fail to see the jelling of a style here. It looks very much as if all the ingredients of what was to become madrigalian style were present in Florence, but the recipe had not yet been fixed. In this view Verdelot, who may have been in Italy as early as 1510 though not in Florence before the early 1520s, acted not so much as innovator but rather as codifier, forming the madrigal into a compact and cohesive genre in much the way that Corelli assembled all the fragments of mid-seventeenth-century instrumental style into a neat package that served as a model for succeeding generations. Layolle, perhaps the most interesting of the native Florentines, shows on occasion Verdelot's compactness of style; at other times one sees in his music some waywardness, suggesting early compositional date or independence of outlook.[54] Corteccia belongs completely in the Verdelot-Arcadelt tradition, as does Rampollini.

To get a clear, if inevitably simplified, picture of the early Florentine madrigal we will look closely at two pieces, representative works by Verdelot and Arcadelt. Verdelot set a variety of textual forms, including some sonnets (or portions thereof), *ottava* stanzas, and madrigals in free form and in patterns related to the canzone or ballata.[55] Occasionally there is music by him for poetry

52. The Italian settings of Carpentras may be seen in Albert Seay, ed., *Elziarii Geneti (Carpentras): Opera Omnia*, vol. 5 (American Institute of Musicology, 1973).

53. See n. 24 above.

54. Layolle left Florence in 1521, but during his years of residence in Lyons he clearly kept in touch with Florentine literary and musical circles. See Agee, "Ruberto Strozzi," pp. 9–11.

55. See Donald Hersh (=Don Harrán), "Verdelot and the Early Madrigal" (Ph.D. diss., University of California, Berkeley), 1963, pp. 70–74, 87–91 and passim.

in traditional forms; an example is Machiavelli's *Amor io sento l'alma*, a ballata addressed to the singer Barbara Salutati.[56] Though only one stanza of text appears in the musical sources, a second stanza exists, and the piece is written so that the *ripresa* can be repeated and a second stanza sung. The pedal-point coda at the end could then be used to finish off the piece.[57] Whether this would have been done in practice I am not sure; it would have been possible of course only for singers who had all the text, not supplied in the surviving partbooks of the musical setting. This problem is a general one in the early madrigal, and indeed even for trecento music, where the musical sources often do not give the whole poem; the case in question is particularly interesting since the composer seems to have provided the means for singing the whole text, something not all the early madrigalists did.

As a general example of Verdelot's style the madrigal *Madonna, per voi ardo* will serve well (Ex. 18).[58] The anonymous poem, the beginning of which was cited earlier, is typical of the numerous "Donna" and "Madonna" texts of the period:

> Madonna, per voi ardo
>   et voi non lo credete;
> perchè non pia quanto bella sete?
>   Ogn'hora io miro et guardo.
> Se tanta crudeltà cangiar volete,
>   Donna, non v'accorgete
> che per voi moro et ardo?
>   Et per mirar vostra beltà infinita
> et voi sola servir bramo la vita.

It is hardly a masterpiece or an example of "high literary quality"; the alternation of long and short lines is nevertheless graceful, and the final couplet, though it lacks the twist of meaning often seen in the madrigal, does serve as a kind of ritornello.

Verdelot's setting, probably written in the mid-1520s, is typical

56. The piece is printed by Slim, *A Gift* 2 : 327.
57. See the fermatas in the music; and note that the music for the *volta* repeats that of the *ripresa* except for the two opening bars. On this point see H. Colin Slim, "Un coro della 'Tullia' di Lodovico Martelli messo in musica e attribuito a Philippe Verdelot," in *Firenze e la Toscana dei Medici nell'Europa del '500*, 3 vols. (Florence, 1980), pp. 509–10.
58. Ex. 18 is given after the Newberry MS as edited by Slim, *A Gift* 2 : 353. I have altered some of the editorial accidentals supplied by Professor Slim.

of his art in its sparingly decorated chordal texture.[59] Points of imitation, absent here, are used elsewhere by Verdelot, though they are less common than might be supposed. The text is set syllabically throughout, with the exception of a few cadential flourishes. Articulation by means of cadence formula is used only for the ends of poetic lines. The third and the last lines of text are repeated in full, one to closely similar and one to identical music; otherwise there is no repetition of text or music. Verdelot divides the poem into units of three plus two plus two plus two lines. The articulation between "Se tanta crudeltà cangiar volete" and "Donna, non v'accorgete" is the only surprise here; its purpose is to emphasize the vocative "Donna" in the same way the opening "Madonna" is stressed. The top voice is still the leading part, and a performance by solo singer with lute accompaniment is possible; such a version indeed exists.[60] All four parts are eminently singable. The rather low range suggests the possibility of performance by four male singers; but the top part could be sung by a woman.[61]

The text is set with due regard for the poetry as it would sound when read. The one exception in the top voice is at "Che per voi" (mm. 25–26). In the lower voices there are occasional departures from this strict standard, as at "non lo credete" (altus and tenor, m. 5); these are always simultaneously "corrected" by at least one other voice. (Even in the later madrigal the individuality of the voices gives way to communal principles of declamation in such places.) If we look closely at the upper voice, line by line, the care with which Verdelot accommodated his melodic writing to the poetry is evident. The opening line is almost motionless except for a slight swell on "Ma*donna*"; only the bit of syncopation at "per voi" differs from the way one would read the verse, and in one source this is smoothed out to ♩ ♩│♩ ♩│♩ ♩ ♩│♩.[62] "Et voi non lo credete" has a change of register for the shift from the opening address

---

59. The Newberry MS can be dated ca. 1527. See Slim, *A Gift* 1:35, 109.
60. It is among the pieces from Verdelot's first book of madrigals chosen by Willaert for intabulation in the *Intavolatura de li madrigali di Verdelotto* (1536). There is a facsimile of this volume (Florence, 1980) as well as a modern edition, edited by Bernard Thomas (London, 1980).
61. See Slim, *A Gift* 1:215, for a portrait of a woman holding this piece in her hand.
62. Florence, Bibl. del Conserv. MS B 2495, no. 2.

to the lover's plaint, expressed in a descending line. This line is a chanson formula, seen in countless French pieces of the period as a six-syllable, six-note figure; Verdelot converts it into madrigalesque formula by adding a seventh note, gracefully opening the cadence at the same time. "Perchè non pia quanto bella sete," repeated to stress the greater intensity of the lover's wail, has a lilting rhythm beginning with a highly characteristic anacrusis of three repeated notes; here the lower voices finish the line with strong delivery of "bella sete" while the soprano provides musical emphasis with an ornamental cadence. The next two lines are almost recited; the melodic lines are carefully shaped but deliberately unmemorable, and the text is declaimed in the most straightforward fashion. By chance or by design the cadential flourish at measure 20 coincides with the words "cangiar volete." The piece reaches its restrained climax at "Donna, non v'accorgete," but even that line droops sighingly to its conclusion. "Che per voi moro et ardo?," divided musically after the fashion of Josquinesque polyphony, seems a bit frivolous in this context, though it does provide good contrast with the intensity of the preceding line. The final couplet, emphasized by the repetition of the last line, is reminiscent tonally and to some extent melodically of measures 5–14. (The opening of the piece is, characteristically, not referred to.) The top voice has the range of an octave, but the melodic line is centered in two fourths, D–G and G–C, tetrachords of the second or Hypodorian mode, seen here in transposition. This mode was in fact much used by madrigalists for the expression of lovers' laments.[63] The frequent use of repeated notes and of even or gently swaying rhythms brings the declamation very close to a reading of the text, an effect heightened by the use of rests and upbeat patterns suggesting slight pauses between lines in that reading.

What has been said here about the top voice could be applied to the other voices as well; even the harmonically conceived skips of the bass rise and fall at just the right places to suit the words. As I have noted, the lower voices correct or emphasize the declamation to the soprano from time to time. Although this piece may be said

63. On this see my "The *Madrigale Arioso*: A Mid-century Development in the Cinquecento Madrigal," *Studi musicali* 12 (1983), 203–19.

to represent primarily a single reading of the poem by four singers acting as one, it might also be seen as four readings by like-minded interpreters who only occasionally give a slightly different emphasis in their voices. Taken as a whole, Verdelot's *Madonna, per voi ardo* represents the early madrigal as a musical genre totally in the service of its text. With regard to its delivery of that text it might be said to achieve a musical realism, within its artificial polyphonic frame, equivalent to the realism of the frescoes of Domenico Ghirlandaio or the portraits of Giovanni Bellini.

Many early madrigals are more elaborate than this one musically, showing much use of imitative counterpoint though almost never without a few phrases declaimed chordally. An example by Verdelot's Florentine successor Arcadelt will show the early madrigal in perhaps its most attractive guise, with a balance of simultaneous and staggered declamation of text, and with some variety of melodic and rhythmic invention within the fundamentally placid style inherited from Verdelot. The madrigal *Quando col dolce suono* (Ex. 19) sets a text that may have been written by the Florentine historian Benedetto Varchi in response to a request from another Florentine, Ruberto Strozzi, then living in Venice; Strozzi asked for a poem in praise of the singer Pulisena Peccorina, the wife of a Florentine resident in Venice, with her name mentioned "del mezo del mandriale in giu."[64] The request is dated 1534, a time when Arcadelt is known to have been in Florence; the musical setting presumably dates from this time.[65]

> Quando col dolce suono
>   s'accordan le dolcissime parole
> ch'escon fra bianche perl'e bei rubini,
>   maravigliando dico: hor come sono
> venuto in ciel che sì dappresso il sol(e)
>   rimiro ed odo accenti alt'e divini.
> O spirti pellegrini,
>   s'udeste Pulisena

64. Agee, "Ruberto Strozzi," pp. 1–2, 11–12.

65. The piece was printed in Arcadelt's *Primo libro*, the lost first edition of which appeared in 1538 or early in 1539; it is also found in Florence, Bibl. Naz. Cent. MS Magl. XIX, 99–102, compiled in the mid-1530s. It is given in Ex. 19, with one or

direste ben ch'udir doppia serena.
Io che veduto l'ho vi giuro ch'ella
è più che'l sol assai lucente e bella.

The opening two lines, the second borrowed from a Petrarchan sonnet, are a kind of motto for the art of the madrigal.[66] Arcadelt sets them with a hymnlike exordium for "Quando col dolce suono," followed by an imitative exchange for the "dolcissime parole," in which is introduced a dotted rhythm to be used a good deal in the piece. Notice that the vocal lines literally imitate rather than exactly reproduce each other in the second line of text; each singer has his own version or reading of the text. In the third line Arcadelt chooses a melodic and rhythmic figuration very close to that of the preceding verse, though here the musical imitation is much more nearly exact. The cadence ending the third line is reminiscent of that articulating the end of the first, as if the composer wanted to mark off the end of a first section of the poem; the text is indeed written in a free adaptation of a canzone, with two three-line *piedi* and a linking rhyme, "pellegrini," to the remainder of the verses.

As the piece continues, the formality of the opening is abandoned in favor of a setting that accommodates the meaning of the text more than its formal outlines. This is a bit surprising; we are used to thinking of the early-cinquecento madrigal as bound by the formal divisions of the poetry, still very much a line-by-line affair. It is in the Venetian madrigal of the 1540s, as practiced by Willaert and Cipriano de Rore, that the sense of the poetry has been thought to gain ascendancy over formal considerations. This repertory will be the subject of another chapter; here I will say only that I think both the formalism of the early madrigal and the irregularity of its second-generation style have been exaggerated. There are many differences between madrigals of the period 1520–35 and those of the 1540s and 1550s, but they do not lie exclusively in the area of formal freedom.

Arcadelt splits the fourth line with an audible break to mark the

two changes of detail, after the edition of Albert Seay, ed., *Jacobi Arcadelt: Opera Omnia*, vol. 2 (American Institute of Musicology, 1970), no. 45.

66. The borrowed line is line 10 of Petrarch's *Candido piè per l'erba fresca* (*Canzoniere*, clxv).

difference between "maravigliando dico" and what is then said; then he rushes through the first part of the speech, from "hor come sono" to the end of line 6 (m. 30), with hardly a break, and with some rhythmic imagery (m. 23) for the repetition of "che sì dappresso" as the infatuated admirer nears the warm sun of his adored one. If one looks closely one sees cadences of sorts to indicate caesuras and line endings (mm. 19, 21, 24), but there are no pauses and there is usually some overlapping, at least one voice beginning the new line as the others finish the old. "Et od'accenti alt'e divini" is reminiscent of "bianche perl'e bei rubini," but in such a subtle way that one hardly notices Arcadelt's acknowledgment of the end of the second *piede* of the poem. At "O spirti pellegrini" (m. 30) one expects a bit of chordal declamation; instead the composer gives each voice an exclamation of its own in imitative style, and the next two lines of text are united in a single musical phrase, hinting in the upper voice at a melodic recitation formula for the words "s'udeste Pulisena" (mm. 34–36). The final couplet is more conventional, yet even here the two lines are blended, so that Arcadelt has to compose a new beginning for the standard repetition of the final line (m. 50).

In its general stylistic vocabulary *Quando col dolce suono* stays within the bounds of the madrigal as Verdelot shaped it; but Arcadelt shows himself possessed of an expertise of technique and a flexibility of response to the text that point the way toward the developments of the mid-century madrigal. After an excursus on the tradition of the *improvvisatori* and the connection between the oral tradition and the madrigal, we will turn to a consideration of some of those mid-century developments.

Finally, although I included the word *humanism* in the title of this chapter I have hardly mentioned it since. The term is overworked in general in scholarly and popular writing on the Renaissance and so often misused in discussions of music that I considered not using it at all. Instead I left it, unexplained, in the title to emphasize the point that in the early madrigal one finds a rhetorically conceived declamation of text, coupled with the beginnings of a musical vocabulary adequate to meeting the intellectual and emotional demands of the verse. This combination went some way toward satisfying by modern standards the humanistic yearning for the perfect blend of word and tone that ancient music was thought to have achieved. It did so as the result of practical experiment almost untouched by humanistic theory, and it is not then surprising to find that the more self-consciously learned critics of the later sixteenth century found the madrigal anything but a fulfillment of humanistic aims. But that is a matter for still another chapter.

· IV ·

Improvvisatori and Their Relationship to Sixteenth-Century Music

WE DO NOT POSSESS all of the repertory of Italian song that was written down during the Renaissance; but for most of the period we have enough to be able to make informed judgments about poetic and musical styles and tastes, and to a lesser extent about modes and techniques of performance. Yet, as Nino Pirrotta has often reminded us, we should not be misled into thinking that we have anything like a complete knowledge of the secular musical culture of the Renaissance.[1] In fact, for the period from the middle of the fourteenth to nearly the middle of the sixteenth century, the music we have in our possession would have been unknown to most Italians of the time. A demographically oriented history of the period would give little attention to polyphonic music, an art cultivated by a small elite. It is difficult to make a study of the music popular in the Renaissance; the evidence is simply not there. Or rather it is not there in the form of written music, for the popular music of the Renaissance, and even some of its courtly manifestations, such as the music for aristocratic dance, was not written down.[2] There is plenty of circumstantial evidence suggesting that

1. The importance of the unwritten tradition in Italian music is a recurrent theme in Pirrotta's work. See, for example, Nino Pirrotta, "Tradizione orale e tradizione scritta nella musica," in *L'Ars Nova italiana del trecento* 2 (Certaldo, 1970), pp. 431–41.

2. A few fourteenth-century dances survive (in London, Brit. Lib. Add. MS 29987); and *bassadanza* tenors from the fifteenth century were recorded, but the music played by an ensemble of dance musicians is not completely recoverable. See W. Thomas Marrocco, *Inventory of Fifteenth-Century Bassedanze, Balli, and Balletti in Italian Dance Manuals*, Dance Research Annual, 13 (New York, 1981); Otto Kinkeldey, "Dance Tunes of the Fifteenth Century," in *Instrumental Music: A Conference at Isham Memorial Library, May 4, 1957*, ed. David G. Hughes (Cambridge, Mass., 1959), pp. 3–30, 89–152.

music and especially song were as much cultivated in this period as in any later one. We are all intrigued by subjects like "Daily Life in the Florence of the Medici";[3] and we would all like to know more about the popular music and song that formed a part of this life—not, I trust, out of a doctrinaire bias or sentimental feeling that popular music was intrinsically better than that patronized exclusively by aristocratic and educated circles, but out of a simple and very natural curiosity.

How can we learn about this side of Renaissance musical activity? Orally transmitted music has not had a very long life in Western culture—unless there were special reasons for preserving it, as was the case with the corpus of plainchant, kept intact and gradually added to for several centuries before it began to be written down in the ninth century. (Nothing survives of the secular music of this period.) Even children's songs change, though slowly; and it is well known that the texts of folk songs survive, not of course unaltered, far longer than their melodies.[4] The unwritten music of the Renaissance is lost and can never be recovered in any substantial way; nevertheless a good deal has been said, and still more can be said, about this vanished art.[5]

There seem to me to be two ways of approaching the subject. One is to collect whatever information can be found about poet-musicians who specialized in *cantari*, the generic name for poetry designed for improvised musical performance. This is not easy to do, for the material is sparse and thinly scattered through letters and archival documents, and the *cantari* that survive in written form—in all probability not very close to their original state—are mostly anonymous.[6] Fortunately the life of Serafino Aquilano, best

3. See, for example, J. Lucas-Debreton, *Daily Life in Florence in the Time of the Medici*, trans. A. Lytton Sells (New York, 1961), which has a few pages on music in Florentine life, more than one ordinarily finds in books of this kind.

4. This may be due largely to the fact that texts could be written down by people who were musically illiterate and could not write down tunes. On this see Charles Seeger, "Versions and Variants of 'Barbara Allen' in the Archives of American Song to 1940," in *Studies in Musicology, 1935–1975* (Berkeley, 1977), pp. 273–320.

5. Much can be written even in the total absence of surviving music. See, for example, Günther Wille, *Musica Romana: Die Bedeutung der Musik im Leben der Römer* (Amsterdam, 1967), an eight-hundred-page book about a culture that has left no actual music behind it.

6. There are a few exceptions, such as the work of Cieco Aretino or of Francesco Cieco, reputed author of the epic *Mambriano*.

known of all poet-musicians in the late fifteenth century, was told by a contemporary, Vincenzo Calmeta, forming the basis for modern study; and the work on the Ferrarese lute singer Pietrobono begun by Emil Haraszti and amplified and corrected by Lewis Lockwood offers a model of modern scholarship; but so far no other figures have fared as well.[7] Famous as many of these men were in their own time—the singer Antonio di Guido was probably the best-known musician in Florence in the mid fifteenth century—details of their careers seem, like their work, to have disappeared, leaving little trace of their existence.

The second approach, somewhat risky but possibly more rewarding, is to search for clues in written music of the material, perhaps even the style, of the improvisatory tradition. I shall try to show that such clues exist, more, I think, for the sixteenth century than for earlier periods, and that they tell us a good deal, though nothing like the whole story.

Many names were used for these poet-musicians: *improvvisatore, dicitore in rima, sonatore, cantore, cantatore, canterino, cantastorie, cantimbanco* (or *cantambanca, cantampanca,* etc.), even *ciarlatano* (or *cerretano*). This warns us that we are dealing not with a single category, perhaps not even with a single professional calling, but with a range of careers, from that of a recognized poet who cultivated a style— an *aria*—of his own, imitating popular culture if not by class background a part of it, through that of a performer valued at court for his skills in playing and singing his own impromptu verse along with the poetry of others (he might also be called a *citaredo*), to that of an itinerant street singer who set himself up in a piazza to entertain the crowd and perhaps sell trinkets and quack remedies. Examples of the first type include Leonardo Giustinian, who gave his name to a genre of fifteenth-century *poesia per musica*, and, at a lower social level, Niccolò d'Arezzo, an *improvvisatore* recognized by

7. Vincenzo Calmeta, *Prose e lettere edite e inedite*, ed. Cecil Grayson (Bologna, 1959), pp. 60–77: "Vita del facondo poeta vulgare Serafino Aquilano"; Emil Haraszti, "Pierre Bono, luthiste de Mathias Corvin," *Revue de musicologie* 31 (1949), 73–85; Lewis Lockwood, "Pietrobono and the Instrumental Tradition at Ferrara," *Rivista italiana di musicologia* 10 (1975), 115–33. In another study Haraszti collected a good deal of miscellaneous information about *improvvisatori*; see his "La technique des improvisateurs de langue vulgaire et de latin au quattrocento," *Revue belge de musicologie* 9 (1955), 12–31.

modern critics as a good poet.[8] Pietrobono, called "dal chitarrino" for his skill in playing stringed instruments but admired also as a singer, is an example of the second type. Though the *ciarlatani* at the bottom of the social scale are mostly forgotten, they were doubtless the most numerous and closest to popular tastes; in the sixteenth century they emerge from total obscurity as a class in the publication, usually anonymous, of *opuscoli*, little booklets of rhymes often based on passages from the epic romances of Pulci, Boiardo, and Ariosto.[9]

Three categories are no doubt insufficient. It is hard to place popular fourteenth-century poets such as Antonio Pucci, or Burchiello and his followers in fifteenth-century Florence, in the first category though their verses may have been sung by others. Not all the singers and instrumentalists gathered around the *signorie* of the Italian peninsula were improvisers, though more may have been, at least on occasion, than we know. And what I have called the lowest level was probably a very mixed group ranging from the literate and musically skilled to miserable hacks. *Canterini*—to use a term frequently seen in documents and corresponding to *cantari*, their work—are mentioned often but not as a distinct class or guild; only rarely, as in Perugia, where they were employed as town servants at the Palazzo dei Priori from the fourteenth through the sixteenth century, were they considered to have a licensed and salaried public function.[10]

The presence of improvisers, here better termed *cantastorie* since they were noted for the performance of chivalric epics based on Arthurian legend, on the *materia di Bretagna* (Tristan stories), and above all on the *materia di Francia* (stories about the court of

8. On Niccolò d'Arezzo see Domenico de Robertis, "L'esperienza poetica del quattrocento," in *Storia della letteratura italiana*, ed. Emilio Cecchi and Natalino Sapegno, vol. 2, *Il quattrocento e l'Ariosto* (Milan, 1966), p. 403.

9. See Giulio Cattin, "Formazione e attività delle cappelle polifoniche nelle cattedrali: La musica nella città," in *Storia della cultura veneta*, vol. 3 (Vicenza, 1981), p. 276n, on the *cantastorie* Antonio Farina and Giovanni detto il Fiorentino, "i quali mandarono alle stampe i testi di loro componimenti." A list of works using material from the *Orlando furioso*, including some pamphlets by *cantastorie*, may be found in G. Agnelli and G. Ravegnani, *Annali delle edizioni ariostee*, vol. 2 (Bologna, 1933), pp. 177–227.

10. See Armando Balduino, ed., *Cantari del trecento* (Milan, 1970), p. 255, where earlier literature on this subject is also cited.

Charlemagne and the feats of Orlando and his fellow knights), is documented from the mid thirteenth century on, sometimes in a negative way: they are forbidden to sing in a certain place or at a certain time, or altogether.[11] Though no clear line of descent can be drawn, these singers are surely the successors of the *giullari* of the troubadour period.[12] As Italy outgrew its feudal past the *cantastorie* indeed served to recreate this past in romantic terms, and an element of nostalgic sentiment, mixed with varying amounts of realism and satire, characterized the epic song of the *cantastorie* through the fourteenth and fifteenth centuries, becoming at last an important ingredient in the chivalric romances of Boiardo and Ariosto.[13]

During the fourteenth century the improvisers were to be heard all over Italy. Some of the *cantari*, based on chivalric, religious, ethical, and even contemporary subjects, were preserved in writing, usually in sources of later date.[14] This alters somewhat our notion of improvisation, though it does not mean that any of this poetry was widely known in written form. There is no reason why the *canterini*, many of whom were blind,[15] could not on occasion have dictated their work; and popular poems must have been sung by people other than their authors. No one thought it necessary to write down the melodies to which this poetry was sung. Indeed, the idea probably never occurred to anyone; "writers" of music belonged to a different class altogether from the *canterini*.

The popularity of this art continued to be great. At Osimo in the late fourteenth century the *cantastorie* in the piazza drew crowds away from church on Sundays and feast days, leading the town government to impose fines on the singers and their audience.[16] And a century later the physician Michele Savonarola, trusted friend of Borso d'Este (himself a lover of the improviser's art), confessed as a sin that he preferred hearing romances sung in the piazza to Ves-

---

11. Francesco Ugolini, *I cantari d'argomento classico* (Florence, 1933), p. 12.

12. Ugolini, *I cantari*, pp. 11–12, cites a thirteenth-century document in which a singer is referred to as *cantator* and also as *ioculator*. See also Balduino, *Cantari del trecento*, p. 12.

13. On this see Giovanni B. Bronzini, *Tradizione di stile aedico dai cantari al "Furioso"* (Florence, 1966).

14. Balduino, *Cantari del trecento*, p. 9.

15. See Pasquale Tuscano, ed., *Cantari inediti umbri e altri testi* (Bergamo, 1974), p. 39.

16. Ugolini, *I cantari*, pp. 12–13.

pers sung in church.[17] The continuing appeal of the *canterini* in the sixteenth century is attested to by many witnesses; the fact that a few of them printed their *poemetti* seems only to have helped them.[18] With some of their material recast as scenarios for the *commedia dell'arte*, the improvisers, who must always have possessed some degree of histrionic skill (just as actors, we are told by Andrea Calmo, were valued for their musical talents), added a new dimension to their art at the close of the sixteenth century.[19] Visitors to Italy in the seventeenth and eighteenth centuries nearly always commented on the poetry and music performed in the piazza. In the early nineteenth century this art was still to be seen and heard; Hans Christian Andersen observed it in the 1830s in Rome and Naples, and was so impressed that he made the hero of the novel he wrote as record of his Italian sojourn an *improvvisatore*, who sang his spontaneous verses at the opera in Naples (after a performance of *The Barber of Seville*!) and, in true Romantic fashion, at Paestum, where the hero leaned against an antique column, strummed his guitar, and sang, to a melody of his childhood, about his life's experience.[20] A twentieth-century scholar tells us that she heard an *improvvisatore*, again with guitar, in the mountains near Pistoia sing endlessly of the Great War of 1914–18.[21] Perhaps one no longer sees this in Italy today, though at street fairs throughout Europe Punch and Judy shows and other improvised entertainment are still popular. The appeal is enduring; I found myself stopping to look and listen in Berkeley's Sproul Plaza when performances of

17. Bronzini, *Tradizione di stile aedico*, p. 2. On Borso d'Este's patronage of *improvvisatori* see Giulio Bertoni, "Il Cieco di Ferrara e altri improvvisatori," *Giornale storico della letteratura italiana* 94 (1929), 272.

18. See above, n. 9.

19. On the musical aspects of the early *commedia dell'arte* see Nino Pirrotta, "La musica," in the article "Commedia dell'arte," in *Enciclopedia dello spettacolo*, vol. 3 (Rome, 1956), cols. 1222–24.

20. Hans Christian Andersen, *The Improvisatore; or, Life in Italy*, trans. Mary Howitt, 2 vols. (London, 1845), esp. 1:69, 75, 240; 2:26, 72, 81, 124. Andersen went to Italy in 1833, and was much struck by the character and appearance of the *improvvisatori* he encountered.

21. Bianca Becherini, "Un canto in panca fiorentino: Antonio di Guido," *Rivista musicale italiana* 50 (1948), 241. On the survival of *cantastorie* in the region around Verona see Giorgio Maria Cambiè, "Testi, problemi, personaggi della musica popolare," pp. 491–572, esp. pp. 557–60, and Marcello Conati, "La musica di tradizione orale nella provincia di Verona," pp. 575–648, esp. pp. 632–35, both in *La musica a Verona*, ed. G. B. Pighi (Verona, 1976).

various kinds were going on—partly to watch the reactions of the crowd and partly out of curiosity mingled with a sense that these performers were for all their occasional oddity somehow close to the center of our own popular culture.

The *cantastorie* were to be seen throughout Italy in the Renaissance, and there were certain places where they performed regularly. One favorite spot was the piazza in front of the Church of San Martino in Florence (Pl. 1), where they mounted a platform (*panca*), drew the audience's attention with some music, and began to declaim their poetic wares. A *cantimbanco* may have looked something like the woodcut illustrations for two sixteenth-century *opuscoli* of popular poetry reproduced in Plates 2 and 3. If the situation were a bit more formal the audience might all be seated, and the performer might be a more distinguished *improvvisatore* singing stanzas from a well-known poem, as shown in Plate 4; the musical instrument depicted here is probably a *lira da braccio*, with which chords could be played to support the song. By the late sixteenth century one might have seen a small group of singer-players, perhaps forming part of a *commedia dell'arte* troupe, as depicted in the Venetian scene shown in Plate 5. And an improvised play could be made from the materials so long sung by *cantastorie*; there is a seventeenth-century scenario based on the deeds of Orlando, illustrated after the fashion of the woodcuts and engravings used in editions of the *Orlando furioso*.[22]

The repertory of the *cantastorie* was large; if the anonymous poet of the fourteenth-century *Cantare di cantari* is to be believed, it ran from dozens of poems on some subjects to hundreds on another (the Round Table) to thousands on yet another (Roman history).[23] Very few of these poems were written down; from those that survive it seems that they were for the most part chains of *ottava rima* stanzas, opening with an appeal for attention and perhaps with a religious invocation, interspersed with remarks like "As I was saying, . . ." and full of changes of topic and characters who are dropped and later picked up, and ending not because the tale is

22. For a reference to this scenario, an "opera reale" on Orlando, see Carlo Grabher, "Ariosto," in *Enciclopedia dello spettacolo*, vol. 1 (Rome 1954), col. 854.
23. See Pio Rajna, "Il cantare dei cantari e il sirventese del Maestro di tutte le arti," *Zeitschrift für romanische Philologie* 2 (1878), 22–54, 419–37.

finished but because, as the authors say, they have gone on quite long enough.[24] However large the repertory of a single performer may have been, some kind of musical dress must have been welcome both to him (for support and as *aide-mémoire*) and to his audience (for variety). We do not know whether improvisers sang in any formal sense or merely declaimed verses to the sporadic sound of a plucked or bowed instrument. If they used preexisting melodies, as seems likely, these must have been stock tunes that were easily varied, easily slipped in and out of. We would of course very much like to have these melodies in written form; and for the sixteenth century it is possible that we do indeed have a few. But if the notated scores of trecento music tell us less than we need to know about how this music sounded, written *arie* on which poetry was improvised tell us far less still. Part of the essence of *aria* was melody, but much of it was style, personal and untranscribable. (The English word *air* has the same double meaning.) The style of *improvvisatori*, often praised, was almost never described in meaningful detail, and this would not have been easy to do even if it had been attempted. How would we, if we had no recordings, describe the personal style of Piaf or Burl Ives? How could we make clear in words the different *arie* of Frank Sinatra and Bing Crosby? Can the music of folk or rock groups, the *cantimbanchi* of today, be adequately described in words?

The uncertainties about the musical side of this art are many, and in certain respects crippling. Still, we know that the musical aspect was important. The improvisers are called not only *dicitori* and *cantori*, which could imply lively declamation without formal melody, but also *cantatori*, *sonatori*, and, more explicitly, *pulsatori*, players of percussion and especially of stringed instruments. They are often depicted with instrument in hand.[25] References to them sometimes name instruments, and one fourteenth-century account

24. On the formulas used in the *cantari* see Maria Cristina Cabani, "Narratore e pubblico nel cantare cavalleresco: I modi della partecipazione emotiva," *Giornale storico della letteratura italiana* 157 (1980), 1–42. Descriptions of the texts may also be found in Ezio Levi, "I cantari leggendari del popolo italiano nei secoli xiv e xv," ibid., suppl. 16 (1914), 1–159.

25. See Pls. 2–5. There is a capital in the Doge's Palace in Venice with the figure of what appears to be a *cantastorie* holding a stringed instrument; for a photograph of it see Pompeo Molmenti, *La storia di Venezia nella vita privata*, 6th ed., 3 vols. (Bergamo, 1902–26), 1:402.

describes improvisers as making "gran colpi pure con l'archetto della viola" to quiet the crowd.[26] The *lira da braccio* can in fact make quite a loud chordal sound, and these poet-musicians, if not virtuosi, must have known how to use their instruments to good effect throughout their performance. In more refined circles the improviser might have played a guitarlike instrument or the lute; in the latter case, since the lute was until the end of the fifteenth century used as a single-line melodic instrument, he would probably have been accompanied by a *tenorista* playing a viol or a large plucked instrument.[27] The mid-sixteenth-century *tenores* of Diego Ortiz are a late reflection of what must have been a long-established tradition of support by a *tenorista*, under a freely elaborated vocal or instrumental part.[28]

There are indications that the skills of some *improvvisatori* were as much musical as anything else. Antonio di Guido, the Florentine *canterino*, impressed everyone who heard him and was said by Luca Landucci (at the time of Antonio's death in 1486) to have "passato ognuno nell'arte di cantare."[29] He was heard singing of the deeds of Orlando by Michele Verino, who said Antonio's verses sounded to him like Petrarch; surely it was the *aria*—music and personal style of performance—and not the words that made this impression.[30] Some improvisers, like Pietrobono, were probably known primarily as musicians; others, like the Niccolò Tedesco who served at the Ferrarese court in the mid fifteenth century, were probably admired for the totality of their skills.[31] And there must have been performers in the piazza who neither had nor required much in

26. Jacopo Passavanti, *Specchio della vera penitenza*, cited in Levi, "I cantari leggendari," p. 20. In a Perugian document of the fourteenth century the name of a *canterino* was followed by the description "cantatoris ac rimatoris et pulsatoris"; his duties included "sonando, cantando, rimas condendo, cantilenas ad iocunditatem omnium pronuntiando et proferendo." See Balduino, *Cantari del trecento*, p. 255.

27. On the use of a *tenorista* to accompany a singer-instrumentalist see Lockwood, "Pietrobono," p. 121.

28. The tenors of Ortiz are given in four-voice texture for a keyboard instrument, but one can easily imagine his viol improvisation over another viol playing the bass line. On Ortiz's method see Howard Mayer Brown, *Embellishing Sixteenth-Century Music* (London, 1976), pp. 33–35 and passim.

29. Luca Landucci, *Diario fiorentino*, cited by Becherini, "Un canto in panca," p. 247.

30. Vittorio Rossi, *Il quattrocento* (Milan, 1933), p. 288.

31. Lockwood, "Pietrobono," p. 119.

the way of musical expertise to hold their audience with the spell of an old story told anew, over some modest strumming.

At this point I remind my "listeners," in the manner of an *improvvisatore*, that I have been speaking mainly of *cantastorie*, singers of epic verse. I will return to this class of performers later; but there were other categories of performers and of poetry sung *all'improvviso* that should be mentioned. The singer Minuccio d'Arezzo spoken of in the *Decameron* is more likely to have performed lyric poems in an early form of an *aria toscana*.[32] Some *cantori* spent their careers in the service of rulers, and this affected what they did. For example, Giovanni Cieco di Parma, at the Ferrarese court in the 1460s and 1470s, is described as having written and sung *capitoli* and even "sonetti petrarcheggianti," for the performance of which he was famous.[33] The poet-singers of Neapolitan court circles were above all *strambottisti*, noted for their skills in singing this lyric genre. And throughout the fifteenth century there are references to demand for singers expert in a local style, such as the oft-mentioned *aria veneziana*.[34] They were not always Italians; some of the best-known singer-instrumentalists were Germans, who may have written and sung verse but who presumably betrayed their origins in their speech and must therefore have been known chiefly as instrumentalists.[35]

On occasion a musician not known primarily as an *improvvisatore* acted in that capacity before a courtly audience. The performance of Pietrobono at the court of Francesco Sforza, probably in 1456, is documented by Antonio Cornazano, who tells us that "Piero Bono, . . . che in musica le stelle havean dotato," sang to the *cetra*,

32. *Decameron*, x, 7. Minuccio, who sang and accompanied himself on the *viuola*, performed a canzonetta by Mico da Siena, "assai buon dicitore in rima." See Howard Mayer Brown, "Fantasia on a Theme by Boccaccio," *Early Music* 5 (1977), 324–39, esp. 333ff.

33. See Giulio Bertoni, "Il Cieco di Ferrara e altri improvvisatori," *Giornale storico della letteratura italiana* 94 (1929), 272f.

34. See Lockwood, "Pietrobono," p. 119, on a certain "Brith," recommended by the *canterino* Niccolò Tedesco as "pulsator e cantor optimus et suavissimus."

35. See above, n. 34, on Brith. A musician from Munich, called "Orbo tedesco," was active in Mantua in the 1470s; he has been tentatively identified as Conrad Paumann. See William F. Prizer, "The Frottola and the Unwritten Tradition: Improvisors and Frottolists at North Italian Courts" (paper read at the annual meeting of the American Musicological Society, 1980).

accompanied by a *tenorista*, a kind of verse described as "ordinata frotta" (this could have been a form of ballata, *terza rima*, or even *ottava* stanzas) on the loves of various fifteenth-century notables, including members of the Sforza family. We are even told that his song was "tucta in semitoni, proportionando e sincoppando sempre, e fugiva el tenore a i suoi cantoni." [36] This description, hard to take at face value, nevertheless informs us that Pietrobono's song was real music, with some melodic *fioritura*, either vocal or on the lute, over a supporting bass.

Nobles and members of ruling families tried their hand at singing *all'improvviso*. Lorenzo de' Medici, though he is recorded as having a poor voice, liked to sing and was of course a poet of some distinction;[37] and Poliziano informed Lorenzo that his son Piero was making excellent progress in this art, of which the poet was a known admirer.[38] The children of Ercole I d'Este received musical training of the kind recommended by Castiglione for the ideal male and female courtier, learning not only to read and perform polyphonic music but also to sing while accompanying themselves and to accompany others. In 1492 Isabella, who may have been taught by Pietrobono or by another *cantore*, Francesco Cieco, the probable author of the epic *Mambriano*, borrowed Francesco from a Gonzaga relative in order to enjoy once more his expert singing.[39] At a later date she spoke of having to practice the *viola* in anticipation of a visit to Ferrara, where she expected to perform with her brother Alfonso.[40] Several aspects of the musical life of the quattrocento come together here: Singing to the "lyre," the humanists' favorite form of music, was practiced both by professionals and by their patrons, noble amateurs. These patrons, especially the rulers

36. The passage, from Cornazano's *La Sfortiade*, is cited and commented upon by Nino Pirrotta, "Music and Cultural Tendencies in Fifteenth-Century Italy," *Journal of the American Musicological Society* 19 (1966), 139–46.

37. See Luigi Parigi, *Laurentiana: Lorenzo dei Medici cultore della musica* (Florence, 1954), pp. 9–21.

38. Pirrotta, "Music and Cultural Tendencies," p. 141.

39. Bertoni, "Il Cieco," p. 276. Francesco had spent the decade of the 1470s at the Ferrarese court.

40. William F. Prizer, "Marchetto Cara and the North Italian Frottola" (Ph.D. diss., University of North Carolina at Chapel Hill, 1974), p. 28. In this letter Isabella speaks of playing *tenore* to whatever it was Alfonso was to do. On the special interest taken by Alfonso d'Este in the viol, on which he became a proficient performer, see Ian Woodfield, *The Early History of the Viol* (Cambridge, 1984), p. 87f.

of Ferrara and Mantua and their relatives, supported the poets and musicians who created the repertory of the frottola; and within this repertory are many pieces suitable for solo singing, including the *arie* designed to fit any sonnet, any *capitolo*, any Latin verse (of the right meter and line length). The frottola is certainly a link between the improvisatory tradition and that of written polyphony.

Petrucci's *arie* must have been commissioned in order to give amateurs material on which to base their own improvised singing. We have already seen one of these *arie*, designed for sonnets (Ex. 14). How close it is to what professional *improvvisatori* actually sang we do not know, but surely it was intended to sound like the real thing. The strambotti printed by Petrucci often contain a lot of vocal *fioritura*, suggesting that they are meant to sound "composed"—though flexibility in performance is always possible since there is usually music only for a single couplet and this music must be repeated four times. Some of the strambotti in the frottola books are so simple melodically and so close to speech and/or dance rhythms that they suggest, even demand, a kind of lively spontaneity in performance that would create at least part of the sense of *aria*. Two examples will help to illustrate this. The first, a setting by Tromboncino, opens with a mock-solemn monotone, followed by a call for attention at a higher pitch, sinking to a half cadence to prepare for the message, which is delivered in bits and pieces and with an amusing imitation in the textless parts, surely playable by a singer-lutenist with a *tenorista* to help (Ex. 20).[41] The second, by Filippo Lurano, contains the alternating triple and duple beats characteristic of the barzelletta; not an actual dance, but full of rhythmic lilt (Ex. 21).[42] The melody, circling around its keynote, F, could hardly be simpler (except for the spontaneous-sounding flourish on "quanto"). Notice that the declamation is faithful to the sound of the words and to divisions within the line but not to the line as a unit; internal repetitions and word splitting in Example 20, and stretching of the line to twelve syllables in Example 21, cause some distortion. As a feature of improvisatory art this seems more

41. *Voi che passati qui fumati el passo*, transcribed from Petrucci, *Frottole libro septimo* (1507), fol. 19.
42. *Vana speranza mia che mai non vene*, from Petrucci, *Frottole libro quarto* (1505), fol. 9.

suitable for short lyric verse, such as strambotti, than for the *ottave* of epic verse, the performance of which one would expect to move rather crisply by the line.

It would be reassuring to think that strambotti such as these represent the improvisatory art of the *strambottisti*—deprived, of course, of the all-important elements of personal style in delivery. The chances of this being so seem a little better than in the case of the *giustiniane* discussed in chapter 2. For one thing, the frottola repertory appears in part to be designed as a reflection of improvised song. Musicians like Pietrobono included frottolas in their repertory; Pietrobono is known to have taught his pupils pieces from the earlier layers of this repertory, among them a *Scaramella* that might be the setting of a "Scaramella" text by Josquin or one by Loyset Compère.[43] Some relationship to popular style can be seen, though less clearly, in strambotti of Neapolitan origin, written down in chansonniers of the 1470s, 1480s, and 1490s.[44] While music of popular cast, presumably unwritten, had been performed along with that of the written polyphonic tradition as early as the first decades of the fifteenth century—Prudenzani's *Solazzo* tells us that[45]—the vogue of improvisatory singing became much more closely intermingled with the practice of "composed" music in the northern-Italian city-states as the century drew to a close. On the other hand, singers famed for their personal style can hardly be expected to have committed their secrets to paper. Those who heard them were free to do so, of course; and some melodic formulas could have found their way into general circulation by this means. We do not possess any music known to be by the much-admired Serafino dall'Aquila. Some texts attributed to him were, however, set by the frottolists; and in a manuscript of Mantuan or Ferrarese provenance is some verse ascribed to Serafino along with anonymous musical settings that may represent at least a reflection

43. This information is from Prizer, "The Frottola and the Unwritten Tradition."

44. See, for example, nos. 119, 128, and 132 in Isabel Pope and Masakata Kanazawa, eds., *The Musical Manuscript Montecassino 871* (Oxford, 1978).

45. Santorre Benedetti, ed., "Il 'Solazzo' e il 'Saporeto' con altre rimi di Simone Prudenzani d'Orvieto," *Giornale storico della letteratura italiana*, suppl. 15 (Turin, 1913), 116–17. The singing of *siciliane* is referred to in the *Paradiso degli Alberti*; see chap. 2, n. 29. On some *siciliane* in the Reina MS see Nino Pirrotta, "New Glimpses of an Unwritten Tradition," in *Words and Music: The Scholar's View*, ed. Laurence Berman (Cambridge, Mass., 1972), pp. 271–91.

of his style. Example 22 shows one of these.[46] Of particular interest is the fact that its melody is very similar to one of the formulas used for singing *ottave* and other kinds of poetry in the sixteenth century.

Arie, identified as such, turn up from time to time in madrigal prints of the sixteenth century, where they are usually designed for *ottave*.[47] In the later part of the century whole collections of *arie*, such as the *Aeri raccolti insieme . . . dove si cantano sonetti, stanze et terze rime* published in Naples in 1577, are to be seen.[48] In the lute-book of the Florentine lute singer Cosimo Bottegari we even have a kind of notebook of *arie* used for a variety of poetic types.[49] These sixteenth-century *arie* are, apart from some inevitable change in harmonic language, not really very different from those published by Petrucci. If one of the latter, written at the beginning of the six-teenth century, is compared to an *aria* from Bottegari's book, which is dated 1573, the melodic and rhythmic similarities are clear—as they would not be if one compared a frottola of circa 1500 to a madrigal of 1570 (Ex. 23).[50]

We know that singing madrigals from partbooks was mixed with solo singing to the lute at informal gatherings, such as that depicted in Antonfrancesco Doni's *Dialogo della Musica* of 1544. The same combination occurred on formal occasions when *intermedi* were sung and played before a crowd of notables, as at the wedding fes-tivities of Cosimo I and Eleanora of Toledo in Florence in 1539. (One assumes that on such occasions the solo singing was not im-provised, except perhaps for details of ornamentation.) We hear

46. *Se'l zapator il giorno se affatica* (Modena, Bibl. Est. MS αF.9.9, fol. 6ᵛ). Ex. 22 is given after Claudio Gallico, *Un libro di poesie per musica dell'epoca d'Isabella d'Este* (Man-tua, 1961), p. 121. Gallico dates the manuscript at shortly after 1500.

47. For some examples see James Haar, "Arie per cantar stanze ariostesche," in *L'Ariosto: La musica, i musicisti*, ed. Maria Antonella Balsano (Florence, 1981), pp. 31–46.

48. This print (RISM 1577⁸), edited by the Neapolitan musician Rocco Rodio, deserves study as one of the largest collections of *aria* formulas of the second half of the sixteenth century. Only two of the four partbooks survive, but fortunately they are the two most important, canto and basso.

49. See Carol MacClintock, ed., *The Bottegari Lutebook* (Wellesley, Mass., 1965); idem, "A Court Musician's Songbook: Modena MS C 311," *Journal of the American Musicological Society* 9 (1956), 177–92.

50. Ex. 23: (a) Marchetto Cara, *Aer de capitoli*, taken from Petrucci, *Frottole libro nono* (1508 [=1509]), fol. 2ᵛ; (b) Cosimo Bottegari, *Aria in terza rima* (Modena, Bibl. Est. MS C 311, fol. 24ᵛ), given after MacClintock, *The Bottegari Lutebook*, p. 75. I have added bar lines and fermatas to Ex. 23b.

the names of famous singers throughout the sixteenth century, praised in terms as glowing as those used earlier. One difference is that fewer of the admired singers of the sixteenth century were improvisers pure and simple; most of them could and did take part in performances of polyphonic music, and thus were expert in the written tradition as well. A figure such as Giulio Cesare Brancaccio, a Neapolitan active as a singer in Rome, Ferrara, and elsewhere for a surprising length of time in the sixteenth century, was famed not just for solo singing but also for his participation in expert madrigal groups;[51] it is much less likely that a fifteenth-century singer known for his soloistic art would have been a member of an establishment devoted to the singing of polyphony.

Improvisers and composers in the written tradition may both have drawn on a repertory of popular song, of which traces are present in quodlibets of the late fifteenth century, in the tenors of a few frottolas, and in the repertory of the *villota*; whether the Neapolitan *villanesca*, which rose to popularity in the 1530s, actually used popular material in addition to imitating popular poetic and musical styles I am not sure.[52] If composers could cite popular song tunes, one wonders if they might also have quoted the melodies of the *improvvisatori*. I think it likely that they did, perhaps often; our failure to recognize this kind of practice is one of the many things separating our rather abstract knowledge of Renaissance music from the multiple resonance it actually had. A quotation of this type could be used where the text quotes or paraphrases a proverb; an example is Giovan Domenico da Nola's *Proverbio ama chi t'ama è fatto antico* (Ex. 24), which uses a form of the melody seen in Example 22 and there associated with a poem by Serafino.[53] There could of course be hundreds of melodic snippets having some topical or local significance hidden in the madrigal. We know that composers quoted one another when a phrase of text that they

51. On Brancaccio see U. Coldagelli, "G. C. Brancaccio," in *Dizionario biografico degli italiani*, vol. 13 (Rome, 1971), pp. 780–84.

52. For popular material in Italian music of the turn of the century see Knud Jeppesen, *La Frottola*, vol. 3, *Frottola und Volkslied: Zur musikalischen Überlieferung des folkloristischen Guts in der Frottola* (Copenhagen, 1970).

53. Ex. 24 is taken from *Madrigali a 4v di I. D. da Nolla* (1545), p. 27. The text of the madrigal is the third stanza of Petrarch's canzone *Mai non vo' più cantar com'io soleva*.

knew in another musician's work turned up in a poem they were setting.[54] If they cited melodies that survive chiefly or only in their citations, identification obviously becomes a rather tricky affair. Nevertheless certain kinds of madrigals seem likely candidates as repositories of melody once widely known and widely used by improvisers.

A promising object of study in this regard is the madrigal cycle, a setting of an entire canzone, sestina, or chain of *ottava* stanzas. The madrigal cycle rose to prominence in the 1540s; it was cultivated throughout the rest of the century but is especially prominent at mid-century. One of the earliest cycles, Jacquet Berchem's setting of the sestina *Alla dolc'ombra delle belle frondi*, has a strong sense of musical unity despite the variation in the number of voices used for individual stanzas and the changes in polyphonic texture from one section to another (see Ex. 25).[55] This unity is not accounted for by the use of a single tonality; still less is it explained by our exaggerated notions of the predictability of early madrigal style. There is melodic continuity from stanza to stanza, often but by no means always more marked in the top voice. And the melody, or rather the melodic formula—which is never given in what must have been its "basic" form but always in a variant—is the one I have already mentioned twice, in connection with Serafino and with a proverbial utterance in a madrigal (compare Exx. 22, 24, and 25). I have found evidence that some kind of basic tune was in the composer's mind in other madrigal cycles of the period, including those of Arcadelt and the young Lasso.[56] This suggests that as composers turned to the setting of multistanza poems, which in an earlier period would have been set to one repeatable musical entity, they were

54. For example, Lasso, in setting Bernardo Tasso's *Vostro fui vostro son et sarò vostro* (*Secondo libro a 5v* [1557]), drew on the four-voice setting of Jacquet Berchem of a similar text, *Vostro fui e sarò mentre ch'io viva* (Arcadelt, *Primo libro a 4v* [1539]). There must be many examples of this kind of allusion in the madrigal repertory.

55. Ex. 25 is from Berchem's setting of *Alla dolc'ombra delle belle frondi*, which appeared in the *Dialogo della Musica* of Antonfrancesco Doni (1544), fol. 27. It is given after the edition of G. F. Malipiero of the *Dialogo* (Vienna, 1965), p. 131.

56. Arcadelt's *Chiare fresch'e dolci acque* (Petrarch) shows clear use of a basic melody in all sections. In Lasso's early madrigal cycles one can see several instances of melodic similarity between sections; see the sestine *Del freddo Reno alla sinistra riva* and *Si com'al chiaro giorno oscura notte* in *Orlando di Lasso: Sämmtliche Werke*, vol. 8, ed. Adolf Sandberger (Leipzig, 1898), pp. 3, 46.

conscious of the varied yet unified art with which the best of the poet-singers treated this poetry, and sought to capture something of the quality of freely varied repetition in their ambitiously planned and carefully written polyphony. In this as in many other respects the madrigal imitated the art of solo song even while, in its polyphony, it provided for simultaneous projection of texts by several reader-singers.

The chief use of melodies that I think can be identified as taken from *improvvisatori* is in settings of *ottava rima* stanzas, especially those drawn from epic romance and in particular from the *Orlando furioso*. Before discussing these tunes I should say something about the tremendous rise in popularity of epic poetry in the late fifteenth century. The materials of the chivalric epic had of course been made use of by *cantastorie* for centuries, and the tradition of singing *ottave* on the exploits of Orlando or Rinaldo was a firmly established one. In the fourteenth and much of the fifteenth centuries epic poetry of an ambitious literary cast was written in Latin, usually on classical themes; Petrarch's once-famous *Africa* is one of the monuments of this genre.[57] Fifteenth-century poets wishing to write about chivalric themes turned to the vernacular—or perhaps it was the other way around. They not only wrote in Italian (not as yet the purified Tuscan of Bembo's readers, of course); they also borrowed conventions of form and style, even turns of phrase, from the *cantastorie*.[58] That the latter should in turn have sung stanzas from these poems, more finished in language, perhaps, than theirs but similar in theme and approach, is only natural. Plate 4, used for a sixteenth-century *cantare* on a sacred text, also served as frontispiece to an edition of Pulci's *Morgante*; without making too much of this coincidence one may still assume that Pulci's stanzas were known to *cantastorie*.[59]

Pulci wrote his poem for the mercantile aristocracy of Florence; but it soon became known elsewhere. Ercole I is said to have gotten hold of a copy of the poem before it was published; and Ferrara is

57. Boccaccio's *Teseide* is of course an early example of a vernacular epic.
58. See Bronzini, *Tradizione di stile aedico*; Cabani, "Narratore e pubblico nel cantare cavalleresco."
59. On Pulci's relationship to the *cantari* see Bronzini, *Tradizione di stile aedico*, pp. 19–31.

one of the places where it would have been most warmly received.
Visitors to the Estense court in the later fifteenth century noticed
that the heroes of Charlemagne's army (from one of whom the
ducal family claimed descent) were to be seen in tapestries and
paintings, that there was much talk of the glories of the chivalric
age, and that poems on this subject enjoyed great popularity—all
this to a much greater extent than in contemporary Florence or
Rome.[60] So infatuated were the Estense with knightly lore that they
began naming their children after heroes and heroines of the *reali
di Francia*, as if to confirm the pedigree they claimed.[61] In this atmosphere, at a court where *improvvisatori* were always present and
much valued, there must have been performances of epic stanzas as
well as eager reading of the latest poems, such as Francesco Cieco's
Mambriano.

Boiardo's *Orlando innamorato* (published while still incomplete in
1484) is usually regarded as the first great epic poem in the Renaissance revival of the chivalric mode. It is in many respects a self-
consciously literary effort, meant to be read in courtly circles rather
than sung in the piazza. But Boiardo, like Pulci, kept much of the
familiar tone of the *cantastorie*; at times he refers to his own verses
as *cantari*, to his writing as *cantando*:

> Ma il lor camino e i fatti e il ragionare
> dirvi a ponto in questo altro cantare.   (I, xxi, 71)

> Per Dio, tornate a me, bella brigata,
> chi volentieri ad ascoltar vi aspetto
> per darvi al mio cantar zoia e diletto.   (I, xxii, 62)

> Cantando qui di sopra, io vi lasciai.   (I, xxi, 1)

60. Bronzini, *Tradizione di stile aedico*, pp. 2–4. See also Werner L. Gunders-
heimer, ed., *Art and Life at the Court of Ercole I d'Este: The "De triumphis religionis" of
Giovanni Sabadini degli Aretino* (Geneva, 1972), pp. 69–70, for a description by
Sabadini of a fresco on chivalric themes at the Estense villa of Belfiore. For an ac-
count of Pisanello's ambitious, never-finished fresco cycle on Arthurian themes,
which was commissioned in the 1440s by Lodovico Gonzaga for the ducal palace in
Mantua, see Joanna Woods-Marsden, "French Chivalric Myth and Mantuan Political
Reality in the *Sala del Pisanello*," *Art History* viii (1986), 397–412.

61. Rinaldo was used as a name by the Estense during the Middle Ages; Marfisa
and Bradamante, names prominent in Ariosto's epic, are among those given members of the ducal family during the sixteenth century. See the genealogical tables in
Edmund G. Gardner, *Dukes and Poets in Ferrara* (1904; repr. New York, 1968). Both
Marfisa and Bradamante d'Este were patronesses of the work of Tasso.

The poem begins with the *cantastorie*'s call for attention:

> Signori e cavallier che ve adunati
> per odir cose dilettose e nove,
> state attenti e quieti, ed ascoltati
> la bella istoria che'l mio canto muove.   (I, i, 1)

And throughout the *Innamorato* Boiardo repeatedly refers to his audience as listeners, not readers. All of this is of course convention; yet, in view of the fact that the audience for Boiardo's epic was the same one that listened to *improvvisatori* sing *ottave* on epic themes, it is not a faraway or dusty convention.

I have found no direct evidence that Boiardo's stanzas were popular among *cantastorie*. The case is quite different for the *Orlando furioso*. Ariosto's observance of the conventional usages of the *cantari*, if less conspicuous than that of Boiardo, is still perceptible;[62] and it is clear that Ariosto knew not only the French romances in the ducal library at Ferrara and the poem of Boiardo, which he said he was continuing, but also a wide range of Italian chivalric verse.[63] No one would suppose that the beautifully wrought stanzas of the *Furioso* were intended for public recitation; we are nonetheless told by the sixteenth-century critic Girolamo Ruscelli that Ariosto's verse was as popular among the common people—who must have heard it declaimed—as among the educated classes.[64] G. B. Pigna, among Ariosto's earliest biographers, says that the poet altered some of his verses after hearing them sung in the street.[65] The theorist Gioseffo Zarlino, no spinner of tales, speaks in the 1550s of "quei modi [by which he means *arie*] sopra i quali cantiamo al presente li Sonetti, o Canzoni del Petrarca, overamente le Rime dell'Ariosto."[66]

Arie designed for *ottave rime* and using stanzas from the *Orlando furioso* as paradigms are to be found in sources of the second half of the sixteenth century; in some of them the choice of stanza suggests

62. See Bronzini, *Tradizione di stile aedico*, pp. 49–65.
63. The fundamental work on Ariosto's sources remains that of Pio Rajna, *Fonti dell'Orlando furioso*, 2d ed. (Florence, 1900). See also Dario Bonomo, *L'Orlando furioso nelle sue fonti* (Bologna, 1953).
64. Girolamo Ruscelli, *Del modo di comporre in versi nella lingua italiana* (Venice. 1558), pp. cv–cvi.
65. G. B. Pigna, *Scontri de' luoghi* (Venice, 1554), Osserv. lii.
66. Gioseffo Zarlino, *Le istitutioni harmoniche* (Venice, 1558), iii, 79.

that the *arie* were to be used for a chain of *ottave* forming a descriptive or emotionally taut scene.[67] But we have no way of knowing whether such *arie* resembled those used by popular *improvvisatori*. If we look for evidence from the poet's lifetime there is not a great deal to be found. Petrucci's prints are too early, and in any event his frottola prints do not contain *arie* for *ottava* stanzas, or indeed any *ottave* (as distinct from strambotti) at all; in the first decade of the sixteenth century this verse form was clearly still the domain of the improviser. *Stanze* do appear in the frottola collections of Andrea Antico in the second decade of the century; there are no *arie*, but there is one setting, by the Mantuan court composer Tromboncino, of a stanza from the *Furioso*, the beginning of Orlando's celebrated lament over his lost love, Angelica (xxiii, 126) (Ex. 26).[68] The date of Antico's print, 1517, is a year after the publication of the first edition of the poem; but the text used by Tromboncino shows several variants from its printed form, suggesting that the composer was given the stanza before the poem was published. We know that Isabella d'Este was eager to see Ariosto's work and that she heard parts of it read before the first version was completed; and the Mantuan court liked to have new poetry set to music whenever possible.[69]

Was Tromboncino's music meant to be a reflection of an improvisatory *aria*? We cannot be sure; but several features suggest that it was: its restricted range, its musical separation between odd and even lines of text, its shift to a higher pitch level for the last couplet. In later settings of textual laments, madrigalists tended to use melodic lines very similar to Tromboncino's, and to employ, as he did, the second (Hypodorian) mode, evidently felt to be lugubrious

67. For a list of chains of stanzas from the *Orlando furioso* set to music during the sixteenth century see Maria Antonella Balsano and James Haar, "L'Ariosto in musica," in *L'Ariosto: La musica, i musicisti*, ed. Balsano (Florence, 1981), pp. 50–51.

68. *Queste non son più lachrime che fuore*. Tromboncino's setting, given in Ex. 26, is in RISM 1517², *Canzoni sonetti strambotti e frottole libro quarto*, fol. 3ᵛ. The version printed in Alfred Einstein, *The Italian Madrigal*, vol. 3 (Princeton, 1949), no. 93, is a somewhat confusing collation of the 1517 print with the lute intabulation in RISM [ca. 1520]⁷, no. 35.

69. On the text used by Tromboncino see A. Zenatti, *Una stanza del Furioso musicata da Bartolomeo Tromboncino* (Florence, 1889). New poetry was often made known through performance by a *citaredo*; on this see the citation from Calmeta given in Pirrotta, "Music and Cultural Tendencies," pp. 141–42.

in quality. The melody used by Giaches Wert for a setting of another Ariostan lament, *Dunque baciar sì bell'e dolce labbia* (xxxvi, 32), is so similar to Tromboncino's that one has to assume either knowledge by the young Wert of the forty-year-old piece or its continuing existence as an *aria* (Ex. 27). This might come to the same thing; Ariosto's stanzas may have been sung to Tromboncino's music in Mantua long after the frottola repertory had passed out of fashion.[70]

Other forms of musical lament may be related to improvisatory practice. One is a kind of recitation approaching psalmody. Verdelot's setting of *Queste non son più lacrime che fuore*, the same stanza Tromboncino had used, is an example of this, despite its six-voice texture, as is Berchem's setting of the same text, and Nolletto's *Non siate però tumide e fastose* (xxvii, 121) (Ex. 28).[71] The melodic figure of the descending fourth, known to us as a seventeenth-century bass formula for lament, appears in sixteenth-century madrigals as a tune, often over what came later to be known as a *Romanesca* bass. It occurs in highly formulaic guise in a mid-century guitar intabulation with the title "Chant d'Orlande";[72] its use in the madrigal may be illustrated by Vincenzo Ruffo's setting of *Deh torn'a me mio sol torn'e rimena* (xlv, 39) (Ex. 29).[73]

The melody discussed above in its use for a setting of Serafino's verse at the beginning of the sixteenth century (see Ex. 22) and recognizable in madrigals by Nola and Berchem (Exx. 24, 25) is often found in music of the middle and even later sixteenth century. Because of its simple, essentially scalar construction there may be many cases of coincidence rather than deliberate intent in its use; when it dominates an entire piece, such as Berchem's *Pungente*

---

70. Ex. 27, from Wert's *Primo libro a 4v* (1561), no. 6, is given after the edition of Carol MacClintock, *Giaches de Wert: Opera Omnia*, vol. 15 (American Institute of Musicology, 1972), p. 19. Wert was in the service of the Gonzaga family (though at first outside Mantua itself) from 1553; see MacClintock, *Giaches Wert (1535–1596): Life and Works* (American Institute of Musicology, 1966), p. 23f.

71. Verdelot's setting of *Queste non son più lagrime che fuore* appeared (unascribed but his by inference) in RISM 1541[16], *La piu divina e piu bella musica . . . a 6v*, p. 13; Berchem's setting is in his *Capriccio . . . sopra le stanze del Furioso* (1561), bk. 1, no. 25; Nolletto's *Non siate però tumide e fastose* is in RISM 1540[18], *Le dotte et eccellente compositioni . . . a 5v*, p. 42.

72. See Daniel Heartz, "Parisian Music Publishing under Henry II: A Propos of Four Recently Discovered Guitar Books," *The Musical Quarterly* 46 (1960), 462f.

73. Ex. 29 is taken from Ruffo's *Libro terzo di madrigali a 4v* (1560), p. 27.

dardo che'l mio cor consumi,[74] or appears in easily recognizable form in the setting of a stanza, particularly one from the *Furioso*, we can be fairly sure that it was chosen for its familiarity as an *aria*.[75] A setting of *Dunque fia ver (dicea) che mi convegna* (xxxii, 18) in an anthology of madrigals printed in 1554 opens with an unmistakable reference to this melody (Ex. 30).[76] Berchem uses it repeatedly in his *Capriccio* of 1561; Example 31 shows one such use, a variant of the melody in which the opening phrases remain on the same tonal level.[77] It turns up in Frescobaldi's *Cappriccio . . . sopra l'Aria di Ruggiero* with the subtitle "Fra Jacopino"—a figure whose identity is unknown to me but whom it would be pleasant to think of as a seventeenth-century *cantastorie*.[78]

The most striking melody that I believe can be identified with the improvisatory tradition is one that turns up first in a Spanish book of songs with vihuela accompaniment, the *Silva de Sirenas* of Enriquez de Valderrábano, published in 1547.[79] Though called a *soneto*, it is an *aria*, meant for the singing of *stanze*; the text given is "Ruggier qual sempre fui tal esser voglio / Fin a la morte e più se più si puote" (xliv, 61), the beginning of Bradamante's celebrated lament. Valderrábano quotes the melody a third lower than its normal pitch elsewhere; the tune at its usual pitch is in the vihuela part.

This melody turns up in a number of madrigalian settings of Ariosto's stanzas, including "Ruggier qual sempre fui"; the stanzas set are usually of a narrative, heroic cast. Alfred Einstein noted its use in a madrigal (to an anonymous text) by Corteccia, and called it *aria di Firenze*, presumably because Corteccia was a Florentine.[80]

---

74. This piece appears in Arcadelt's *Primo libro* (1539) without ascription; in editions of that volume from 1546 on it is ascribed to Berchem. It is printed in Albert Seay, ed., *Jacobi Arcadelt: Opera Omnia*, vol. 2 (American Institute of Musicology, 1970), no. 41.

75. On this see James Haar, "The *Madrigale Arioso*: A Mid-century Development in the Cinquecento Madrigal," *Studi musicali* 12 (1983), 203–19.

76. RISM 1554²⁸, *Il quarto libro di madrigali . . . a note bianche*, p. 24.

77. *Ch'aver puo donna al mondo più di bono* (viii, 42), in Berchem's *Capriccio*, bk. 1, no. 14.

78. A text associated with this tune in the seventeenth century is "Fra Jacopino a Roma se n'andava / bordon in spalla e in col una schiavina"; see Guido Pannain, "Francesco Provenzale e la lirica del suo tempo," *Rivista musicale italiana* 32 (1925), 516–17. I am grateful to Professor Anthony Newcomb for giving me this reference.

79. See Haar, "Arie per cantar stanze," p. 39.

80. Alfred Einstein, "Ancora sull'aria di Ruggiero," *Rivista musicale italiana* 41 (1937), 169.

What drew his attention was the fact that the melody is treated as an *aria*, repeated four times without change, while the polyphonic texture of the other three voices is through-composed. Several other composers set Ariosto using the same melody in the same way. Example 32 gives the tune as used by Berchem; it is found in identical form in the work of other composers of the period.[81] The madrigals based on this use of the melody are, it seems to me, "composed" *arie*, with a tune heard intact but surrounded by changing accompaniment; in some settings the melody passes from voice to voice, giving each singer a chance to play the *improvvisatore*. A number of madrigals setting Ariostan stanzas, while they do not give this melody intact, make clear reference to it (see Ex. 33, from one of the settings of "Ruggier qual sempre fui");[82] in some ways I find this use of the melody even more suggestive of the improvisatory art than its quotation as a fixed tune.

I think this melody has some right to be called the *aria di Ruggiero*.[83] Its origin is unknown, but it must have been in general circulation for some time before reaching Spain in the 1540s, and the special circumstances of its use strongly suggest that it was a pre-existent tune known to madrigalists rather than something composed by one of them. Whether it is related to the tenor given by Ortiz in his *Tratado de glosas* of 1553, there untitled but later to become known as the *Ruggiero*, I am not sure.[84] The melody in fact fits that tenor (or bass) quite well except in one crucial place, the end of the first phrase—a full stop in the melody, a half cadence in the bass. Although one might well be a variant of the other, I have not found a form of the melody fitting Ortiz's tenor used in the madrigal literature, or a variant of the *Ruggiero* bass that would precisely support the melody. Perhaps the melody and bass were

81. *Ricordati Pagan quando uccidesti* (i, 27), in Berchem's *Capriccio*, bk. 1, no. 4.
82. Ex. 33 is the opening of Francesco Bifetto's setting of *Ruggier qual sempre fui* from his *Secondo libro a 4v* (1548), p. 2.
83. A form of the tune turns up in London, Brit. Lib. MS Royal App. 74, there called "Rogier." See John Ward, "Music for 'A Handefull of Pleasant Delites,'" *Journal of the American Musicological Society* 10 (1957), 172.
84. See Max Schneider, ed., *Diego Ortiz: Tratado de glosas sobre clausulas y otros generos de puntos en la musica de violones, Roma, 1553,* 3d ed. (Kassel, 1936; repr. Kassel, 1961), pp. 134 and, for the original in facsimile, xxvii. Ortiz adds a fifth, ornamental part to a four-part harmonization of the *Ruggiero* bass.

one in the oral tradition—possibly in Naples, the likely source of Ortiz's tenors—from which, I think, both are derived.

As I have said, madrigalists of the mid sixteenth century frequently use melodic formulas that may come from the art of the *improvvisatori*, especially in settings of the narrative stanzas of the *Orlando furioso*. This connection between the oral and written traditions reaches its apogee in the enormous madrigal cycle of Jacquet Berchem, called *Capriccio* (1561), consisting of three books of ninety-odd stanzas from Ariosto's poem. Berchem chose a sequence of texts that makes narrative sense, reducing the poem to some of its major themes—especially those involving Orlando himself, Ruggiero, and Bradamante. This was deliberately done; attention is called to it by the printing of single-line plot synopses as running heads in the partbooks. The madrigal cycle is thus equated with a choice of stanzas such as that a *cantastorie* might make out of Ariosto's vast poem. In this sense Berchem's division of the *Capriccio* into three books is like a three-day performance by an *improvvisatore*. Even the unexplained title *Capriccio* might refer to the composer's attitude, one of playful (though often highly contrapuntal) adaptation of the art of the piazza. As if to underscore his intention by musical means, Berchem makes much use of the melodic formulas I have been talking about. One final example may be cited (Ex. 34); in a setting of lines 3–8 of the first canto, stanza 41, subtitled "Lamento di Sacripante per la fugga d'Angelica," Berchem introduces in the upper voice alone a lament tune (a), the "Ruggiero" tune (b), a descending-fourth lament formula (c), and the melody we first saw used in a setting of verses of Serafino (d).[85]

Berchem's *Capriccio* is dedicated to Alfonso II of Ferrara (it may have been composed in Ferrara), and this seems no haphazard choice. Ariosto's great poem glorifying the Estense was here set, in a carefully chosen selection, to music in up-to-date madrigalian style mixed with references to the venerable and much-loved art of the *improvvisatori*. This remarkable work may be seen as an attempt by a composer to do for its musical side what Ariosto had done for the verse of the *cantastorie*.

85. *Che debbo far perch'io son giunto tardi*, in Berchem's *Capriccio*, bk. 1, no. 6.

·*V*·

Italian Music in the Age of the
Counter-Reformation

ONE OF THE INTERLOCUTORS in Antonfrancesco Doni's *Dialogo della Musica* of 1544 says, on being given a madrigal by Arcadelt to sing, "Che volete fare di tanta musica? Questo è troppo vecchio."[1] Since Arcadelt's music had been in print for only five years when this remark was made (his *Quinto libro* was in fact issued in 1544), Doni's attitude seems surprising; we would expect that in the 1540s these madrigals would just have been approaching the height of their popularity. Very little of what Doni says, in this work or elsewhere, can be taken at face value; but if we credit this statement as being in some degree representative of what actively interested amateurs of the madrigal were thinking, it tells us several things.

First of all, the madrigal, which circulated in manuscript copies from the mid-1520s, chiefly in Rome and Florence but perhaps elsewhere as well,[2] must have been known to a good many people before it first appeared in print, and hence was not altogether a novelty when Venetian publishers began to put it out in 1533.[3]

---

1. Antonfrancesco Doni, *Dialogo della Musica* (1544), ed. G. F. Malipiero (Vienna, 1965), p. 35.

2. The manuscript sources for the early madrigal are chiefly but not exclusively Florentine. For example, the MS Venice, Bibl. Marc. cl. ital. 1795–98, a set of partbooks dating from the mid-1520s and containing a few madrigals in addition to frottolas and *villote*, was copied in the Veneto. Individual madrigals circulated freely; the work of Arcadelt had become well known through this means before it was published. On this see Richard J. Agee, "Ruberto Strozzi and the Early Madrigal," *Journal of the American Musicological Society* 36 (1983), 9.

3. The celebrated first appearance of the term *madrigal* in a music print is in the *Libro primo de la Serena*, published in Rome in 1530. But this volume is a mixed one resembling the miscellaneous printed collections of the 1520s; the real history of the

Nonetheless the printing of part music of all kinds and especially of madrigals in large numbers, which began in the late 1530s, when the new technique of single-impression printing reached Venice, brought about great changes in Italian musical life. The consumers of this art, formerly small groups of cognoscenti, now included anyone who could afford to buy the prints. From inscriptions on surviving copies we see that ordinary people, often a group indicated by a single name followed by the phrase "e degli amici," did acquire them.[4] Individual printings were not large by modern standards but immense compared to the making of manuscript copies; and popular collections were reprinted as often as publishers thought it feasible to do so.[5] There was a constant demand for new madrigals, but established names had commercial importance; publishers used the well-known names of composers such as Verdelot, Arcadelt, Festa, and Willaert to sell volumes containing only a few pieces by these musicians and filled out with music by lesser-known and sometimes very young madrigalists.[6] Composers who had already appeared in print were asked by or on behalf of publishers to send in more of their music.[7] Although we do not know as much about how printers got hold of music as we would

madrigal in print begins with Verdelot's *Primo libro*, printed from Antico's woodcuts in Venice in 1533.

4. Hubert Naich's *Exercitium Seraficum*, a volume of madrigals printed in Rome ca. 1540, was written, says the composer in the dedication, "in maggior parte à richiesta di questa e di quello," members presumably of the "accademia degli amici" that Naich lists himself as belonging to.

5. Prints of music were described as "nuovamente stampati" or "ristampati," the latter indicating either reprints or new editions. But reprintings were also made without indication; on this see Stanley Boorman, "The 'First' Edition of the *Odhecaton A*," *Journal of the American Musicological Society* 30 (1977), 183–207. For an example of a famous work printed incomplete, then with the completion inserted in the same edition, see Alvin H. Johnson, "The 1548 Editions of Cipriano de Rore's Third Book of Madrigals," in *Studies in Musicology in Honor of Otto E. Albrecht*, ed. John W. Hill (Kassel, 1977), pp. 110–25, esp. pp. 117–19.

6. Verdelot's volumes of five- and six-voice madrigals, for example, are full of music by other composers. An extreme case of disingenousness on the part of publishers is the *Libro primo a 3v* of Costanzo Festa, "ristampato" in 1541 "con la Gionta de Quaranta Madrigali di Jhan Gero"; this volume contains at most one piece by Festa.

7. Thus in 1544 Antonfrancesco Doni wrote, on behalf of the publisher Girolamo Scotto, to Claudio Veggio, whose *Primo libro* had been issued by Scotto in 1540, begging the composer to send another set of madrigals to be printed. See Doni, *Lettere* (Venice, 1544), fol. 110ᵛ.

like, it is clear that the Venetian firms of Girolamo Scotto and Antonio Gardano had agents in Rome and elsewhere and were always on the lookout for new material.[8]

To a certain extent the publishers had thus become patrons of the madrigal, paying or taking on a commercial partner to pay the cost of printing and distribution (though at times they may have entered into partnership with a composer, or even printed music at the composer's expense).[9] Music prints were like other books regularly dedicated to rulers and secular or ecclesiastical aristocrats; it is not clear, however, that the dedicatees were always or even very often genuine patrons. A new age of amateur consumption of music, fed by commercial enterprise, had begun. As a result, much of the music published in the 1540s tended to echo the formulas so successfully used by Verdelot and Arcadelt. (The latter's *Primo libro* was probably the most often reprinted volume of music by a single composer in the whole of the life of the madrigal.)[10] Books designed for beginners and used for teaching purposes were also popular; the duos of Jhan Gero and of Bernardino Lupacchino were reprinted over and over again.[11] To some extent the popularity of the madrigal was a matter of text independent of musical setting; poems known in settings for four or five voices were printed in collections of easier music in newly written compositions for two or three voices, such as the series of volumes that appeared under the name of the publisher Girolamo Scotto.[12] The new public of

8. We shall know much more about the activities of Venetian music printers in this period when the comprehensive work of Mary Lewis on Gardano and of Jane Bernstein on Scotto is published.

9. For a rare example of a contract between typesetter, printer, and publisher, see Donna G. Cardamone, "*Madrigali a tre et Arie napolitane*: A Typographical and Repertorial Study," *Journal of the American Musicological Society* 35 (1982), 439–41. An example of a contract involving a composer (Morales) is discussed by Suzanne G. Cusick, *Valerio Dorico: Music Printer in Sixteenth-Century Rome* (Ann Arbor, 1981), pp. 95–103.

10. See Thomas W. Bridges, "The Publishing of Arcadelt's First Book of Madrigals" (Ph.D. diss., Harvard University, 1982).

11. See Lawrence F. Bernstein and James Haar, eds., *Ihan Gero: Il Primo Libro de' Madrigali italiani et Canzoni francese a due voci* (New York, 1980), pp. xxiv–xxxi. The first edition of this work was probably the Palermo copy mentioned on pp. xxv–xxvi; the date of this print was almost certainly 1540, as I learned from a personal communication from Professor Jane Bernstein.

12. Whether Scotto himself was the composer of the various volumes of two- and three-voice madrigals that appeared under his name in the 1540s and in subsequent reprints is uncertain. We know that Gero wrote at least some of his own two-

madrigal singers, for the most part untroubled either by literary-musical theory or by aristocratic notions of conservative decorum, simply and very naturally craved novelty—not just new pieces but music offering something new in the way of style or expression. In this context Doni's remark makes excellent sense.

Of course the old sources of musical patronage did not disappear. Madrigals were written, sometimes to poetry of local origin, for the Ferrarese court by Alfonso and Francesco della Viola, by the French composer Maître Jhan, and later by the great Flemish musician Cipriano de Rore; and for the Gonzaga by Hoste da Reggio in the 1540s and later by Giaches Wert, just as their predecessors had written frottolas. Francesco Corteccia served as a court composer to the first Medici dukes, and in the next generation Stefano Rossetti and the Mantuan nobleman Alessandro Striggio wrote madrigals, for private entertainment and for spectacular *intermedi*, at the Florentine court. Much of the repertory of the madrigal still originated in aristocratic circles, and sometimes the music was withheld from publication at the patron's request. The madrigals and motets of Willaert's *Musica nova*, written in the 1540s but not printed until 1559, are one example of this; the Ferrarese court pieces of Luzzasco Luzzaschi, written for the virtuoso singers of Alfonso II but not published until after the duke's death, are another.[13]

There were also new sources of patronage. Musicians who held posts at cathedrals and churches in towns where there was no resident court wrote madrigals and got them into print; their patrons were prominent clergymen, individual noblemen, and groups of interested amateurs who shared in the now universal vogue of the madrigal.[14] Academies, some of them short-lived and loosely orga-

---

and three-voice pieces for Scotto and/or Gardano; the publishers may have hired other musicians to produce this kind of thing.

13. For the *Musica nova* see Anthony Newcomb, "Editions of Willaert's *Musica nova*: New Evidence, New Speculations," *Journal of the American Musicological Society* 26 (1973), 132–45, with citation of earlier literature on the subject; Helga Meier, "Zur Chronologie der *Musica nova* Adrian Willaerts," *Analecta Musicologica* 12 (1973), 71–98. On Luzzaschi's volume see Adriano Cavicchi, ed., *Luzzasco Luzzaschi: Madrigali per cantare e sonare, a uno, duo e tre soprani (1601)* (Brescia, 1965).

14. Examples include the madrigals of Bertoldo Bertoldi of Castel Vetro (1544), dedicated to Laura d'Este; Francesco Bifetto of Bergamo (1547–48), dedicated to Ruggiero Conte di Calepio; Giandomenico Martoretta of Calabria (1548–54), one of whose volumes is dedicated to a "nobile cavaliero de l'isola di Cipro"; and Anselmo Reulx (1543–46), whose place of activity is unknown and whose prints lack

nized but others of substance and of real importance in the cultural life of their communities, were being formed all over Italy. Not all of them had musical interests, but many did combine literary and musical activity. Among the most important and longest-lived was the Accademia filarmonica of Verona, founded (or refounded as the successor to earlier groups) in 1543, and still in existence today.[15] Composers, among them the well-known madrigalists Giovan Nasco and Vincenzo Ruffo, were hired by the Filarmonica to give its members instruction in music and to compose on request. These kinds of corporate patronage are strong testimony to the newly widened scope of composition and performance of polyphonic music. Although the academies were probably all-male, performance of madrigals by mixed groups became common. From the first days of the madrigal we hear of women singers, and by mid-century there were women composers as well.[16] As we shall see, the role of women as performers became central in the last quarter of the sixteenth century, at least in places where Counter-Reformation severity was not the rule.

Except for the *rime spirituali* that began to appear in print at mid-century, there is no drastic change in the poetry of the madrigal as the genre began to outgrow its earliest stages. Petrarch, not at first used as much as one would have thought, began to appear with more frequency, and this will call for further comment. *Petrarchisti* such as Luigi Cassola were still in vogue, and the pastoral verse of Sannazaro and his imitators was popular. After the publication of its final version in 1532, the *Orlando furioso* became a favorite source for settings of *ottave*, and imitators of Ariosto supplied quite a few *stanze*; until the appearance of Tasso's *Gerusalemme* the popu-

dedications. See Emil Vogel, Alfred Einstein, François Lesure, and Claudio Sartori, *Bibliografia della musica italiana vocale profana pubblicata dal 1500 al 1700* (=*Il nuovo Vogel*), 3 vols. (Pomezia, 1977), nos. 352, 364–65, 1738–41, 2336–39.

15. See Giuseppe Turrini, *L'Accademia filarmonica di Verona dalla fondazione (maggio 1543) al 1600 e il suo patrimonio musicale antico* (Verona, 1941).

16. Machiavelli's mistress, Barbara Salutati, was well known as a singer; she may have performed the canzoni of Verdelot written for Machiavelli's comedies. See H. Colin Slim, *A Gift of Madrigals and Motets*, 2 vols. (Chicago, 1972), 1:85, 92–95. Doni's *Dialogo* has a woman interlocutor-singer in its second part; and Doni speaks admiringly in one of the prefaces of the work of the singing and playing of Polissena Pecorina. As the century went on, references to female singers multiplied. Maddalena Casulana (b. ca. 1540) was a well-known singer as well as a madrigalist, whose compositions appeared in collected volumes and mid-century anthologies.

larity of the Ariostan *ottava* was unchallenged. Local poets offered texts, or commissioned their setting, just as the Florentine patrons of Verdelot had done; there is often little overlap between texts set by composers active in different cities.

If we consider the madrigal repertory as it stood in the 1540s, when it was becoming widely popular throughout Italy, we see that its initial Florentine stage had already been followed by activity in Rome, under Clement VII and Paul III; in the Ferrara of Alfonso I and Ercole II; in Venice, where a circle of musicians was forming around the *maestro* of San Marco, Adrian Willaert; and in Naples, where the versatile and prolific Giovan Domenico da Nola was well launched into his long career. Within a very few years Verona, Milan, and a host of smaller cities could boast of resident madrigalists.

At first it seems hard to account for the madrigal's evident popularity. It is not popularesque in tone like the frottola, and in fact madrigal prints contain rather few pieces of popular cast.[17] The real successor to the frottola, the *canzone alla villanesca*, began to appear in print in the late 1530s, playing parent to a whole group of popular genres that achieved success alongside but not intermingled with the madrigal. Judging from Italian tastes of earlier periods, one would think that music in four, five, or six partbooks calling for fully vocal performance would have appealed little to a wide public. And the prevailingly melancholy, often elegiac tone of the music (more serious than much of the verse it sets) would seem less than ideal for frequent performance in company. Not all madrigals were doleful, of course; and performers doubtless varied the diet with the new *villanesche*, remnants of the frottola repertory, and solo singing of popular materials.

Reasons that might be advanced for the success of the madrigal in print are not, however, hard to find. First of all, most early madrigals are not very difficult to sing; their range is small, rhythmic patterns are simple, vocal ornament is absent or modest. The music is actually easier to perform than much of the frottola literature. Like the frottola, the madrigal in print offered the public

17. There are a few exceptions. For one, see Don Harrán, "*Chi bussa*? Or the Case of the Anti-madrigal," *Journal of the American Musicological Society* 21 (1968), 85–93.

some access to music associated with aristocratic tastes; the element of snobbery, evident in the attitude of Antonfrancesco Doni, surely contributed to the madrigal's success.[18] Then, the ability to read music, in part increasing as a result of the development of music printing and in part stimulating its growth, had evidently become much more general by the fourth decade of the sixteenth century. Partbooks of printed music were designed to be read from, not as repositories of pieces to be memorized and then sung in freely varied manner. There is much visual evidence to support this assertion: paintings show performances from partbooks, with finger tapping of the *tactus* evident, and many partbooks show correction of printers' errors and especially the addition of bar lines, usually dividing the music by breves (though one cannot be sure that these were not drawn in much later).[19] And above all the partbooks themselves seem designed for ease of reading: canons when they exist are resolved, the music is spaced so that the text can be underlaid without undue crowding, and as the century goes on the text underlay becomes more and more precise, dividing words carefully and leaving few problems even for modern readers of this music.

That a book is designed to be read from is less self-evident than it sounds, if by reading one means proceeding at sight and at a reasonable speed. This is true of sixteenth-century books in general but especially true of musical notation in the period. If one compares a page of fifteenth-century notation (often less clear in text underlay than the manuscripts containing the trecento repertory) first with a frottola print and then with a later-sixteenth-century partbook (Pls. 6–8), the difference seems clear, and is not due sim-

18. Music for state events such as weddings or ceremonial entries occasionally reached the public in print, an example being the festival madrigals by Corteccia and others for the wedding of Cosimo I de' Medici in 1539; see Andrew C. Minor and Bonner Mitchell, *A Renaissance Entertainment: Festivities for the Marriage of Cosimo I, Duke of Florence, in 1539* (Columbia, Mo., 1968). Doni liked to pose as a man of the world, a connoisseur, even a collector of music. He did manage to get hold of a fair amount of unpublished music for his *Dialogo*, and he once addressed himself to Cosimo I as a collector and patron, hoping for ducal support. See James Haar, "A Gift of Madrigals to Cosimo I," *Rivista italiana di musicologia* 1 (1966), 167–89.

19. Curiously, many sixteenth-century partbooks look unused, with obvious errors uncorrected. But these often come from princely libraries where they were simply stored away; volumes in regular use by singers would have been marked up, but because of the circumstances of their purchase and use had a much smaller chance of survival.

ply to the fact that the more recent notation is easier for most of us to read right off. Musical notation in earlier periods served to record a repertory, as a memory aid to those who already knew the piece in question, or as a page to be studied closely and memorized, *then* performed; or at least that is what the surviving sources look like. (We do not know how the individual sheets that early performers are sometimes depicted using were notated.) Sixteenth-century music, and in particular secular music, was written down for all those reasons plus an additional one, that of providing a repertory of material to be read through. Readers of music needed clarity of visual appearance on the page; they also required a large number of pieces in a familiar style—though they were eager for novelty as well. The whole process of reading, or reading through, music seems to me fundamentally different from other forms of music making; and when readers of music, once few in number and possessed of an almost secret skill, became many, the whole of musical culture changed. Later in the sixteenth century one even sees the publication of music in "study scores," intended for silent reading.[20] And in the late sixteenth century a book of madrigals could sometimes be conceived as a *canzoniere* or a series of dramatic excerpts meant to be read in sequence from start to finish, and was thus a book in every sense of the word. I hope I do not simply sound here like a latter-day convert to the theories of Marshall McLuhan; the point I am making seems essential if we are to understand both the popularity of the cinquecento madrigal and the restless air of novelty seeking that marks its middle years.

If the users of madrigal prints read through a good deal of music, were they conscious of reading the poetry as well? Not all singers of today are, certainly; and from another remark by the useful Doni we gather that some sixteenth-century singers of madrigals might as well have performed the music to solmization or nonsense syllables. But Doni adds that to persons of discernment the authorship and character of the text meant something.[21] At the very least

---

20. For example, in 1577 Angelo Gardano published a volume containing thirty-five pieces by Cipriano de Rore in score format, designed for study or keyboard performance, under the title *Tutti i madrigali di Cipriano de Rore a quattro voci spartiti et accomodati per sonar d'ogni sorte d'instrumento perfetto, et per qualunque studioso di contrapunti.* See *Il nuovo Vogel*, no. 2388.

21. *Dialogo*, p. 82.

singers were aware of key words and of textual imagery; the success of the inventive musical vocabulary we call "madrigalisms" depends mainly on the singers' recognition of musical imagery matched to that of the text, whether or not the musical devices used are clearer to the eye than to the ear. But did singers of madrigals finish a piece with the sensation that they had given a "reading" of the poem? The question cannot of course be answered with a flat monosyllable. It is easy to say that singing can never be the same thing as reading or speaking; but if we look ahead to the end of the sixteenth century and the concept of *recitar cantando*, we are reminded that at the close of the Renaissance at least some people thought it could be. In certain respects the early madrigal, with its basically syllabic declamation and its gently curved (sometimes nearly flat) melodic lines, seems meant for the singers to treat the verse as if they were reading aloud, using repetitions of words and phrases for rhetorical emphasis; single parts diverge into imitative counterpoint as if to emphasize the individuality of each reader within the framework of a harmonious single interpretation of the text. Or the reading may be, as in the case of madrigals intended for *intermedi*, a choral one in the antique sense of the term, the voicing of communal sentiment.

Although recent work on the fifteenth-century chanson has moved away from the view that its text and music are only loosely connected,[22] there is nevertheless a noticeable change in vocal music composed in the second and third decades of the sixteenth century; if not a perfect marriage of words to music, then at least a "meaningful relationship" becomes evident. This can be seen in manuscript and printed sources of the music, though not always with perfect clarity; scribes and typesetters may have lagged behind composers in disposition of text, as indeed I believe they occasionally did in other matters (such as visual layout of the music and consistent use of accidentals that amateur singers could not readily have supplied in the way that professionals did). Further evidence is offered by writers commenting on the relationship of text and notes. Trecento definitions of *poesia per musica*, such as the remark

22. An example of a newer approach is the study by Don Randel, "Dufay the Reader," in *Music and Language*, Studies in the History of Music, vol. 1 (New York, 1983), pp. 38–78.

that ballatas are "verba applicata sonis,"[23] suggest the kind of intent that the result actually seems to show; whether or not texts were put to preexisting music adapted for the purpose, melody and text existed in conceptually different planes, and this remained the case for a long time, except in pieces showing the influence of popular song styles. From the mid fifteenth century through most of the cinquecento, theorists offering advice on the subject of text setting did so in a prescriptive vein. Some distinctions of practice between sacred and secular music are suggested, though not treated in detail. Common-sense advice is mixed with an increasingly explicit set of caveats about avoidance of barbarisms such as setting unaccented syllables to prominent notes; but until the middle of the sixteenth century the approach is always that of setting text to music. In the famous set of rules given by Zarlino, writing in the 1550s, we see the order reversed for the first time; Zarlino's precepts are for composing music to suit the text.[24] We should not make too much of this, for Zarlino's rules were not newly conceived but adapted from those given by an older contemporary.[25] Nevertheless Zarlino holds the correct humanistic position, that music should be consequent upon and subservient to the words it clothes.[26] At the simplest level this means that words when sung should sound like the spoken word, and a poem set to music should sound like verse read aloud.

Conscious preoccupation with mechanically correct declama-

23. Santorre Debenedetti, "Un trattatello del secolo xiv sopra la poesia musicale," *Studi medievali* 2 (1906–7), 67.

24. Gioseffo Zarlino, *Le istitutioni harmoniche* (Venice, 1558), iv, 33.

25. See Don Harrán, "New Light on the Question of Text Underlay prior to Zarlino," *Acta Musicologica* 45 (1973), 24–56. The theorist in question is Giovanni Lanfranco.

26. *Istitutioni harmoniche*, iii, 26: "Che l'harmonia, che si contiene in essa sia talmente accomodate alla Oratione, cioè alle Parole, che nelle materie allegre l'harmonia non sia flebile; & per contrario, nella flebile, l'harmonia non sia allegra." Zarlino goes so far as to say that musical syntax is, or should be, close to verbal syntax; see Harrán, "New Light," pp. 33–34. The idea that music should be the servant of poetry, usually identified with the period of Monteverdi, was already current in mid-century. See, for example, the language of Marc'Antonio Mazzone in a dedicatory letter of 1569: "Il corpo della musica son le note, & le parole son l'anima, e si come l'anima per essere più digno del corpo deve da quello essere seguita, & imitata, cosi ancho le note devono seguire, & imitare le parole" (cited in Emil Vogel, *Bibliothek der gedruckten weltlichen Vocalmusik Italiens aus den Jahren 1500–1700* [1892], *mit Nachträgen von Prof. Alfred Einstein* [Hildesheim, 1962], 1:441). See also the letter of Giovanni del Lago on the subject (1541), cited in Walther Dürr, "Zum Verhältnis von Wort und Ton im Rhythmus des Cinquecento-Madrigals," *Archiv für Musikwissenschaft* 15 (1958), 90.

tion can be seen at the beginning of the sixteenth century in the pedagogical experiments conducted by German musicians and schoolmasters, setting Latin text to quantitatively corresponding musical values.[27] The influence of these exercises ought not to be exaggerated, at least for the early sixteenth century. (Quantitatively precise music of more importance was written later in the century for humanistic Latin texts and for the experimental French verse of Baïf's academy, but Italian song was affected only indirectly by such experiments.) And the matching of musical and verbal accent is in itself no great achievement. On the more important problem of how the music can match the individual life and sense of the text it accompanies the theorists offer little advice, just as they limit their precepts on musical matters to how to write counterpoint, hinting only occasionally at how these basic materials are to be used in creative composition.[28] They say nothing about how poetic caesuras and enjambements are to be treated in the music, or about how rhyme or internal symmetries of poetic design should be reflected. Happy and sad texts should receive appropriate musical dress; that we are told, though not how to achieve this correspondence other than through choice of melodic mode in accord with the ancient belief in the varying ethos of the modes.[29] As the century goes on there are more remarks about the matching of verbal *affetti* with corresponding musical inventions, the result being a

27. In 1507 Petrus Tritonius published a collection of Horatian odes in metrically precise block chords; his example was followed by later German composers, including Ludwig Senfl and Paul Hofhaimer. See Rochus von Liliencron, "Die Horazischen Metren in deutschen Kompositionen des XVI. Jahrhunderts," *Vierteljahrsschrift für Musikwissenschaft* 3 (1887), 26–91.

28. This is not to say that theorists confused counterpoint with composition. In the late sixteenth century the two are clearly distinguished, as in the work of Ludovico Zacconi. For a study of the difference between composition and counterpoint in the work of Tinctoris, see Margaret Bent, *"Resfacta* and *Cantare super librum," Journal of the American Musicological Society* 36 (1983), 371–91.

29. See the general statement of Zarlino cited above, n. 26. The fourth book of Zarlino's *Istitutioni harmoniche*, which deals separately with each of the twelve modes, characterizes each of them by a set of ethical qualities. The effectiveness of this approach is lessened by the fact that Zarlino renumbered the twelve modes between editions of his treatise, starting on D in the 1558 edition, on C in that of 1573. (The modes of course retained the ethical qualities they had to start with; that is, the D mode is described the same way whether it is the first or the third. But to those who associated modal number with modal ethos Zarlino's shift must have been confusing.) See Richard L. Crocker, "Perchè Zarlino diede una nuova numerazione ai modi?," *Rivista italiana di musicologia* 3 (1968), 48–58.

1. Florence, Church of San Martino (fifteenth century).

2. A *cantastorie* (fifteenth/early sixteenth century).

3. A *cantastorie* (fifteenth/early sixteenth century).

4. A *cantastorie* (late fifteenth century).

5. *Ciarlatani* in the Piazza di San Marco, Venice (late sixteenth century).

6. *Canto de' sartori: De sartor nui siam maestri* (ca. 1480).

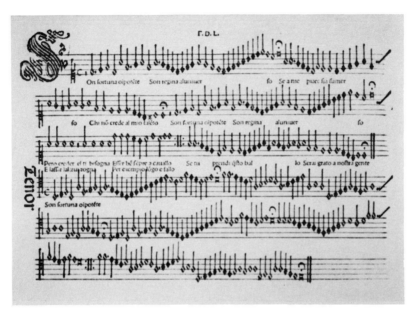

7. F. D. L. (=Filippo Lurano?), *Son fortuna omnipotente* (1505).

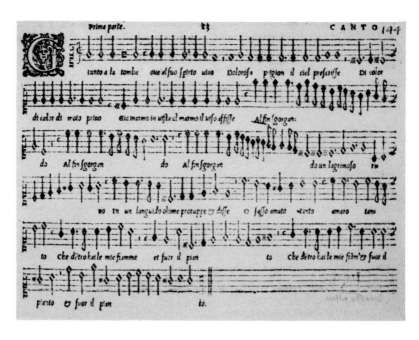

8. Giaches Wert, *Giunto alla tomba ove al suo spirto vivo* (1581).

heightening of the affective properties of the text and more intense operation on the affections of singers and listeners—what we call in our own very limited vocabulary the expressive side of musical language.[30] None of this was generalized into aesthetic theory, nor was there any need to do so. By universal agreement, the aesthetic basis for both poetry and music was the Aristotelian doctrine of imitation of nature; the method for achieving successful results, a use whenever possible of the Ciceronian precepts of imitation of recognizably excellent models.

In creating a musical style that would appear to rise from the demands of the text and hence to sound in performance like a reading of that text, the first madrigalists turned to established genres like the French chanson and to a lesser extent the Latin motet for models. Mixed with traditional ways of setting poetry line by line, and of alternating chordal and staggered textures to achieve the *varietas* praised by theorists, are genuine responses to the texts at hand. Musical repetitions correspond to poetic symmetries within a through-composed framework; caesuras and, less often, enjambements are reflected in musical ebb and flow; exclamations and direct address are set off; easily musicalized images of flight, of rise and fall, of audible emotional tics such as sighs are made use of. Interspersed with these are musical puns, such as melodies using solmization-syllable notes when *lasso* or *mi fa* occurs in the text, or the employment of blackened notes when *notte* comes along. We see in this apparently naive combination several kinds of response to words in tone, where, I think, the sixteenth century saw only one, with appearance, sound, and meaning all fused rather than being distinct characteristics; and I think we must be careful not to look with a patronizing eye on an attitude toward verbal and musical language different from our own. To the end of the Renaissance, composers went on thinking that the way to capture the essence of a poem was to bring to musical life the *affetti* of individual words and phrases, and they continued to use a mixture of what we consider naive and sophisticated methods to do so.

30. This kind of statement is found more often in prefaces and dedications to collections of music than anywhere else. See James Haar, "Self-consciousness about Style, Form, and Genre in Sixteenth-Century Music," *Studi musicali* 3 (1974), 219–32.

There were critics of madrigalistic pictorialism in the late sixteenth century, though few if any disinterested ones. But at the time Antonfrancesco Doni made his remark about Arcadelt no one saw a need to reform madrigalistic excess; it was something in the opposite direction that was wanted. The madrigal as cultivated by Verdelot is, for all its sweetness of sound and justness of declamation, slightly monotonous, its reading of the text inflected in so gentle a manner as to be nearly lacking in persuasive rhetoric—or so at least it may have come to seem to its contemporary singers and audiences. In the search for novelty that overtook the genre beginning around 1540 was a clearly evident if for a long time unstated attempt at heightening the individuality and urgency of musical rhetoric, at giving greater variety and dramatic force to the sung word. This can already be seen in the later madrigals of Arcadelt, particularly in those that I think were written after the composer left Florence for Rome in 1539.[31]

The first extension of musical language in this direction was rhythmic. The 1540s saw the appearance of a number of madrigal prints advertised as written *a misura breve* (in a short measure, according to the semibreve rather than *alla breve*) or *a note nere* (with many black or short-value notes), or called *madrigali cromatici* (here meaning "colored" in a rhetorical sense, by the introduction of many short, also blackened, notes).[32] Various reasons have been advanced in explanation of this phenomenon, including the publishers' desire for something novel to advertise on title pages; and composers used these short note values (presumably at a tempo somewhat slower than that of the white-note *alla breve* madrigal) in different ways, sometimes producing a fussily syncopated style that pitted voice against voice in slightly-out-of-balance imitation, not always in response to a textual suggestion.[33] One effect of this new way of writing outweighed the others in importance: the text could

31. These madrigals appeared for the most part in anthologies of the 1540s; Arcadelt's own five volumes are nearly all the work of his Florentine residence in the 1530s.

32. The series of volumes devoted by the publishers Gardano and Scotto to madrigals of this type have been edited by Don Harrán, *The Anthologies of Black-Note Madrigals*, 5 vols. (American Institute of Musicology, 1978–81).

33. See James Haar, "The *Note Nere* Madrigal," *Journal of the American Musicological Society* 18 (1965), 22–41.

now be declaimed to a range of rhythmic values extending from the breve to the *fusa* or *chroma* (in the usual modern transcription from the whole note to the sixteenth note). The full range was not always used, but in place of Verdelot's steady succession of semibreves and minims, making for a nearly uniform rate of declamation, there could be marked retardations and accelerations, allowing for a more dramatic reading of the text. Example 35 shows two samples (a, b) of the old and three (c–e) of the new declamatory patterns.[34] After its initial wave of popularity the black-note madrigal appeared less often, and its declamatory range is found in music notated *alla breve*; in later-sixteenth-century music one sees the two notational systems used to characterize settings of different kinds of texts, the long measure preferred for more serious poetry and the short one reserved for lighter, sometimes ironic or satirical verse.[35]

Although one of the most important volumes of black-note madrigals is the *Libro primo* for five voices of Cipriano de Rore (1542), presumably written in or near Venice, the main center of cultivation of the new style was Rome, among musicians of the papal choirs and composers in the service of cardinals and wealthy laymen resident there. Even more closely associated with Rome is an outgrowth of the black-note style, the *madrigale arioso* of the 1550s.[36] A series of madrigal anthologies with this title, containing work by a number of Roman composers and including pieces by Palestrina and the young Orlando di Lasso, was collected and published by the Roman singer-composer-printer Antonio Barrè in the years 1555–63. Use of the adjective *arioso* would suggest that these pieces make use of *arie*, the stock melodies of the *improvvisatori* that I spoke of in the last chapter; they do so to a limited extent, but I think these pieces show another application of the concept of *aria*.

34. (a) Verdelot, *Ogn'hor per voi sospiro* (*Libro secondo a 4v* [1534], no. 14); (b) Costanzo Festa, *Dur'è'l partito dove m'astringete* (Verdelot, *Libro secondo a 4v* [1534], no. 12); (c) Reulx, *S'io credessi per mort'esser scarco* (Petrarch) (RISM 1542[17], *Il primo libro . . . a misura di breve*, no. 15); (d) Naich? Rampollini? Berchem?, *Che giova saettar un che si muore* (Bembo) (RISM 1542[17], no. 25); (e) anon., *Sì vivo è lo splendore* (RISM 1549[30], *Libro terzo . . . a notte negre*, no. 28).

35. See Alfred Einstein, *The Italian Madrigal* (Princeton, 1949), pp. 400, 511, 633, 659 and passim.

36. James Haar, "The *Madrigale Arioso*: A Mid-century Development in the Cinquecento Madrigal," *Studi musicali* 12 (1983), 203–19.

One of the consequences of the rhythmic variety allowed in the black-note madrigal was the development of a dramatically heightened mode of declamation; another, related yet distinct, was the freedom given composers to use a kind of *parlando* musical language, not necessarily urgent in its rhetoric but possessed of a conversational ebb and flow quite unlike that of the early madrigal's regular pace of delivery. This *parlando* declamation is carried to a further degree of development in the *madrigale arioso*. The text is spoken to a subtle alternation of rhythmic values that gives the effect not of first-time reading but of spontaneous delivery of well-known lines, with retardations and anticipations for emphasis, even pauses for breath (see Ex. 36).[37] The top voice tends to predominate, and though imitative staggering of voices and some independence of material in the lower parts are used for variety, the texture is basically chordal, all the singers thus participating in the *arioso* quality of the writing.

In madrigals of this type I sense that an aspect of the improviser's art hard to capture in writing was aimed at. The frottola shows qualities related to improvisatory style, but for the most part in too regular and dancelike a way; the early madrigal does not, to me, suggest improvisation at all. The most intimate connection between words and music had always been in the *arie* of *canterini* and *citaredi*; in the otherwise unpretentious repertory of the *madrigale arioso* I see an effort to gain for the polyphonic madrigal something of that close connection, the words being not so much sung as spoken in music. That this should be attempted within the framework of four-voice polyphony shows the power of the madrigalian convention of representing the song of one person by the harmonious blend of a company of singers.

Pitch as well as rhythm was an area of musical experiment at mid-century; this can be seen in the motet as much as in the madrigal, and in both genres it is connected with strivings after a musical vocabulary of increased vividness. Chromaticism—now used in the modern sense—is the general term covering the tonal

37. Ex. 36: (a) Nola, *Tosto ch'il sol si scopr'in oriente* (RISM 1555[27], *Primo libro delle muse a 4v*, no. 16 in reprint of 1557[17]); (b) Paolo Animuccia, *La fiamm'ove tutt'ardo* (RISM 1558[13], *Secondo libro delle muse a 4v*, no. 13); (c) Palestrina, *Perch'al viso d'amor portava insegna* (Petrarch) (RISM 1562[7], *Terzo libro delle muse a 4v*, no. 24).

ventures seen in some of the music of Rore, of the young Lasso, of lesser-known composers such as Pietro Taglia in Milan and Hoste da Reggio in Mantua, and of the theorist-composer Nicola Vicentino.[38] There is more than one kind of chromatic experiment at this time. For many musicians it was a matter of accentuating and being more explicit about coloristic juxtaposition of sonorities, such as major triads based on notes a third apart. In a certain sense this is not genuine chromaticism since the movement of each vocal part might be conventionally diatonic; the iridescent tonal palette of Lasso's *Prophetiae Sibyllarum* is accomplished, for example, without very much use of chromatic movement by any single voice.[39] Many madrigalists used this coloristic device—at first self-consciously but later in the century as a normal rhetorical gesture—to set off key words or phrases, as can be seen in Example 37.[40] Its roots are in earlier-sixteenth-century music; the novelty in its use is partly increased frequency, partly the choice of unexpectedly remote sonorities, and partly its position in the musical fabric, given emphasis by rhythmic means.

Another type of chromatic practice was that espoused by Nicola Vicentino, who attempted to bring to modern life the chromatic and enharmonic *genera* of ancient music, which had fallen out of use some thousand years earlier.[41] Strictly construed, the chromatic genus calls for use of two sizes of semitone and avoidance of the diatonic whole tone—hard to do in the context of Renaissance polyphony; but Vicentino meant to be strict, and wrote some music

38. The best general study of this phenomenon remains that of Theodore Kroyer, *Die Anfänge der Chromatik im italienischen Madrigal des XVI. Jahrhunderts* (Leipzig, 1902). See also Henry W. Kaufmann, "Vicentino and the Greek Genera," *Journal of the American Musicological Society* 16 (1963), 325–46.

39. On Lasso's *Prophetiae* (especially its often-discussed opening piece) see Karol Berger, *Theories of Chromatic and Enharmonic Music in Late-Sixteenth-Century Italy* (Ann Arbor, 1980), pp. 104–15, and the studies cited there.

40. Ex. 37: (a) Rore, *Se ben il duol che per voi donna sento* (*Libro secondo a 4v* [1557], no. 19); (b) Rossetti, *Soleano i miei pensier soavemente* (*Libro primo a 4v* [1560], no. 4); (c) Wert, *Quando non più d'amor gl'aurati strali* (*Libro terzo a 5v* [1563], no. 12, *2ª parte*, mm. 18–27). The doubtless deliberate resemblance of Rossetti's opening to that of Arcadelt's *Il bianco e dolce cigno cantando more* makes the chromatic shift at "soavemente" all the more effective (see Ex. 43a).

41. The title of Vicentino's treatise, *L'antica musica ridotta alla moderna prattica*, refers to this effort at resuscitation of the ancient genera. For a study of the treatise see Henry W. Kaufmann, *The Life and Works of Nicola Vicentino* (American Institute of Musicology, 1966), chap. 3, as well as the article cited above, n. 38.

doing just this while at the same time working on the design of instruments that could play chromatic and enharmonic intervals. His claim that modern music was actually a blend of the ancient genera led in 1551 to a public debate on the subject, one of the more extraordinary recorded demonstrations of sixteenth-century interest in musical problems.[42] Most relevant here, however, is Vicentino's basic aim: he wanted to enrich what he saw as the insufficiently expressive musical language of his time through the addition of elements of ancient music that had been said to have special qualities of *ethos*. Vicentino's humanistic experiment achieved less of what we can recognize as affective textual expression than did the less radically conceived chromaticism of his contemporaries, but even they tended to use it in a more neutral way than we would expect. Later in the century composers did of course succeed in using chromatic language for striking rhetorical effect.

By about 1550 the madrigalian style of Verdelot and Arcadelt had thus been subject to a good deal of experiment, but its fundamental outlines remained the same. During the 1540s, however, a quite different approach to writing madrigals had developed in a circle of musicians centered in Venice and for the most part made up of colleagues and students of the revered *maestro* of San Marco, Adrian Willaert. One might say without simplifying matters too much that by mid-century there was a Roman madrigal, identified with Arcadelt and his followers, and a Venetian one, with Willaert and Rore its leading figures. This Venetian madrigal is characterized by seriousness of musical language corresponding to the texts, which include some of Petrarch's most melancholy and contemplative sonnets, set in their entirety; by adoption of a densely polyphonic texture, most often composed of five voices; and by use of subtle, half-hidden techniques of musical resemblance among the voices that give new meaning to the concept of imitation. In all this it resembles the contemporary motet far more than did the chansonesque madrigal of 1530.

We can only guess at the reasons for this change of style and mode of expression. Willaert's earlier madrigals, some of which could have been written in Ferrara or Rome, are within the stylistic limits of the Florentine-Roman madrigal, though his solid north-

---

42. See Kaufmann, *Vicentino*, pp. 22–32.

ern training as a polyphonist may be a bit more in evidence than is the case with Verdelot and Arcadelt. In matters purely musical Willaert may have been influenced by Rore, although he is said to have been the latter's teacher; when Rore arrived in Venice, presumably around 1540, he was already a mature composer, fully trained in the polyphonic technique favored by Nicholas Gombert and his contemporaries, a style marked by closely woven imitative texture and staggered rather than simultaneous cadential articulations. All of this can be seen in Rore's first madrigal book, published in 1542; he could not have learned this style quickly. There is no reason to think that these madrigals were not written in Venice, or at least in the Veneto; Rore seems to have made use of a musical style he had already mastered, brilliantly adapting it to Italian and to the setting of poetry favored in Venetian academic circles.

Willaert and his fellow musicians are known to have composed and performed madrigals for a private *accademia* of patrons; to an outsider who heard some of this music it was stunning in its novel beauty.[43] But it is clear that the intended novelty was not just musical. It is often said that Willaert and Rore sought to elevate the tone of the madrigal to meet the quality of the Petrarchan poetry it set. I think this should be stated in another way. Venetian literary circles in the closing years of Bembo's life and throughout the following decades were active in discussion of the kinds of topics that appealed to the critical mind of the cinquecento.[44] One matter frequently, sometimes hotly discussed throughout Italy in the middle and later years of the century was that of genre; the subjects debated included, for example, the distinction between epic and romance and why Ariosto should be thought to have written the latter rather than the former.[45] I do not know of any discussions of liter-

43. See Doni's remarks about the music of Willaert's circle in the dedication to the tenor partbook of his *Dialogo della Musica*, p. 5 in Malipiero's edition.

44. For a survey of literary debates in the period see Bernard Weinberg, *A History of Literary Criticism in the Italian Renaissance*, 2 vols. (Chicago, 1961). Martha Feldman's "Venice and the Italian Madrigal, ca. 1535–1550" (Ph.D. diss., Univ. of Pennsylvania, 1986), sheds new light on the relationship of Venetian literary criticism to music.

45. Tasso's *Apologia in difesa della "Gerusalemme liberata"* (*Opere*, ed. Bruno Maier, vol. 5 [Milan, 1965], pp. 625–720) carries on an argument begun by Camillo Pellegrino, whose *Carrafa o vero dell'epica poesia* (1584) placed Tasso above Ariosto as a true epic poet; this drew a defense of Ariosto from Bastiano de' Rossi and Leonardo Salviati. Among other defenders of Ariosto was Giovanni de' Bardi, who particularly admired the suitability of Ariosto's verse for music. See Claude Palisca, "The 'Camerata fiorentina': A Reappraisal," *Studi musicali* 1 (1972), 211.

ary genre that deal more than in passing with music in this period; musical theorists such as Vicentino and Zarlino do hint at distinctions of genre, and in the later sixteenth century it became usual to talk of linked musical and literary categories. It seems to me that a conscious decision must have been made—though perhaps not explicitly recorded—in Venetian academic circles where music played a part; a decision to treat the madrigal not as *poesia per musica* but as serious literature for which a suitably serious musical style was to be cultivated, the whole adding luster to the image of the vernacular as the equal of ancient literature. There could be and indeed was occasional relaxation of this standard, but not a wholesale one. What Alfred Einstein calls the "lighter forms"—the *villanesca, mascherata, villota*, and so on—were then to be the designated refuge of the whole tradition of *poesia per musica*, and a musical style fitting them was also to be deliberately created. If there is any truth in my hypothesis that music in Venice followed the dictates of literary theory, the somewhat puzzling double careers of Willaert and many of his followers, as composers of highly serious polyphony for the madrigal and of cheerfully unpretentious musical patter, carefully remade from its Neapolitan models, for the *villanesca*, make sense: the *villanesca* existed less as comic relief from the now very serious madrigal than as its deliberately and artificially created literary and musical companion, at a lower level. It is as if a new version had appeared of *De vulgare eloquentia*, using madrigals (actually mostly sonnets) and *villanesche* to typify Dante's tragic and comic styles.

The most important compositions in the new Venetian style are the contents of Willaert's *Musica nova*, written for four, five, six, and seven voices, and Rore's volumes of five-voice madrigals. In Willaert's collection the four-voice pieces, though they partake of the new style, are not fully characteristic of it; the pieces for seven voices are dialogues with consistent alternation of three or four against four, all seven being used only for repetition of the final poetic line. The madrigals for five and six voices show the Venetian style at its most characteristic. Verdelot and Arcadelt had written madrigals for five and six voices, but it is in the work of the Venetians that a stylistic separation can be seen, one that persists through the rest of the century, between the four-voice madrigal, tending toward economy of declamatory texture, and the full-blown polyphony favored in five- and six-voice pieces. Since four-voice writing had for some time been regarded as a classic norm, the decision of Willaert and his circle to set their most serious compositional efforts in a thicker polyphonic texture was an important one, different in direction from but comparable in importance to Beethoven's choice of Haydn's quartets rather than the string quintets of Mozart as models for his most serious contrapuntal style.

L'aura mia sacra al mio stanco riposo, like all but one of the madrigals in the *Musica nova* the setting of a Petrarchan sonnet, is typical of Willaert's new approach (Ex. 38).[46] It is divided into two parts in the manner of the contemporary motet; Willaert's closeness to the poetry is reflected in the comparative lengths of the sections, which, despite use of textual repetitions, correspond to the verse lengths of the sonnet's octet and sestet. The end of the first part is marked by an effectively sudden cadence on A, the dominant of its prevailing sixth or Hypolydian mode; and the second section opens with a kind of "developmental" tonal passage leading through the final of the mode to an area on its flat side. This bit of tonal architecture is appropriate to the close of the octet, "Amore m'ha roso," and the opening of the sestet ("e di pietà dipinta"); it also gives musical impetus and variety to an otherwise tonally static piece. Willaert's closely woven texture sets the poetry by its syntactical structure rather than by the poetic line, almost making a mannerism of this approach in its emphasis of caesura rather than line ending. Still, one can hear the sonnet structure in the cadences at the end of the fourth line (mm. 32−35) and the end of the sestet's third line (mm. 91−92). Strong cadences are otherwise avoided; even the clearly audible articulation separating the two halves of the second poetic quartet (at "Poi seguo," m. 49), though it cadences firmly, is denied musical finality by the simultaneous entry of the next poetic line.

This feature of Willaert's music, related to the motet style of Gombert, has often been commented on, and it is of course in strong contrast to the musical phraseology of the earlier madrigal.

46. Ex. 38, *L'aura mia sacra al mio stanco riposo*, is taken from Willaert's *Musica nova* (1559), p. 84. The madrigal is printed in Adrian Willaert, *Opera Omnia*, ed. Hermann Zenck and Walter Gerstenberg, vol. 13 (American Institute of Musicology, 1966), no. 8.

Its intended effect in the madrigal is surely to force upon performer and listener alike a close reading of the text, close to the point of resembling, in a necessarily figurative sense, a silent reading as opposed to a conventional reading aloud of the poem. This approach to text setting is intensified by Willaert's choice of material; there is little that is melodically striking in this madrigal, and very little exact melodic correspondence among the voices. The musical ideas are chiefly rhythmic, each phrase of text receiving an undemonstrative but precise setting emphasizing both sound and meaning in the words. Each voice retains the rhythmic shape allotted a particular textual phrase, but the lines pass in and out of melodic resemblance to one another in a free flow of musical consciousness. They combine into a single reading of the poem, but one marked by a collective pondering of its meaning and of its verbal music. That Willaert's great skills in counterpoint and vocal orchestration combine to form a tonally unified, darkly sonorous musical fabric of great distinction is not, certainly, beside the point; but the main purpose of it all is in how the text is read. Instead of intensifying rhetorical drama or declamatory *parlando*, Willaert has chosen to intensify the seriousness of purpose with which the words are set—in an almost literal sense set deeply—into the music.

The madrigals of Cipriano de Rore show virtuoso command of all the elements seen in Willaert's *Musica nova*. To these Rore adds an element of melodic grace and individuality, present in a subtle way in the madrigals of his first two books for five voices, more noticeable in his later work. Rore effectively uses distinctive melodic gestures to begin pieces, providing elements of a rhetorical exordium meant not merely to get attention but to aid in forcing an attitude of serious concentration on both performers and listeners. Some examples of these exordia are given in Example 39.[47]

Rore's madrigals were enormously influential, not only on Venetian composers but also on everyone who took the writing of madrigals seriously; this includes Vincenzo Ruffo, a number of other northern-Italian composers, and the younger "Roman" composers, such as Palestrina, Lasso, and Philippe de Monte, who blended

47. Ex. 39: (a) *Tu piangi e quella per chi fai tal pianto* (*Libro primo a 5v* [1542], no. 9); (b) *O sonno o della queta humida ombrosa* (*Libro secondo a 4v* [1557], no. 5); (c) *Mia benigna fortuna è'l viver lieto* (*Libro secondo a 4v* [1557], no. 9, 2ᵃ *parte*).

Rore's techniques with the clearer harmonic palette and more defi-
nitely articulated cadential structure of the Roman madrigal as carried forward in their music. Like the work of Josquin in the early
decades of the century, that of Rore served, if not as a direct model,
then as an ideal toward which serious musicians continued to look
during the middle generations of cinquecento musical culture.[48]

Among the Petrarchan texts chosen by Venetian madrigalists
were the canzone *Vergine bella* and the sonnets *Padre del ciel dopo i
perduti giorni* and *Io vo piangendo i miei passati tempi*. These are "spiritual" madrigals *avant la lettre*, at once religious in message and an
integral part of Petrarch's *Canzoniere*. Texts such as these, not set by
the first generation of madrigalists, are found scattered in madrigal
prints of the late 1540s and 1550s, well before the first advertised
collection of *madrigali spirituali*, published in 1563.[49] The appearance of such texts suggests, of course, the influence on the madrigal
of Counter-Reformation poetic currents. Printed collections of
rime spirituali were in circulation by mid-century;[50] and if one assumes that composers chose texts freely—or, what seems to me
more probable, that patrons of the madrigal wished to have religious texts sung alongside poetry of an unreformedly secular
nature—there is nothing very surprising about their appearance in
madrigal collections.

Madrigals could be made into devotional music simply by sub-
stituting religious texts of similar meter and form, or by rewriting
the texts to "spiritualize" them. This was an established tradition;
laude had been made from trecento ballatas and from strambotti,
barzellette, and carnival songs in the fifteenth century, and the

---

48. A summary of Rore's posthumous reputation is given by Alvin H. Johnson,
"Rore," in *The New Grove Dictionary* 16:187. See also the remarks of Adriano Banchieri, who saw Rore as the most important composer between Josquin and Marenzio, cited below in chap. 6, p. 129.

49. There are a few earlier settings, such as Scotto's three-voice composition of
Padre del ciel in his *Madrigali a 3v, libro primo* of 1541 and Arcadelt's *Io vo piangendo*,
published in 1554 (*Il quarto libro . . . a 4v a note bianche*) but probably written some
years earlier.

50. See Elena Ferrari Barassi, "Il madrigale spirituale nel cinquecento e la rac-
colta monteverdiana del 1583," in *Congresso internazionale sul tema Claudio Monteverdi
e il suo tempo*, ed. Raffaello Monterosso (Verona, 1969), p. 230n, where there is men-
tion of two volumes of *rime spirituali* printed in Venice in 1550. Katherine Powers of
the University of California, Santa Barbara, is preparing a dissertation on the early
madrigale spirituale.

practice was an ongoing one.[51] Petrucci printed two books of laude, keeping them distinct from his frottola anthologies; but many frottolas could easily have been "spiritualized." After Petrucci's volumes no laude were printed for some time; but they were certainly still sung, and may occasionally have been included in the repertory of madrigal singers.[52] In 1563 two collections of laude appeared in print. One is Serafino Razzi's large miscellany of pieces of varying age and character, supplied with devotional texts and used, says Razzi, in Florentine churches after Vespers and Compline.[53] The other is Giovanni Animuccia's first book of laude, intended by the author for "devout persons," whether clerics or laymen, but probably written for performance at the Roman oratory of San Filippo Neri.[54] The lauda as a genre intended for performance in a religious setting is really outside the limits of our subject; but the line between lauda and madrigal may not have been very precisely drawn in the mid sixteenth century. In 1565 Animuccia published a volume of three-voice madrigals that included some motets and spiritual madrigals, all written in a simple, easily singable style; he dedicated them to two young men associated with Neri's oratory.[55]

The singing of madrigals on religious texts may have become a part of the musical life of academies in the early years of the Counter-Reformation, when oratories, which could be described as academies of exclusively religious bent, were being founded. The first published anthology of spiritual madrigals, the *Musica spirituale* of 1563, was put together by Giovanni dal Bene of Verona, himself a writer of religious poetry.[56] Bene could have been a mem-

51. Federico Ghisi, "Strambotti e laude nel travestimento spirituale della poesia musicale del quattrocento," *Collectanea Historiae Musicae* (Florence) 1 (1953), 45–78; Domenico Alaleona, "Le laudi spirituali italiane nei secoli xvi e xvii e il loro rapporto coi canti profani," *Rivista musicale italiana* 16 (1909), 1–54.

52. Several laude are included at the end of an early manuscript anthology of madrigals, Florence, Bibl. del Conserv. MS B 2495. They appear to be somewhat later additions to the manuscript, but their presence is nonetheless suggestive.

53. RISM 1563⁶, *Libro primo delle laude spirituali . . . raccolte dal R. P. Fra Serafino Razzi Fiorentino* (facs. Bologna, 1969).

54. *Libro primo delle laude di Gio. Animuccia. Composte per consolatione, et a requisitione di molte persone spirituali, et devote, tanto religiosi, quanto secolari.* On Neri and the spiritual madrigal see Barassi, "Il madrigale spirituale," pp. 222–26; on Animuccia's connections with Neri's oratory see Lewis Lockwood, "Giovanni Animuccia," in *The New Grove Dictionary* 1:437.

55. *Il primo libro de madrigali a 3v . . . con alcuni motetti, et madrigali spirituali*, dedicated to "M. Marco: Et Piero del Nero."

56. RISM 1563⁷, *Musica spirituale. Libro primo di canzon et madrigali a 5v . . . rac-*

ber of the Accademia filarmonica in Verona; he included in his volume pieces by Nasco, Ruffo, and Lambert Courtois, all composers associated with that academy in the 1540s and 1550s.[57] Musicians were certainly asked to write new music for devotional madrigal texts. A letter of 1565 from Cardinal Carlo Borromeo, one of the most important figures in the final deliberations of the Council of Trent, to his vicar in Milan states this clearly: "I am much pleased with your plan to make a collection of devout madrigals [madrigali honesti] such that every good man can sing them; and if worthy men could be found to compose the music it would be easy to have someone here [in Rome] write the words on spiritual and devout subjects." [58]

Composition of madrigals to religious texts becomes a marked feature of later-sixteenth-century musical culture; nearly every madrigalist published individual pieces if not whole volumes of madrigali spirituali.[59] And the process of trasvestimento, by which single pieces or whole collections were "spiritualized" with rewritten texts, continued throughout the century, either informally, as at the Filippine oratory in Rome, where the madrigal anthology L'amorosa Ero (1588) had its pastoral verse replaced by one dealing with St. Peter, or in printed versions, such as the books of Monteverdi madrigals spiritualized by Aquilano Coppini.[60]

It is not clear that the madrigale spirituale developed a musical language of its own. The major preoccupation of reform-minded composers of sacred music, intelligibility of the text for believing

colta gia dal reverendo Giovanni dal Bene nobil veronese à utilità delle persone christiane, e pie. . . .

57. See Lewis Lockwood, The Counter-Reformation and the Masses of Vincenzo Ruffo (Venice, 1970), p. 97.

58. Cited, and the Italian text given, in Lockwood, The Counter-Reformation, p. 94.

59. Barassi, "Il madrigale spirituale," pp. 217–52, mentions a number of composers and prints. So far as I know, no one has attempted a complete listing of examples of the genre. For an interesting study distinguishing the musical character of the madrigale spirituale from that of the secular madrigal in the work of Palestrina, see Agostino Ziino, "Testi laudistici musicati da Palestrina," in Atti del Convegno di studi palestriniani, 28 settembre–2 ottobre 1975, ed. Francesco Luisi (Palestrina, 1977), pp. 381–408.

60. Leo Schrade, Monteverdi, Creator of Modern Music (New York, 1950), p. 208. On the contrafactum of L'amorosa Ero see Harry B. Lincoln, ed., The Madrigal Collection L'amorosa Ero (Brescia, 1588) (State University of New York Press, 1968), pp. ix–xii.

listeners, affected the madrigal only marginally. Animuccia could say in the preface to his second book of laude that he tried to minimize use of *fughe* and other contrapuntal *inventioni* so as not to "obscure the meaning of the words" while at the same time supplying musical variety.[61] But no madrigalist went to the lengths that Ruffo did in his Tridentine Masses, allowing contrapuntally staggered entrances only by truncating the text so that as each voice came in it got only the part of the text reached by the voices already present.[62] The madrigal continued to be written primarily for its performers, not for an audience needing to hear the text with uncontrapuntal clarity.

And yet the development of the madrigal was affected by Counter-Reformation thought, and not simply in matters of social context, what kind of thing was sung where. In choosing texts by Gabriel Fiamma or Angelo Grillo or—in his penitential vein—Luigi Tansillo, madrigalists had to be fully serious, to use their battery of musical rhetoric in a genuine rather than playful effort at persuasion. In reaction to the rise of devotional madrigals was the development in the secular sphere of frankly hedonistic *poesia per musica*, verse for which the increasingly vivid musical language of the madrigal was more than adequate technically and far more than sufficient emotionally. Some of the stresses and strains caused by this mismatching of poetic and musical intent, and some of the solutions found by musicians for it, will be the subject of the final chapter.

61. *Laude libro secondo* (1570); see Vogel, *Bibliothek* 1:25. On the whole matter of the lauda and spiritual madrigal in Rome during this period see Howard E. Smither, *A History of the Oratorio*, vol. 1 (Chapel Hill, 1977), pp. 47–76.
62. Lockwood, *The Counter-Reformation*, pp. 188–89, 276 (Ex. 6).

·VI·

The Rise of the Baroque Aesthetic

NEAR THE END OF Tasso's *La Cavaletta*, a dialogue on formal structures and aesthetic levels in Italian poetry, the author (here as elsewhere called "forestiero napolitano") turns to music, speaking of it in Dantesque manner as a necessary "condiment" for most kinds of poetry. Having asked rhetorically whether one should prefer the sort of music pleasing to lascivious young people or that suiting the taste of mature and thoughtful men and women, Tasso continues thus: "Let us then put aside all this degenerate music that has grown soft and effeminate; and let us beg Striggio and Wert and Luzzaschi, and any other excellent musician who wants to join them in the effort, to recall music to that gravity of style from which it has strayed—or which it has often betrayed through excess, so much so that it is better to be silent than to talk about it."[1]

What was Tasso complaining about in the music of his time? (The dialogue was written in 1587.) At first it seems that he was striking a common humanistic pose, especially since he continues by saying that proper music should be what Aristotle calls "Doristi"—in the Dorian ethos—and in its simple magnificence should be written in a manner "accomodato a la cetera," for which a Frenchman of the time would say "mesuré à la lyre." But Tasso was not asking for a musical return to antiquity; in the dedicatory letter to

---

1. Torquato Tasso, *La Cavaletta overa de la poesia toscana*, in *Opere*, ed. Bruno Maier, vol. 5 (Milan, 1965), p. 150: "Dunque lasciarem da parte tutta quella musica la qual degenerando è divenuta molle ed effeminata, e pregheremo lo Striggio e Iaches e'l Lucciasco e alcuno altro eccelente maestro di musica eccelente che voglia richiamarla a quella gravità de la quale traviando è spesso traboccata in parte di cui è più bello il tacere che'l ragionare."

this dialogue he says that Tuscan poetry is so excellent, its best writers so worthy of emulation, that with it in mind one might contest the vaunted superiority of ancient writers.[2] Nor was Tasso the kind of poet who, like Goethe, wanted to hear his verse sung in as unobtrusive and uncompetitive a setting as possible. Wherever he lived, but especially in Naples and Ferrara, Tasso counted musicians among his friends and wrote poems for them; and it must have been gratifying to him to see his poetry chosen repeatedly by the leading composers of the period.[3] He may not have been overpleased to see isolated stanzas from his *Gerusalemme* set to music; in his discussion of literary genres Tasso says that *epopeia* or heroic verse has no need of music.[4] But this reservation is not the basis for his complaint. Earlier in the *Cavaletta* Tasso speaks with favor of musicians whom he had heard singing canzoni in such a way that one could hear the "replicazione del modo"—the internal symmetry of the opening section or *fronte*—after which the music proceeded freely.[5] He liked, then, to be able to hear poetic structure in musical settings; his complaint about modern music may have been based partly on his perception of its emphasis on setting words and phrases of text as graphically and affectively as possible, with the frequent result that the poetic structure became all but inaudible.[6] The "soft and effeminate" qualities he found distasteful may be

2. *La Cavaletta*, p. 88: "La poesia toscano è tanto nobile per la bellezza de la favola quanto per l'eccelenza de gli scrittori: laonde potrebbe far dubbia la palma de gli antichi Grechi e Latini."

3. See the references to musicians in *La Cavaletta*, p. 129. For poems by Tasso on musical subjects see nos. 192, 193, 531, 617, 643 (addressed to a composer), and 717–22 in *Rime*, ed. Angelo Solerti (Bologna, 1898–1902). For a study of Monteverdi's use of and response to Tasso, see Nino Pirrotta, "Scelte poetiche di Monteverdi, I," *Nuova rivista musicale italiana* 2 (1968), 10–42. Marenzio's choice of Tassonian texts may be seen in James Chater, "Fonti poetiche per i madrigali di Luca Marenzio," *Rivista italiana di musicologia* 13 (1978), 60–103.

4. *La Cavaletta*, pp. 148–49. A list of madrigals on texts from Tasso's epic may be found in Alfred Einstein, "*Orlando furioso* and *La Gerusalemme liberata* As Set to Music during the Sixteenth and Seventeenth Centuries," *Music Library Association Notes*, 2d ser., 8 (1950–51), 629–30.

5. *La Cavaletta*, pp. 128–29.

6. On this tendency in the madrigal of the late sixteenth century see Lorenzo Bianconi, "Struttura poetica e struttura musicale nei madrigali di Monteverdi," in *Congresso internazionale sul tema Claudio Monteverdi e il suo tempo*, ed. Raffaello Monterosso (Verona, 1969), pp. 337–48, esp. pp. 338–39. For an effort to show that composers created a structure analogous to but not identical with that of the poetry they set, see Walther Dürr, "Zum Verhältnis von Wort und Ton im Rhythmus des Cinquecento-Madrigals," *Archiv für Musikwissenschaft* 15 (1958).

something else as well, perhaps the somewhat *galant* style of the canzonetta that became pervasive in the madrigal in the 1570s and 1580s. For whatever reasons—and some of these may be far from obvious—one of its most astute and sympathetic critics found something seriously wrong with the late-sixteenth-century madrigal in regard to concept and style.

Expressions of concern, of conservative reaction to musical innovation, can be seen from time to time in the second half of the sixteenth century, from Zarlino's attack on the chromaticism of Vicentino to Artusi's complaints about Monteverdi and the "defects" of modern music. From another direction, that of the humanistic vanguard, with Vincenzo Galilei as its self-appointed spokesman, came attacks on the "laceramento della poesia" in madrigalistic polyphony, leading to the conclusion—or, rather, from the assumption—that only in soloistic monody could the affective power and meaning of poetry be successfully captured.[7] At the same time there was continuing pressure on composers of madrigals to invent ever more vivid and daring forms of musical speech to match the *affetti* of the words they set. In part this pressure was that of emulation among musicians themselves. The expressive vocabulary of one brief generation of composers soon lost its punch—came to seem unexceptional or even passed into the general language shorn of its original rhetorical intent.

This constant renewal of musical gesture formed the history of what Monteverdi called the *seconda pratica*, a word-centered musical language the origins of which he saw in the madrigals of Cipriano de Rore.[8] The traditional polyphonic devices of Renais-

---

7. Galilei's sustained criticism of contrapuntal music may be found in his *Dialogo della musica antica e della moderna* (Florence, 1581), pp. 80–90; for an English translation see Oliver Strunk, *Source Readings in Music History* (New York, 1950), pp. 302–22. On the Florentine circles in which Galilei moved see Nino Pirrotta, "Temperaments and Tendencies in the Florentine Camerata," *The Musical Quarterly* 40 (1954), 169–89, esp. 172–74; Claude Palisca, "The 'Camerata fiorentina': A Reappraisal," *Studi musicali* 1 (1972), 203–36.

8. In the preface to his *Quinto libro* (1605) Monteverdi, while defending his work, speaks of a *seconda pratica*; his brother Giulio Cesare glossed this preface at some length in a "declaration" attached to Monteverdi's *Scherzi musicali* (1607), saying of this second practice that it is a style in which all musical values are subordinated to the demands of the text—a style originating, he says, in the music of Cipriano de Rore. The term *seconda pratica* has perhaps been used more loosely by modern writers than it should. Though Monteverdi cites Rore as its "rediscoverer," all the other composers he lists are his own contemporaries or near-predecessors, the oldest

sance music, the various forms of imitative counterpoint that had themselves been conceived as musical response to words, were now the domain of conservative sacred polyphony and of textless instrumental music; only if used in some exceptional way could they serve the madrigalist's purpose. The rules governing the "science" of music, treated by theorists as if they were of immemorial antiquity and changeless character, even though by the end of the cinquecento they had been observed in full detail for less than a century, were accepted by composers no less than by theorists as the given basis for musical composition, but they were regarded in a new light: correct procedures could be amplified, rules could be bent, in the service of the text. For all his pedantry Artusi was in a way right to concentrate on technical detail; the kind of expressive novelty that, while occasionally using illicit melodic intervals or surprising juxtapositions of sound and texture, contented itself with observance of contrapuntal rules was one thing; music that literally broke the rules was another. Thus as the sixteenth century drew to a close the madrigal was regarded as effete and lacking strength of fiber by some, as a gothic holdover that continued to frustrate humanistic expectations by others, and as a dangerously revolutionary suborner of established practice by a third group.

Still, the madrigal in its newest guises had many admirers, and ones who counted: Guglielmo Gonzaga and his family in Mantua; Marenzio's Roman circle of patrons and friends; to some extent the Habsburg and Wittelsbach courts (though they were not really centers of innovation for the madrigal, despite the great artistic achievements of Monte and Lasso); the *ridotti* of Count Bevilacqua in Verona; academic and aristocratic circles in Naples; and above all the court of Alfonso II of Ferrara. Madrigals continued to sell; the number of reprints of volumes by Rore, Lasso, Wert, and Marenzio is as impressive as the continuing large amount of new music published in the last four decades of the sixteenth century. Even the theorists on the whole approved; they were not always or even often Beckmessers. Adriano Banchieri saw in Marenzio's work a per-

---

among them being Giaches Wert. One view of the salient features of the *seconda pratica* is that of Denis Arnold, "*Seconda Pratica*: A Background to Monteverdi's Madrigals," *Music & Letters* 38 (1957), 341–52.

fection of "chamber" or madrigalian style equal to that of Palestrina in the realm of sacred music.[9] In 1614 Banchieri, reviewing the musical history of the remote and then the recent past, noted with approval that many of the innovations of secular music had passed into general musical circulation. His view of what we call the Renaissance begins with the school of Josquin, who composed "with diverse proportions and variety of tempo." Next is that of Cipriano, who, seeing music of such complexity, "reduced music into sweet harmony." To Rore succeeded the school of Marenzio, who invented new and charming ideas "di portar bene le parole sotto le note." Even Marenzio was now outdone by a new school (no head of it is named, but Banchieri was of course himself a prolific composer), which when setting *parole volgari* could imitate their *affetti*, "of sadness, harshness, untruths, questions, cries, joy, laughter, music itself," in so natural and consequent a way that "one hears declaimed the complete meaning of the whole text." And Banchieri saw this progress toward an ever-increasing linguistic power of music as still on the ascendant in his own generation.[10]

The public liked to see madrigalists competing in the game of musical wordplay. I see no other explanation for such a phenomenon as the collection called *Sdegnosi ardori*, thirty-one settings of a single madrigal by Guarini, collected by an Italian musician at the Bavarian court and published in Munich in 1585; this text, *Ardo sì ma non t'amo*, was set to music over sixty times in all.[11] Guarini's *Tirsi morir volea* was also chosen repeatedly for musical setting, as were

9. In a letter addressed to Artusi, Banchieri congratulated Artusi for criticizing the destroyers of "buone regole" but not the work of Palestrina in church music or Marenzio "nella stile da Camera," for both were "esemplari di perfetta Armonia, elettori di vaghe parole . . . gravi nelle modulationi, copiosi nelle inventione . . . zelanti delle buone regole." (The letter is cited in Giuseppe Vecchi, "L'opera didattico-teorica di Adriano Banchieri in rapporto alla 'Nuova prattica,'" in *Congresso internazionale sul tema Claudio Monteverdi e il suo tempo*, p. 385.) Artusi does cite Marenzio with favor; see *Seconda Parte dell'Artusi overa delle imperfettioni della moderna musica* (Venice, 1603; facs. Bologna, 1968), pp. 16, 18.

10. Adriano Banchieri, *Cartella musicale nel canto figurato, fermo & contrapunto*, 3d ed. (Venice, 1614; facs. Bologna, 1968), pp. A3–A4.

11. RISM 1585[17], *Sdegnosi ardori. Musica di diversi auttori sopra un istesso soggetto di parole, a 5v*. The work is said to have been "commissioned" by G. B. Galanti and assembled by Giulio Gigli da Imola. There are at least thirty settings of the original text in addition to those in the 1585 print. The poem drew forth a *risposta* by Tasso, then a *contrarisposta* and a further reply; settings of these bring the number of madrigals on the subject to about ninety-five.

madrigal texts drawn from his *Pastor fido*.[12] Competing settings of a single text can be seen even in the earliest days of the madrigal, but they are rare in occurrence and modest in number.[13] In the late sixteenth century an increasing virtuosity of compositional technique and an increasing sense of commercial venture in music publishing combine in the case of *Sdegnosi ardori* to give us something like a Diabelli competition.

There is evidence that commercial factors were important; amid the flow of new madrigals appear collections such as Zuan Jacomo Zorzi's *Eletta di tutta la musica*, a volume of pieces that had already been printed individually and met with success, and Angelo Gardano's *Musica di xii autori*, said to contain "i più belli Madrigali i che hoggidi si cantino."[14] Near the turn of the century such collections, representing the taste of the early 1580s in Italy, were issued with some frequency by German and Flemish printers.[15] Anthologies described as representing the musical taste of individual cities, or the repertory performed at aristocratic *ridotti*, can also be found, along with an increasing number of collections said to be suited for singing to the lute or the cembalo.[16] It is clear that consumers

12. Alfred Einstein counted twenty-six settings of *Tirsi morir volea* (*The Italian Madrigal* [Princeton, 1949], p. 542), and there are more; see Emil Vogel, Alfred Einstein, François Lesure, and Claudio Sartori, *Bibliografia della musica italiana vocale profana pubblicata dal 1500 al 1700*, 3 vols. (Pomezia, 1977), 3:561. For a preliminary list of madrigals drawn from the *Pastor fido* see Arnold Hartmann, Jr., "Battista Guarini and *Il pastor fido*," *The Musical Quarterly* 39 (1953), 415–25. *Ah, dolente partita!* (III, iii), for example, was set over thirty times.

13. For an example see James Haar, "*Altro non è il mio amor*," in *Words and Music: The Scholar's View*, ed. Laurence Berman (Cambridge, Mass., 1972), pp. 93–114.

14. RISM 1569[20], 1576[5]. See also the *Musicale essercitio* of Ludovico Balbi (1589[12]), consisting of the soprano part of a number of celebrated madrigals with newly added lower voices composed by Balbi.

15. Examples include 1588[21], 1589[8], and 1590[20], three volumes of *Gemma[e] musicalis* (Nuremberg); 1596[8], *Madrigali a 8v de . . . famosi autori* (Antwerp); 1596[10], *Paradiso musicale . . . a 5v* (Antwerp); and 1597[13], *Fiori del Giardino di diversi . . . autori* (Nuremberg). One of the first of the northern anthologies of madrigals, RISM 1583[14], *Harmonia celeste . . . nelle quale si contiene una scielta di migliori madrigali che hoggidi si cantino* (Antwerp), features some newer music, such as Marenzio's *Tirsi morir volea* and the madrigals of Stefano Felis, along with older music, including pieces by Lasso that had appeared in print more than twenty years earlier.

16. Collections designed "da cantare et sonare" are very common in the late sixteenth century and do not require special notice here. Madrigal books devoted to a single person or theme begin to appear in the last third of the century; examples include RISM 1568[16], *Corona della morte dell'Illustre Signore . . . Anibal Caro*, with a dedicatory letter by Giulio Bonagiunta saying that "io raccolto alquanti sonetti composti sopra la morte dell'ecc. Sig. Anibal Caro dal Sig. Gio. Battista suo amantissimo

needed to be stimulated to go on buying madrigal prints. In the early years of the seventeenth century the number of publications decreased; this seems to me not so much a sign that the madrigal was going out of fashion as an indication that the public was surfeited, had acquired about all the madrigals it needed.[17] Collections of monodies were now of course becoming common; and sets of laude and other forms of *musica spirituale*, not very numerous in the third quarter of the century, appeared more often at its close, evidently meeting a demand that publishers had been slow to grasp.

Madrigal volumes calling special attention to their texts also became more common in the late sixteenth century. Isolated early examples such as Pisano's *Musica . . . sopra le canzone del Petrarcha,* Jacques Ponte's cycle of Bembo stanzas, and Rore's third madrigal book, advertised as containing the *Vergine* of Petrarch, can be found; but they did not immediately start a trend. In such a simple matter as giving the names of the authors of the texts music printers were curiously obtuse; in the first half of the century I know only one example, Giovantommaso Cimello's *Libro primo di Canti a quattro voci sopra madriali & altre Rime con li nomi delli authori volgari . . .* (1548), and the publisher's use of this title clearly shows what a novelty it was.[18] Even in the later sixteenth century one rarely finds poets'

---

nipote, li quali havendo fatto vestire da eccellenti Compositori d'una Musica, che rende concente molto proprij alli concetti delle parole"; 1570[15], *I dolci frutti . . . a 5v,* which includes an eleven-part canzone, set by eleven chosen musicians, on the theme of a Venetian military victory; and 1579[3], *Trionfo di musica . . . a 6v,* with a sestina set by six composers in honor of the wedding of Francesco I de' Medici. Madrigal volumes of strongly local character also become prominent; among them are RISM 1569[19], *Musica de' virtuosi della florida capella dell' . . . S. Duca di Baviera;* 1582[5] and 1583[10], the *Lauro secco* and *verde* books of Ferrarese (and other) composers; 1582[4], *Dolci affetti . . . a 5v de div. ecc. musici di Roma;* 1586[7], *Armonia di scelti authori a 6v sopra altra perfettissima armonia di bellezze d'una gentildonna Senese in ogni parte bella;* 1586[10], *I lieti amanti . . . a 5v,* dedicated to Mario Bevilacqua by Hippolito Zanluca, who says, "La qual dedicatione fanno meco insieme tutti quei gentilhuomini che ordinariamente si riducono in casa mia per cosi fatto trattenimento"; and 1609[17], *Sonetti novi di Fabio Petrozzi Romano sopra le ville di Frascati . . . a 5v.*

17. The pages of Emil Vogel, *Bibliothek der gedruckten weltlichen Vocalmusik Italiens aus den Jahren 1500–1700* (1892), *mit Nachträgen von Prof. Alfred Einstein* (Hildesheim, 1962), 2:774ff., show this falling off from 1600 on, particularly on the part of Venetian printers, who issued laude and monodies but very few madrigal collections.

18. The title page of this print also promises "le piu necessarie osservanze instromentali, e piu convenevoli avvertenze de toni accio di possano anchora sonare, & cantare insieme"; unfortunately these *osservanze* and *avvertenze* are not to be found in the single surviving copy of the book.

names in madrigal books;[19] the situation is just the reverse of that in seventeenth- and eighteenth-century opera and cantata libretti, where the composer of the music is mentioned in fine print or not at all. This should not be taken to mean that music counted for little in Baroque opera, or poetry for little in the madrigal. Sixteenth-century lyric poetry had its own life in print; apart from the collected works of individual poets, there were many anthologies of *Rime diversi*, with as precise ascription of authors' names as the publishers could manage.

There is every indication that musicians and their patrons were increasingly concerned about choice of poetic text in the later sixteenth century; studies of the poetic choices of Marenzio and Monteverdi show this, and other composers, among them Giaches Wert and Philippe de Monte, were also clearly conscious of new poetic currents, though they often continued to set older poetry as well.[20] An increasing tendency to compose sets of madrigals devoted to single poets, forming musical *canzonieri* arranged in a deliberate order, can be seen in the last two decades of the century. And poets show a new interest in, and a new respect for, musicians, writing verse that celebrates composers as well as performers.[21] If one compares the attitude of Michelangelo toward Arcadelt, one of indifference bordering on disdain, with the admiring friendship of Tasso toward Wert and later Gesualdo, one sees clearly that musicians had risen in the estimate of other artists, and that music of serious character was no longer viewed as a minor decorative art.[22]

19. There are some exceptions, among them the amusing RISM 1564[16], *Di Manoli Blessi il primo libro delle greghesche con la musica di sopra, composta da diversi autori*, with a preface by the author (Antonio Molin) saying, "Chesta musica per me fada cumponere de multi Eccellendi Autturi del Musica sora li mie Versi e Rime della Rumeca lingua nostra." On Manoli Blessi / Molin see Paolo Fabbri, "Fatti e prodezze di Manoli Blessi," *Rivista italiana di musicologia* 11 (1976), 182−96. The collection of 1564 has been edited by Siro Cisilino, *Manoli Blessi: Greghesche Libro I, 1564* (Padua, 1974).

20. See above, n. 3.

21. Tasso, for example, wrote a poem in praise of a composer, possibly Giaches Wert, verse for the *donne cantatrici* of Ferrara, and poetry for Gesualdo in Naples; see his *Rime* 1 : 389ff. and the references in n. 3 above. Guarini's first appearance in the madrigal literature, in Giulio Fiesco's *Musica nova a 5v* of 1569, is in a volume written, says its composer, "ad instanza del S. Batt. Guarini"; see Vogel, *Bibliothek* 1 : 237; Einstein, *Italian Madrigal*, pp. 555−58.

22. For Michelangelo's attitude toward Arcadelt's setting of his verse see Einstein, *Italian Madrigal*, pp. 161−62. One can see something of this change in the way

The madrigal could be, and indeed was, discussed by literary theorists without more than passing references to music.[23] In the last third of the sixteenth century the poetic madrigal underwent a noticeable change in character, the result of and also a cause for literary theorizing about the genre. The "discursive" content, straightforward syntax, and restrainedly Petrarchan language characteristic of the madrigal of the first half of the century were replaced by a self-conscious return to the idyllic content of the trecento madrigal, by an artificial, somewhat convoluted syntax, and by an increasingly mannered vocabulary emphasizing word repetition and assonance, with special attention to deliberately clustered dark and light vowel sounds. Madrigals tended to become shorter and more concise, with a high proportion of seven-syllable lines and an avoidance of multiline internal groupings. The gently epigrammatic final couplet seen in the early madrigal was replaced by ever sharper, wittier, more surprising conclusions. A madrigal by Torquato Tasso placed alongside one of about the same length by Ariosto will show something of this change of poetic style.

Oh, se quanto è l'ardore	Là dove sono i pargoletti Amori,
tanto, Madonna, in me fusse	ed altri ha teso l'arco,
l'ardire,	altri saetta al varco,
forse il mal c'ho nel core—osarei	altri polisce la quadrella d'oro,
dire.	voi parete un di loro
A voi devrei contarlo,	scherzando in verde colle o'n
ma per timor, oimè! d'un sdegno,	riva ombrosa
resto,	fra la turba vezzosa;
che faccia, s'io ne parlo,	e se voi non avete auree saette,
crescerli il duol sì che l'uccida	le dolci parolette
presto;	e i dolci sguardi son facelle e
pur io vi vuo' dir questo;	strali
che da voi tutto nasce il mio	e i bei pensieri in voi son piume ed
martire,	ali.
e se'l more, il fate voi morire.	(Tasso)[25]
(Ariosto)[24]	

---

other artists regarded music; Cellini, though trained as a musician, scorned the art as ignoble, whereas Venetian painters of the late sixteenth century were proud to be considered musicians as well.

23. See Ulrich Schulz-Buschhaus, *Das Madrigal: Zur Stilgeschichte der italienischen Lyrik zwischen Renaissance und Barock* (Bad Homburg, 1969), passim.

24. Ludovico Ariosto, *Lirica*, ed. Giuseppe Fatini (Bari, 1924), p. 12.

25. *Rime*, ed. Solerti, 4:68.

The sonnet and the *ottava* stanza were affected in much the same way in language and syntax; Tasso's heroic *stanze* in particular are stylistically quite different from those of Ariosto. But the poetic madrigal of the later sixteenth century shows the greatest change. Its mannered syntax and virtuosic wit approach "baroque" poetic extravagance, and its deliberate emphasis on verbal musicality shows an almost startling attention to the sound of words.[26]

All of this posed a new challenge to composers. Their musical syntax had been developed to suit comparatively straightforward narrative; their affective rhetoric was better matched to verbal images of light or movement—physical or emotional—than it was to the sound of words. Bembo's theories about sound in poetry were best realized by musicians when verbal sound was linked with clear-cut meaning that could be externalized through use of high and low, major and minor, consonant and dissonant, fast and slow musical ideas. The challenge was great, almost like that posed for composers by Symbolist poetry in the late nineteenth century. I am not sure that sixteenth-century musicians ever met this challenge with complete success; they responded not so much with a new vocabulary of affective devices as with an increased ability to shift quickly from one device to another, and an increased willingness to interrupt the "discursive" flow of their musical syntax with sudden changes of figure and texture.

Alfred Einstein says of later-sixteenth-century composers that they had "a supply of ready-made formulas, a sort of musical rhyming dictionary or handbook of musical rhetoric."[27] These formulas may have been numerous and varied in use, but, in comparison with what poets could draw on, musicians had only a few categories or types of devices: high or low pitch areas, for individual voices or the whole contrapuntal texture; wide or narrow spacing of voices; fast or slow motion; melodic movement up, down, static, or circular, by step or by leap; chordal texture or contrapuntal staggering of voices; melodic or contrapuntal inversion; hexachordal puns and *inganni*; melodic progressions foreign to the mode of the piece; unusual or oddly juxtaposed chordal sonorities; citation of a

26. For a survey of the "melic" and epigrammatic madrigal and their contrast with the earlier "discursive" madrigal see Schulz-Buschhaus, *Das Madrigal*.
27. *Italian Madrigal*, p. 554.

familiar bit of music from a well-known work; textures, such as *fauxbourdon*, that had associative meanings; visual puns such as white versus black notes, or paired semibreves for "occhi." This list grew as I wrote it down, and it is probably not complete; perhaps it is a bit unfair to say that composers had a limited rhetorical vocabulary in comparison with that of writers. But I stick to my assertion that musicians could portray only general emotional states; things like jealousy, self-doubt, and wavering belief, or the complex states of mind and emotion in the thought and language of a poet like Tasso, were beyond their capacity to depict—despite Banchieri's confident assertion that music could do everything the words said or implied. In the solo *recitar cantando* of Jacopo Peri and Monteverdi greater subtlety of expression could be achieved, but only fleetingly. In my opinion—and I use the phrase deliberately, for I do not feel confident enough to state it as fact—the total fusion of word and tone at the most refined psychological level was bound to remain incompletely fulfilled in Renaissance music.

Composers had a more basic problem to overcome. The syntactical structure of sixteenth-century music was a flowing one, designed for setting poetic lines or even groups of lines without sudden disruption of style or logic. Individual words and phrases could be repeated, and varying degrees of cadential articulation could be used to subdivide musical sentences, but the classical musical language of the mid sixteenth century, whether Roman or Venetian in style, could not respond easily to quicksilver changes in poetic imagery. Several modifications of musical language, not in themselves closely related to matters of textual expression, gave the madrigal of the later sixteenth century some of the flexibility it needed.

First, there is an observable change in harmonic usage, hard to define but immediately apparent if one contrasts either the chordal patter of the frottola with that of the villanella after about 1560 or the imitative polyphony of Palestrina, Lasso, and Andrea Gabrieli with that of Willaert and Rore. Einstein speaks of the "clearing-up of the harmonic style."[28] He is concerned with the rise of modern tonality, and though we now decry this concern as unhistorical, he

28. *Italian Madrigal*, p. 606.

is of course not altogether wrong in his perception of the phenomenon. By a process that was not conceptualized at the time and that we cannot really trace step by step, composers began to use a vocabulary of solidly rooted chords related to one another in clearly functional ways, not always or exclusively those favored in the "rational" music of the late-seventeenth and eighteenth centuries. The vertical and horizontal aspects of musical thought were changing, in a way suggestive of the changing relationships of line, color, and volume in mid- and late-sixteenth-century painting. This new emphasis on chordal definition in the madrigal has often been thought to reflect the influence of popular vocal genres such as the villanella; equally important, I think, was the influence of instrumental dance music. If we compare the vocal *arie* of the early sixteenth century with the instrumental tenors of Ortiz, also used for *arie* but organized in symmetrical periods and moving in regular alternation of strongly functional triads, the difference is clear and telling. Composers of vocal music could use their chordal vocabulary in an evenly spaced harmonic rhythm if they so chose, or they could change chordal sonorities with iridescent rapidity, then pause to let a sequence of florid melisma or imitative counterpoint flow over an unchanging chord. Example 40, borrowed from Einstein, shows the change in chordal vocabulary used for setting the same text in the 1540s and the 1560s.[29] In Example 41, a setting by Giaches Wert of an impressively gloomy, then passionate stanza from Tasso's *Gerusalemme liberata*, the slowly measured but darkly colorful chordal sonorities, combined with a low tessitura, contrast strikingly with the melisma for "Al fin sgorgando."[30] This phrase, although its harmonic underpinnings are hardly less slow-moving than the preceding chords, seems to come from a different source of expressive rhetoric (note that Wert takes almost as long to get through the fifth line of the stanza as he spends on the first four lines put together); only the curiously academic final measure of the passage (m. 23) pulls it back into the everyday musical world. In

29. Ex. 40: (a) Veggio, *Donna per acquetar vostro desio* (Doni?) (Doni, *Dialogo della Musica* [1544], no. 1); (b) Andrea Gabrieli, *Donna per acquetar vostro desio* (*Libro primo a 5v* [1566], no. 12). Both are cited by Einstein, *Italian Madrigal*, p. 532.

30. Ex. 41, *Giunto alla tomba ove al suo spirto vivo* (*Libro settimo a 5v* [1581], no. 9), is given after the edition of Carol MacClintock, *Giaches de Wert: Opera Omnia*, vol. 7 (American Institute of Musicology, 1967), no. 9.

this piece Wert still observes the poetic line as a unit, bending but not breaking the narrative pace of the *ottava* stanza. Similarly, contrasting chordal and figural textures are used for smaller textual units in settings of poetic madrigals.

Another general stylistic change in later-sixteenth-century music is one of rhythmic usage. Ruth DeFord has pointed out that regular use of the *fusa* (the modern eighth note, or a sixteenth in two-to-one reduction) as a text-bearing rhythmic unit can be seen in madrigals of the 1570s and 1580s, particularly in the canzonette of Girolamo Ferretti and Giovanni Conversi.[31] This is an extension of the rhythmic experiment in the *note nere* and *arioso* madrigals of the preceding generation; but its introduction is accompanied by a general change in text rhythm. The *parlando* style of the *arioso* madrigal was smoothed out into a hierarchy of rhythmic patterns subordinate to the semibreve *tactus*, which now resembled the modern accentual beat. Even the smallest rhythmic units in what has been called the canzonetta style tend to be grouped evenly; free speech rhythms are much less in evidence. A prominent signpost of this new rhythmic style is the dactylic pattern ♩ ♪ ♪, called by Einstein "narrative" rhythm.[32] It may have come into the madrigal directly from the French chanson, where it had been prominent for half a century; or, as I think more likely, it may have been taken over from the instrumental *canzona francese*. The new rhythmic patterns may also reflect an academic interest in quantitative verse setting; but the regularity of the patterns does not really echo the cadence of Italian speech even if long and short note values are used so carefully as to avoid any hint of "barbarisms." The result of this new rhythmic style is that the madrigal, often in whole pieces but certainly in actively patterned sections contrasting with slow-moving chords and chains of suspensions, becomes more regular, more "musical" in an instrumental sense, more dancelike. (The *balletti* of Orazio Vecchi and Giovanni Gastoldi are the most obvious end result of this usage.) Example 42, the opening of a setting by Wert of a Guarini madrigal, shows this rhythmic style, still supple

31. Ruth I. DeFord, "The Evolution of Rhythmic Style in Italian Secular Music of the Late Sixteenth Century," *Studi musicali* 10 (1981), 43–75.

32. Alfred Einstein, "Narrative Rhythm in the Madrigal," *The Musical Quarterly* 29 (1943), 475–84.

and graceful but far more regular than the declamatory rhythms of the *arioso* madrigal of the 1550s.[33] This new rhythmic style, imposed on the text rather than growing out of it, is associated primarily with lightweight poetry in the pastoral vein so popular in the last third of the sixteenth century. Its use can also be seen in the most serious madrigals, where its presence is at first surprising.

This suggests that it might be a good idea to reexamine our assumptions about the basic character of early Baroque music. We used to think of Baroque art as extravagantly florid, unrestrainedly expressive, naturalistically irregular in form—in contrast to the serenely balanced, classically tempered realism of Renaissance art. The falseness of this view, created by the Romantics' concentration on what they saw as extraordinary purity and balance in the work of Raphael and of Palestrina, then supported by the polarities set up by Ernst Wölfflin and Curt Sachs, has long been evident—but perhaps longer to historians of art and literature than to musicologists. In our discipline we have come to realize the absurdity of the term *baroque* as applied to the highly disciplined art of Corelli, Vivaldi, and Bach; but many of us have tended to cling to a view of seventeenth-century music that depicts movement from a wayward, expressively irregular language at the century's opening to the fully controlled tonal polyphony of its last years. In this view the madrigals of Gesualdo are representative of the Baroque spirit, rising to prominence just as Palestrina breathed his last; and the melodic and harmonic audacities of the monodists—Baroque disruptions of Renaissance polyphony—are just around the corner.

In fact both monodic experiment and the expressionistic madrigal, though taken to extremes in the years around 1600, antedate the turn of the century by about a generation. And both monody and the rhetorically intense madrigal use as a point of departure stylistic premises that include a firmly defined chordal vocabulary and a regularized, quasi-instrumental set of rhythmic patterns. The straining after ever more startling madrigalistic effects, ever more naturalistic solo song, is not something new but rather an intensification of late-Renaissance aesthetic postures; what is "Baroque" is the sharpening of generic divisions and the use of independently

33. *O primavera gioventù de l'anno* (*L'undecimo libro a 5v* [1595], no. 2), given after MacClintock, *Opera*, vol. 12 (1972), no. 2.

musical, instrumentally derived patterns as a framework. Thus what I see as the "Baroque aesthetic" in music has more to do with principles of order and categorization than with "free" expression.

In the madrigal of circa 1580–1620 there is nothing like a uniform or even very orderly succession of stylistic and rhetorical changes. Composers continued to set old poetry along with the newer madrigal, often mixing new musical techniques with older verse; the pastoral poetry of Sannazaro was, for instance, set in very much the same way as that of Guarini and even Marino. Occasionally a musician could give evidence of a kind of historically determined stylistic sense. Monteverdi set Pietro Bembo's *Cantai un tempo e se fu dolc'il canto* in a way that seems deliberately intended to reflect the musical vocabulary of the generation of Rore, that most immediately affected by Bembo's poetic doctrine, just as he returned to the *prima prattica* in writing a Mass based on a motet by Gombert; but his setting of Petrarch's *Hor che'l ciel e la terra*, admittedly a later work, is a compendium of the most up-to-date rhetorical devices, used in an affectively disruptive "modern" fashion.[34]

Local schools of madrigalists went their own way, though not of course without regard for the novelties they could observe in some of the centers of madrigalistic experiment. Mantua, offering the madrigals of Giaches Wert and Benedetto Pallavicino, out of which came much of Monteverdi's approach to the genre, was one such center. Ferrara, where one could hear the elaborate soloistic style of Luzzaschi and others, with its emphasis on virtuoso female voices, was another. In Naples there was a tendency toward rhetorically intense harmonic experiment, out of which Gesualdo began to develop his peculiarly mannered brand of madrigal (and Gesualdo's connections with Ferrara in the 1590s provide a good instance of cross-fertilization in madrigalian style). Naples was also a center of cultivation of the *aria*, monody in all but name. Roman madrigalists tended to prefer pastoral verse and canzonetta-like musical style, carried to heights of perfection and incorporating other stylistic currents with Mozartian virtuosity in the work of Marenzio. Venice was more conservative, despite its justly famed use of concerted vocal and instrumental forces; the essentially moderate style of the

---

34. *Cantai un tempo* appears in Monteverdi's *Secondo libro a 5v* (1590), no. 21; *Hor che'l ciel* is in the *Madrigali guerrieri et amorosi . . . libro ottavo* (1638), no. 2.

1570s, of which the madrigals of Andrea Gabrieli are the best representative, continued to be cultivated through the turn of the century. Florentine madrigalists seem on the whole to take an imitative rather than an innovative stance in this period (though the precursors of Marco da Gagliano have not as yet been studied thoroughly); the splendor of Medicean festival music is rooted in a style close to that of the Venetian and Roman madrigal of the third quarter of the sixteenth century. The sonorous ritornelli and sinfonie of the early Florentine opera, as well as its chorus, alternating lilting chordal declamation with canzonetta patterns, are of course a direct continuation of this festive category. Florentine operatic monody, that of Jacopo Peri in particular, is a more self-consciously innovative style, though its originality was long exaggerated even as its artistic worth was underestimated.[35] But here, as in the monodies of Giulio Caccini and his contemporaries, rhythmic movement is quite regular, with anacruses landing strongly and predictably on the beat; the effect of free *parlando* has to be achieved through performance—Caccini's famous *sprezzatura*—since it is not, except for some rapid syncopation in ornaments, written into the music as it was in the earlier *arioso* madrigal.[36] Even for monody the influence of instrumentally conceived patterns seems pervasive; in the practice of *recitar cantando* one could take great liberties, and make the most of affective dissonance and coloristic harmonic juxtaposition, but the mid-century efforts of composers to achieve textual rhythms as freely varied as those of a skillful reader of the text seem to have been redirected.

The late madrigal is hard to characterize briefly. Not only were there various local tastes and practices, but the genre developed by accretion rather than by clear-cut stylistic change, and composers

35. On the aesthetic and stylistic premises of Florentine opera see the works cited above, n. 7, and also Nino Pirrotta, "Early Opera and Aria," in *New Looks at Italian Opera: Essays in Honor of Donald J. Grout*, ed. William W. Austin (Ithaca, 1968), pp. 39–107.

36. This statement is subject to modification by the findings of Stephen Willier on manuscript vs. printed copies of Caccini's work, published in "Rhythmic Variants in Early Manuscript Versions of Caccini's Monodies," *Journal of the American Musicological Society* 36 (1983), 481–97; but the essentially regular nature of Caccini's notational practice is visible in all the versions cited by Willier. How unwritten rhythm such as the simple long value under which Monteverdi set a whole line of text in *Sfogava con le stelle* (*Quarto libro a 5v* [1603], no. 4) was performed we do not know; modern singers tend to treat it like plainchant, which seems an improbable solution.

felt free to work in a variety of styles. This becomes evident shortly after mid-century; the later music of Rore, for example, shows more interest in chordal declamation and external effect than one might have expected. A number of composers, including distinguished musicians such as Striggio, Lasso, and Costanzo Porta, continued to write in a polyphonic idiom that differed from that of Rore only in its clearer and firmer harmonic basis. Elements of the *arioso* madrigal were retained in declamatory madrigals setting *ottave* by Ariosto and then Tasso, and this declamatory style, often incorporating canzonetta rhythms, was used for other poetic genres as well. As the canzonetta blended into the serious madrigal, new forms of light music developed, including the *balletto* of Gastoldi and Vecchi, so beloved of English madrigalists. The "contrast" madrigal, with its alternation of chordal or chain-of-suspension passages, often heavily pathetic in tonal color, and chirping diatonic figuration in cheerfully pastoral style, was perhaps the most fashionable type of the 1580s and 1590s; it can be seen everywhere. A particularly instructive example is Vecchi's reworking of the old Arcadelt favorite *Il bianco e dolce cigno*, which begins with citation of Arcadelt's opening phrase and then introduces contrasting roulades in rapid, rhythmically regular *parlando*, making Arcadelt's melancholy *fauxbourdon* seem very slow-moving, almost an *ars antiqua* of the madrigal (Ex. 43).[37] The best examples of this mixture of the pathetic and the pastoral are the madrigals of Marenzio, too well known to need illustration here.

Two examples of the serious madrigal at the end of the sixteenth century will show something of how composers then responded to texts, in one case in the traditional manner of treating poetic lines as entities, in the other by fragmenting the text into sharply contrasting segments. The first example, a setting by Giaches Wert of a madrigal from Guarini's *Pastor fido*, uses a traditional mode of procedure coupled with modern elements of melody, harmony, and declamatory rhythm (Ex. 44).[38] Guarini's madrigal is typical of

37. Ex. 43: (a) Arcadelt, *Il bianco e dolce cigno cantando more* (*Primo libro a 4v* [1539], no. 1); (b) Vecchi, *Il bianco e dolce cigno cantando more* (*Libro primo a 5v* [1589], no. 1).

38. *Ah, dolente partita!* (*Pastor fido*, III, iii) (*L'undecimo libro a 5v* [1595], no. 1), given after MacClintock, *Opera*, vol. 12, no. 1. This text was also set by Marenzio and Monteverdi. For an instructive comparison of the three settings see Pierluigi Petro-

the poetic taste of the period in its compact handling of an old Petrarchistic oxymoron on life-renewing death, in its preference for seven-syllable lines, and in its carefully placed alternation of light and dark vowel sounds. Wert is a bit more expansive than the poet, though very economical in his use of musical material. He finds musical equivalents for Guarini's "vivace morire" and "vita al dolore" (mm. 23–28) in quickly adjusted rhythmic and harmonic movement. "Vita" and "dolore" even show an effort on the composer's part to match harmonic tint to vowel color. Only "La pena della morte" (m. 14ff.) seems perfunctorily set, and this only because we may misread the expressive intent of its harmonic shift.

The descending line of "Ah, dolente partita!," with its two sopranos linked in parallel thirds, is a characteristic pattern of lament; also characteristic is Wert's choice of the second mode on G, the most frequently used of sixteenth-century tonal types for expressions of lament.[39] Wert's use of the poem's second line as countersubject, both musically and poetically, to the first is a late-sixteenth-century device beloved of Marenzio and often used with great effect by Monteverdi; here it is especially well suited to the poem's structure and meaning. In the fourfold repetition of poetic and musical material that occupies the first ten measures of the piece, only the final one uses the second line of text alone. Connoisseurs of the madrigal doubtless noticed this musical wordplay while at the same time admiring the invertible counterpoint (at the twelfth) that allows each voice to proceed without exact repetition. "Da te parto e non moro?" is a musical as well as a verbal question in the shape of the top line's melody, even if one asked in the rhythmic language of instrumental music. Wert separates "E pur i' provo" from the phrase that precedes it, though both are part of one poetic line; this is the only exception to his otherwise complete adherence to Guarini's line units, and it is something that even Arcadelt might have done; but one should remember that Guarini knew all about madrigals as music, and wrote his poetry in a consciousness of musical technique that no poet set by Arcadelt could have had—going

belli, "'Ah dolente partita': Marenzio, Wert, Monteverdi," in *Congresso internazionale sul tema Claudio Monteverdi e il suo tempo*, pp. 361–76.

39. For the term *tonal type* see Harold S. Powers, "Tonal Types and Modal Categories," *Journal of the American Musicological Society* 34 (1981), 428–70.

so far, it is claimed, as to write the text for a *ballo* in the *Pastor fido* by underlaying music already composed by Luzzaschi.[40] In other words, late-sixteenth-century composers often adhered to the line structure of the new poetry they set—more than Rore and Willaert had done for Petrarch, for instance—because the poetry was written with a concept of musical ebb and flow of just the kind the madrigalists liked. In all the talk of composers responding to poetry in the sixteenth century there should be room for at least a few words about poets responding to music.

If we are surprised by the turn to B♭ for the poet's experience of the "pena de la morte" we should remind ourselves that this tonal area is not only the relative major of the later tonal system's G minor but also the dominant of the transposed Hypodorian mode, and that this harmonic shift may in Wert's time have had a gently pathetic effect now unappreciated by our tonally tainted perception. At "E sento nel partire / Un vivace morire" Wert gets as close to *arioso* rhythms as late-sixteenth-century rhythmic conventions allowed; and if one looks more closely at the melodic lines in the upper two parts one sees that they are derived from the material of the piece's opening rhymed couplet. This reference becomes more obvious as the madrigal nears its end; the melodic line setting "Che dà vita al dolore," given in its prime form in the tenor and in inversion in the top voice, is then used as poetic and musical counterpoint to the final line, a clearly audible variant of "Ah, dolente partita!" Wert takes his time in ending the madrigal, following the old custom of nailing down the madrigal's epigrammatic point through repetition; but he adds to the poet's *acutezza* by reusing the material with which he set the opening of the madrigal. In this work we can see in microcosm almost the whole history of the sixteenth-century madrigal.

40. Battista Guarini, *Il pastor fido e il compendio della poesia tragicomica*, ed. Gioachino Brognoligo (Bari, 1914), p. 306n: in the *Annotazioni* to the edition of 1602 we are told that for the *ballo* in act III, *Cieco Amor non ti credi' io*, a dance expert made up the steps in imitation of the "giuoco della cieca"; then "fu messo in musica da Luzzasco, eccellentissimo musico de' nostri tempi. Indi sotto le note di quella musica il poeta fe' le parole, il che cagionò la diversità dei versi, ora di cinque sillabe, ora di sette, ora di otto, or di undeci, secondo che conveniva servire alla necessità delle note. Cosa che pareva impossibile, e, se egli non l'avesse fatta molte altre volte, con tanta maggiore difficoltà quant'egli negli altri balli non era padrone dell'invenzione, come fu in questa, non si sarebbe forse creduto."

Gesualdo's setting of the anonymous madrigal *Ecco, morirò dunque* seems at first to represent a quite different approach to verse that, if less elegant than that of Guarini, is equally typical of the period (Ex. 45).[41] Every poetic line is divided into contrasting musical phrases; little effort at continuity in melody, harmony, or texture is evident—or perhaps we should say that a good deal of effort has gone into thwarting the listener's expectations. But if we admit this, and then digest the harmonic audacities and textural discontinuities for which Gesualdo is all too famous, what remains is a piece that shares some strong similarities of stylistic premise, if not of surface result, with that of Wert. And the difference between the two settings is only in part the result of Gesualdo's aim to shock singers and listeners by use of textural disruption and harmonic law-breaking; there is also a great difference in quality. Next to the professional and artistic security of Wert's music Gesualdo's seems not so much shocking as amateurish, like that of a number of early-seventeenth-century monodists whose affective strivings break rules that appear to have been imperfectly grasped in the first place.

The *prima parte* of *Ecco, morirò dunque* is made up of contrasting ejaculations dividing each of the three lines of poetry and alternating chords with slightly staggered but still syllabic articulation; the whole is then repeated in rather inexact invertible counterpoint—Wert's method without his contrapuntal control. A little coda (mm. 15–17) finishes off the first part of the piece. The second section proceeds in much the same way, dividing each poetic line and using roughly executed invertible counterpoint in the course of repeating each musical-poetic segment. Gesualdo's technique resembles Wert's in more than the use of contrapuntal inversion to get repetition at varied pitch levels. His rhythmic patter is if anything even more regular, beat-dominated, than that of Wert. In matters of harmony the relationship is less clear; here comparisons of Gesualdo to Marenzio would yield more tangible results, for both composers are constrained through use of chains of suspensions, resolved at different rates of speed, to mix chord inversions with the strong root progressions that dominate Wert's music. Again

41. *Ecco, morirò dunque* (*Libro quarto a 5v* [1596], no. 12) is given in Ex. 45 after the edition of Wilhelm Weismann, *Gesualdo di Venosa: Sämtliche Madrigale für fünf Stimmen*, vol. 4 (Hamburg, 1958), no. 16.

the comparison, were we to make it in detail, would, I think, show Marenzio's mastery of harmonic materials as a standard against which Gesualdo's music looks and sounds sadly amateurish. Certain of Gesualdo's harmonic dares are effective, to be sure; and in fairness it should be said that some of Gesualdo's music shows greater expertise than does *Ecco, morirò dunque*. But with composers like Wert and Marenzio one never has to apologize.

I did not choose a madrigal by Gesualdo in order to suggest that there was a general decline in standards at the end of the sixteenth century; it was on the contrary an age of great virtuosity in both composition and performance. But much of Gesualdo's music is evidence of the dangers of virtuosity, especially when mixed with expressionist, even exhibitionist rhetoric: one has to be very good to bring the whole thing off. Gesualdo was not without influence on his contemporaries and successors; but the extremes of his style were no more imitated than was the contrapuntal intensity of the Venetian madrigal of Willaert and Rore in the hands of their successors. Many composers of the turn of the century were able to cultivate an expressionist vocabulary without succumbing to extremes. Monteverdi's madrigals are not only inventive and individually distinctive but also a brilliant summary of the whole of late-Renaissance musical rhetoric, recapitulated with great dramatic force.

The use of contrapuntal music to suggest layers of textual interpretation thus continued through the beginning of the seventeenth century; and the pleasure taken by musicians in making individual thought and character sound through the medium of part music had a delightful late bloom in the madrigal comedies of Vecchi and Banchieri. But the tendency to separate musical discourse into categories, which I see as one of the most important aspects of the emerging Baroque aesthetic, was all in the direction of giving the expression of personal thought and individual emotion to solo song, reserving polyphony for choral commentary. As the madrigal was transformed into the continuo song this happened gradually and more or less naturally, though the shift was at the end a radical one. Composers like Monteverdi and Marco da Gagliano continued to enjoy and to expand on the possibilities for verbal interplay offered in madrigals using poetic and musical countersubjects like those seen in Wert's *Ah, dolente partita!*. And certain affective madrigalian techniques, such as chains of suspensions and contrasts of register, were not easy to achieve in solo song. But for impassioned narrative, soloistic recitation was increasingly favored, even within the traditional five-voice framework. Some of Monteverdi's later madrigals are really harmonized monodies or solo songs with choral interjections; and it is not very surprising that Monteverdi and others actually made polyphonic madrigals out of preexisting monodies, the reverse of earlier-sixteenth-century practice.[42]

In the early Florentine-Mantuan *favola in musica* there was deliberate and self-conscious separation of solo song from choral pieces, most of the latter being dance songs or choral commentary on the action. Within the solo song there was further distinction of genre, with speech depicted by *recitar cantando* and properly "musical" texts (in the sense of a character's having a song to sing) by strophic continuo song. From the first some *arioso* moments occurred even in pieces in the most severely recitative style, but the separation of emotional state from narrative through the division of aria from recitative lay in the future. The mid-seventeenth-century division of musical speech into *recitativo* and *aria* might be seen as a negation of the humanistic striving for unity of word and tone, a clear victory of music over poetry (though one should remember that libretti were written with the intention of separating narrative from portrayals of emotional states). But even in the dramatic work of Jacopo Peri and the young Monteverdi the solo recitative is governed by the rhythms and to some extent the melodic and harmonic vocabulary of the later madrigal; the solo song follows patterns of organization derived from the instrumental dance. At a certain point in the later sixteenth century the course of the development of musical language aimed at representing a reading of the text was altered by the introduction of a framework of pat-

42. The most famous example is of course Monteverdi's *Lamento d'Arianna*, the sole surviving piece from his opera *L'Arianna* of 1607–8, recomposed as a five-voice madrigal (*Sesto libro* [1614], no. 1); on the difficulties Monteverdi encountered in doing this see Gary Tomlinson, "Madrigal, Monody, and Monteverdi's 'Via Naturale alla Immitatione,'" *Journal of the American Musicological Society* 34 (1981), 96. In 1614 Pietro Maria Marsolo published a set of four-voice madrigals that are reworkings of monodies by other composers; see Lorenzo Bianconi, ed., *P. M. Marsolo: [Secondo libro de'] madrigali a quattro voci ed altre opere* (Florence, 1973).

terns that, even while appearing to allow unlimited freedom, put a kind of extraverbal element of control into song.

It might be going a bit far in the direction of paradox to suggest that Renaissance excess was replaced by Baroque regularity, but, as a corrective to an unthinking acceptance of the reverse view, one might consider some such claim. For most of the sixteenth century, secular song was on the whole chamber music, intimate in character as well as in mode of performance. In the Baroque period a third category, that of theater or drama, was added to the old distinctions of church and chamber. Only if we confuse the emotive and the dramatic will we see the later madrigal as breaking the bounds of chamber style; its standardization or regularization of musical language instead furnished a vocabulary suited for stage declamation rather than intimate reading. This leads me to a final paradoxical statement: The great age of Renaissance polyphony is also that of private reading—by turns thoughtful and impassioned—of poetry in music. With the rise of Baroque monody comes the age of public, dramatic speech making in music.

APPENDIX
MUSICAL EXAMPLES

Ex. 1.   Giovanni da Cascia, *O tu, cara scienzia mia, musica* (Florence, Bibl. Med.-Laur. MS Pal. 87, fol. 5ᵛ)

con   va‑ghi can‑

con   va‑ghi can‑

ti,   Che,

ti,   Che,

che fa ri‑no‑vel‑lar tut‑tor gli a‑man   ‑

che fa ri‑no‑vel‑lar tut‑tor gli a‑man   ‑

ti,   Che fa   ri‑no‑vel‑

ti,   Che fa ri ‑ no‑vel‑

lar tut‑tor gli a‑man ‑

lar tut‑tor gli a‑man ‑

[Ritornello]

ti,   Pe   ‑

ti,   Pe   ‑

152

ro ri - tor - no a te mu - si - ca   ca

ro ri - tor - no a   te mu - si - ca   ca

ra,

ra,

Ex. 2.   (*a*) Jacopo da Bologna, *Non al suo amante più Diana piacque*
(Petrarch) (Florence, Bibl. Naz. Cent. MS Panciatichi 26, fol. 71);
(*b*) Keyboard intabulation of (*a*) (Faenza, Bibl. Com. MS 117,
fol. 78, after Dragan Plamenac, ed., *Keyboard Music of the Late
Middle Ages in Codex Faenza 117* [American Institute of Musicology,
1972], p. 94)

(a)

Non

(b)

Non na el so amante

Ex. 3.   Maestro Piero, *Quando l'aere comenza a farse bruna* (Rome, Bibl. Ap. Vat. MS Rossi 215, fol. 7ᵛ): types of ornaments

Ex. 4.   *Lucente stella che'l mio cor desfai* (Rome, Bibl. Ap. Vat. MS Rossi 215, fol. 22, after W. Thomas Marrocco, ed., *Polyphonic Music of the Fourteenth Century*, vol. 11 [Monaco, 1978], no. 45)

2. I   a –   ti to - i   dol –   ce   pro –
3. E   bei   o - chi toi la –   dri   e

me - ton   sa –   lu - te.   A
il va – go   ri - so   Fu –

chi se   spe - chia   nel –   lo
ran mi   a vi – ta   per

Da Capo

to   bel   vi – so.
lor   ver –   tu – te.

Ex. 5. *Per tropo fede talor se perigola* (Rome, Bibl. Ap. Vat. MS Rossi 215, fol. 19, after W. Thomas Marrocco, ed., *Polyphonic Music of the Fourteenth Century*, vol. 11 [Monaco, 1978], no. 62)

1.10. Per   tro - po
4. El   ben se
7. On   –   de la
9. Sì   che de

fe - de ta - lor se   pe - ri   –   go - la.
ta - ci_e lo mal pur se ci   –   go - la.
mor - te spe - so se   ne spi   –   go - la.
do - glia lo mio cor for - mi   –   go - la.

2. Non   è   do – lor   nè
3. Co   –   me, sen – ça   fa –
5. Las   –   so   co – lui   che
6. Chè   l'a - mor   so   ve –
7. Oi   –   mè, ch'a – mor m'à
8. On   –   de con – vien me_o–

più	mor	–	ta	–	le	spa	–	se – mo.
lir,	ca	–	der	en		bia	–	se – mo.
mai	se		fi	–	dò_in	fe	–	me – na,
ne –	no_a	–	ma	–	ro	se	–	me – na,
pos –	to_in		co	–	tal	ar	–	çe – re,
gnor	la	–	gre	–	me	spar	–	çe – re,

Ex. 6.   Francesco Landini, *Non avrà ma' pietà questa mia donna* (Donati) (Florence, Bibl. Naz. Cent. MS Panciatichi 26, fol. 30ᵛ, as printed in Leo Schrade, ed., *Polyphonic Music of the Fourteenth Century*, vol. 4 [Monaco, 1958], p. 144)

Ex. 7.   Anthonius Zachara da Teramo, *Ciaramella, me dolçe Ciaramella!* (Lucca, Arch. di Stato MS 184, fol. 80ᵛ, after Gilbert Reaney, ed., *Early-Fifteenth-Century Music*, vol. 6 [American Institute of Musicology, 1977], p. 20)

Fra Ma - çan-te sot-to, po - li - to̱ e bel - lo
to' dà si gran bot-to, to - sto m'a - braz - za,

Fra Ma - çan-te sot-to, po - li - to̱ e bel - lo
to' dà si gran bot-to, to - sto m'a - braz - za,

Fra Ma - çan-te sot-to, po - li - to̱ e bel - lo
to' dà si gran bot-to, to - sto m'a - braz - za,

con la chier-cha ra - sa;
stren-gi̱ e pur me ba - sa,

con la chier-cha ra - sa;
stren-gi̱ e pur me ba - sa,

con la chier-cha ra - sa;
stren-gi̱ e pur me ba - sa,

Da Capo

4. chè'n que - sta ter - ra de me n'è più bel - la.

4. chè'n que - sta ter - ra de mi n'è più bel - la.

4. chè'n que - sta ter - ra de me n'è più bel - la.

161

Ex. 8. Prepositus Brixiensis, *O spirito gentil, tu m'ay percosso*
(Oxford, Bodl. Lib. MS Canon. misc. 213, fol. 25, after Gilbert
Reaney, ed., *Early-Fifteenth-Century Music*, vol. 5 [American Institute of Musicology, 1975], p. 85)

Ex. 9. Nicolaus Zacharie, *Già per gran nobiltà triumpho et fama*
(Oxford, Bodl. Lib. MS Canon. misc. 213, fol. 125ᵛ, after Gilbert
Reaney, ed., *Early-Fifteenth-Century Music*, vol. 6 [American Institute of Musicology, 1977], p. 137)

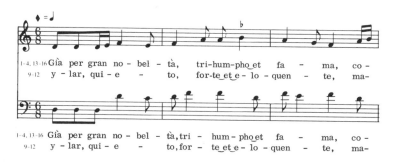

mo   li ciel   da   di – o,   se – re – no si – gnor
gna – ni –mo e   to' ni   –   do,   con – tem – pe – ra –to e

mo   li ciel   da   di – o,   se – re – no si – gnor
gna – ni –mo e   to' ni   –   do,   con – tem – pe – ra – to e

mi   –   o,   l'al – te – za   di   toa   ca – xa   che o –
fi   –   do   de   la fer – ma   col – lo   –   na   che'l

mi   –   o,   l'al – te   za di toa   ca   –   xa   che o –
fi   –   do,   de   la   fer – ma col – lo   –   na   che'l

gn'om   chia   –   ma.
ciel   bra   –   ma:

gn'om   chia   –   ma.
ciel   bra   –   ma:

5-6. Toy chia – ri   pre – ces – sor,   da   Io – ve e   Mar – te
7-8. ju – sto,   be – ni – gno, au –da – ze in   o – gne   par – te,

5-6. Toy chia – ri   pre – ces – sor,   da   Io – ve e Mar – te
7-8. ju – sto,   be – ni – gno, au –da – ze in   o   –   gne   par – te,

Ex. 10.   Johannes Ciconia, *O rosa bella, o dolce anima mia* (Rome, Bibl. Ap. Vat. Cod. Urb. lat. 1411, fol. 7ᵛ, with corrections of detail from Paris, Bibl. nat. MS n. acq. fr. 4379, fol. 46ᵛ)

1) extra E in MS.

2) Corrupt in MS; reading from concordance.

3) Text phrase "per villania" inserted in MS.

Ay lassa me dolente deco finire
  per ben servire e lealmente amare.
Soccorimi ormai del mio languire
  cor del cor mio non mi lassar penare.
O dio d'amor che pena e questa amore
  vide che io mor tuto hora per questa iudea.

O rosa bella . . .

Ex. 11.   John Dunstable(?) or John Bedyngham(?), *O rosa bella*
(Porto, Bibl. Mun. MS 714, fol. 54ᵛ, as printed in Nino Pirrotta,
"Ricercare e variazioni su 'O rosa bella,'" *Studi musicali* 1[1972], 75)

Non me las - sar mo - ri — re in cur - te -
a, Non me las - sar mo - rir in cur - te - si - a, in
si - a, in cur - te - si - a, in cur - te - si - a, in cur - te - si - a.
cur - te - si - a, in cur-te - si - a, in cur - te - si - a.

Ex. 12. Guillaume Dufay, *Credo*, tenor, mm. 168–70 (Bologna, Civ. Mus. Bibl. Mus. MS Q 15, fol. 34)

La vil-la - nel - la non è bel - la se non la do - mi - ni - ca.

Ex. 13. (a) *Ayme sospiri non trovo pace* (Escorial MS IV.a.24, fol. 85ᵛ);

(b) *Ayme sospiri* (Petrucci, *Frottole libro sexto* [1506], fol. 4ᵛ, after Walter H. Rubsamen, "The Justiniane or Viniziane of the Fifteenth Century," *Acta Musicologica* 29 [1957], 180)

(c) *Moro di doglia e pur convien ch'io dica*: hypothetical tune;

(d) *Moro di doglia* (Petrucci, *Frottole libro sexto*, fol. 3ᵛ)

glia   e   pur con - vien

glia   e   pur chon-vien

ch'io   di – cha,   con – vien   ch'io   di – cha

ch'io   di, – chon – vien   ch'io'l   di – cha

Ex. 14.   *Modo di cantar sonetti* (textless) (Petrucci, *Frottole libro quarto* [1505], fol. 14)

Ex. 15.   Bartolomeo Tromboncino, *Se gran festa me mostrasti* (Carretto) (Petrucci, *Frottole libro quinto* [1505], fol. 38ᵛ)

sti.

Le careze che me festi
  assai più del consueto
con parole e dolzi gesti
  più che pria non me far lieto,
perche dissi nel secreto
  fiamma verde pocho dura;
e perhò non feci cura
  se poi presto te cangiasti.

Se gran festa

El dì primo tutto'l mondo
  era in festa et io d'argento,
l'altro poi che fo el secundo
  fui di piombo in un momento.
Per mi poi cangiosi el vento
  che mai fui dopo ben visto
ma si come fusse un tristo
  di me poi non te cerrasti.

Se gran festa

Ex. 16.   Antoine Brumel, *Noé noé* (Petrucci, *Canti B* [1502], fol. 28ᵛ, after Helen Hewitt, ed., *Canti B numero cinquanta*, Venice, 1502 [Chicago, 1967], pp. 161–63)

No - é, no - é, no - é,

No - é, no - é, no - é, no -

No - é, no - é, no - é, no -

No - é, no - é, no - é, no -

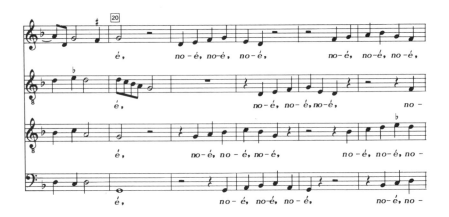

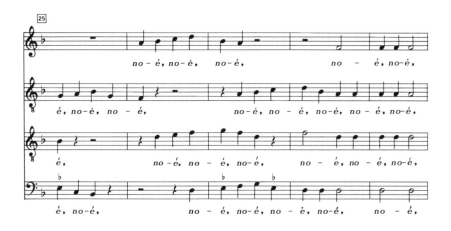

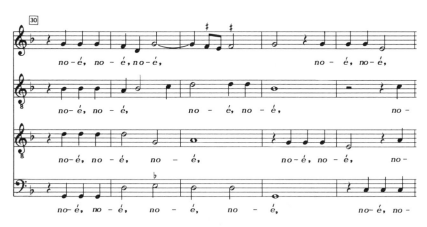

Ex. 17.   Antonius Patavinus(?), *Vrai dieu d'amor chi mi conforterà*
(Bologna, Civ. Mus. Bibl. Mus. MS Q 21, no. 46)

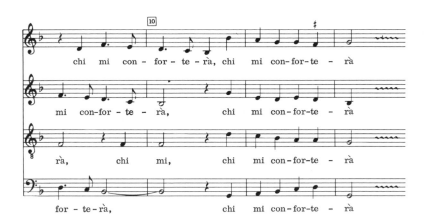

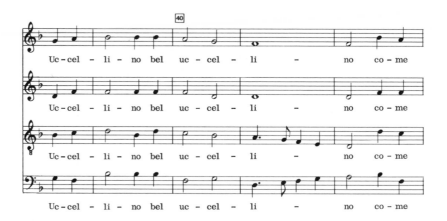

Uc-cel - li - no bel uc-cel - li - no co - me

Uc - cel - li - no bel uc - cel - li - no co - me

Uc-cel - li - no bel uc-cel - li - no co - me

Uc - cel - li - no bel uc - cel - li - no co - me

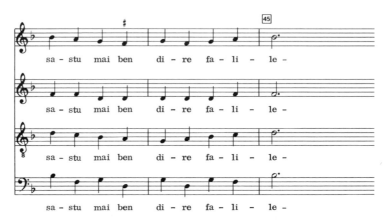

sa - stu mai ben di - re fa - li - le -

sa - stu mai ben di - re fa - li - le -

sa - stu mai ben di - re fa - li - le -

sa - stu mai ben di - re fa - li - le -

Ex. 18. Philippe Verdelot, *Madonna, per voi ardo* (Chicago, Newberry Lib. Case MS VM 1578, M91, sec. 3, fol. 13, after H. Colin Slim, *A Gift of Madrigals and Motets*, vol. 2 [Chicago, 1972], p. 353)

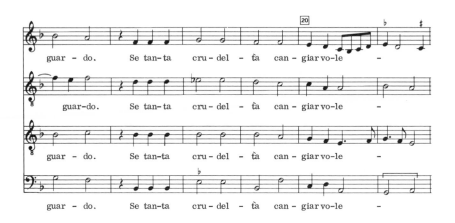

guar - do. Se tan- ta cru - del - tà can - giar vo- le -

guar-do. Se tan- ta cru- del - tà can - giar vo- le -

guar - do. Se tan- ta cru - del - tà can - giar vo- le -

guar - do. Se tan- ta cru - del - tà can - giar vo- le -

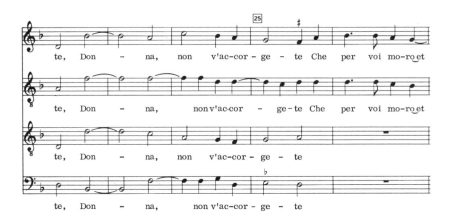

te, Don - na, non v'ac-cor- ge- te Che per voi mo-ro et

te, Don - na, non v'ac-cor - ge- te Che per voi mo-ro et

te, Don - na, non v'ac-cor - ge - te

te, Don - na, non v'ac-cor- ge - te

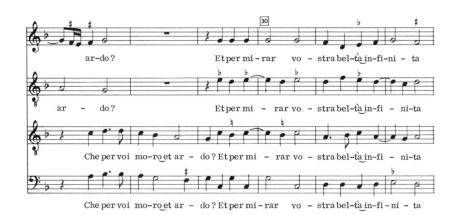

ar- do? Et per mi - rar vo - stra bel- tà in-fi - ni - ta

ar - do? Et per mi - rar vo - stra bel- tà in-fi - ni-ta

Che per voi mo-ro et ar - do? Et per mi - rar vo - stra bel- tà in-fi - ni-ta

Che per voi mo-ro et ar - do? Et per mi - rar vo - stra bel- tà in-fi - ni- ta

Ex. 19.   Jacques Arcadelt, *Quando col dolce suono* (*Primo libro a 4v* [1539], no. 15, after Albert Seay, ed., *Jacobi Arcadelt: Opera Omnia*, vol. 2 [American Institute of Musicology, 1970], no. 45)

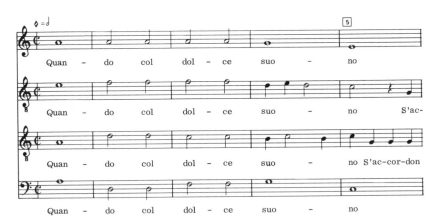

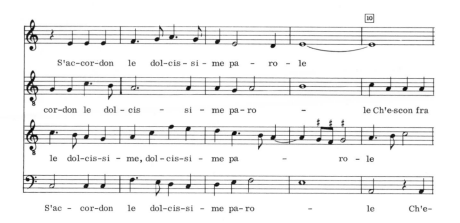

S'ac-cor-don le dol-cis-si - me pa - ro - le

cor-don le dol-cis - si - me pa-ro - le Ch'e-scon fra

le dol-cis-si - me, dol-cis-si - me pa - ro - le

S'ac - cor-don le dol-cis-si - me pa-ro - le Ch'e-

Ch'e - scon fra bian - che perl' e bei ru - bi -

bian - che per - le, ch'e-scon fra bian-che perl' e bei ru - bi -

Ch'e-scon fra bian - che perl' e bei ru - bi -

scon fra bian - che perl' e bei - ru - bi -

ni, Ma - ra - vi-glian-do di - co: hor co - me so -

ni, Ma - ra - vi-glian-do di - co: hor co - me so -

ni, Ma - ra - vi-glian-do di - co: hor co - me so -

ni, Ma - ra - vi -glian-do di - co: hor co - me so -

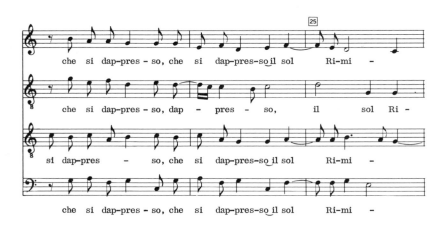

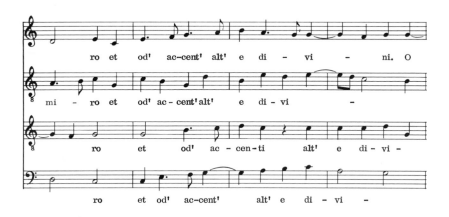

giu-ro ch'el - la, vi giu-ro ch'el - la È più che'l sol as-sai lu-

vi giu-ro ch'el - la È più che'l sol as - sai lu - cent' e

giu-ro ch'el - la È più che'l sol' as - sai

vi giu - ro ch'el - la È più che'l

cent' e bel - la, è

bel - la, lu - cent' e bel - la, è più che'l

lu - cen - te e bel - la, è

sol' as - sai lu - cent' e bel - la,

più che'l sol as - sai lu - cent' e bel -

sol as - sai lu - cent' e bel - la, lu - cent' e

più che'l sol' as - sai lu - cen - te e

è più che'l sol' as - sai lu - cent' e

Ex. 20.   Bartolomeo Tromboncino, *Voi che passati qui fumate el passo* (Petrucci, *Frottole libro septimo* [1507], fol. 19)

1) Notes in brackets are editorial suggestions for a vocal line adapted to the demands of the text.

Che'n ter-ra ia - ce, che in ter - ra ia - ce.

Et queste membre poste in freddo sasso
  Per seguitar amor sempre fallace.
Io son qui posto in loco umido e basso
  Per donna altiera e cruda senza pace.
Pero fugite amor e sua mercede
  Che porge altrui un fin che non si crede.

Ex. 21.   Filippo Lurano, *Vana speranza mia che mai non vene*
(Petrucci, *Frottole libro quarto* [1505], fol. 9)

Va-na spe-ran-za mi-a che mai non ve - ne Va-no soc-cor-so

mi - o quan - to sei tar - do.

Pato ogni male per aspectar el bene
  In questo mezo me consumo ed ardo.
Hai dispietato amore hor chi te tene
  Che fai che non despari el crudo dardo.
Meglio e morir e uscir d'affanni e pene
  Che viver e sperar quel che non vene.

Ex. 22. *Se'l zapator il giorno se affatica* (Modena, Bibl. Est. MS αF.9.9, fol. 6ᵛ, after Claudio Gallico, *Un libro di poesie per musica dell'epoca d'Isabella d'Este* [Mantua, 1961], p. 121)

Ex. 23.   (*a*) Marchetto Cara, *Aer de capitoli* (Petrucci, *Frottole libro nono* [1508 (=1509)], fol. 2ᵛ)

Nas - ce la spe-me mia   da in dol-ce ri - so   O - gni mio ben da un

hu - mil sguar-do pen - de   La mia fe-li-ci - ta sta in un bel vi - so.

(*b*) Cosimo Bottegari, *Aria in terza rima* (Modena, Bibl. Est. MS C 311, fol. 24ᵛ, after Carol MacClintock, ed., *The Bottegari Lutebook* [Wellesley, Mass., 1965], p. 75)

Ex. 24.   Giovan Domenico da Nola, *Proverbio ama chi t'ama è fatto antico* (Petrarch) (*Madrigali a 4v di I. D. da Nolla* [1545], p. 27)

Pro - ver-bio a - ma chi t'a - ma è fatt' an - ti - co

Io   so ben quel ch'io di - co hor lass' an - da - re

Ex. 25. Jacquet Berchem, *Alla dolc'ombra delle belle frondi* (Doni, *Dialogo della Musica* [1544], fol. 27, after the edition of G. F. Malipiero [Vienna, 1965], p. 131)

Ex. 26.   Bartolomeo Tromboncino, *Queste non son piu lachryme che fore* (Ariosto) (RISM 1517², fol. 3ᵛ)

Ex. 27.   Giaches Wert, *Dunque baciar sì bell'e dolce labbia* (Ariosto) (*Primo libro a 4v* [1561], no. 6, after Carol MacClintock, ed., *Giaches de Wert: Opera Omnia*, vol. 15 [American Institute of Musicology, 1972], p. 19)

Ex. 28. (a) Philippe Verdelot, *Queste non son più lacrime che fuore* (Ariosto) (RISM 1541[16], p. 13);
(b) Jacquet Berchem, *Queste non son* (*Capriccio* [1561], bk. 1, no. 25);
(c) Nolletto, *Non siate però tumide e fastose* (Ariosto) (RISM 1540[18], p. 42)

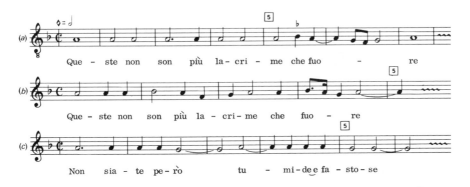

Ex. 29. Vincenzo Ruffo, *Deh torn'a me mio sol torn'e rimena* (Ariosto) (*Libro terzo di madrigali a 4v* [1560], p. 27)

lo-sa e ne - ra

Ex. 30. *Dunque fia ver (dicea) che mi convegna* (Ariosto) (RISM 1554[28], p. 24)

Dun - que fia ver (di - cea) che mi con - ve - gna

Ex. 31. Jacquet Berchem, *Ch'aver puo donna al mondo più di buono* (Ariosto) (*Capriccio* [1561], bk. 1, no. 14)

Ch'a-ver puo don-na al mon-do più di buo - no ij

Ex. 32. Jacquet Berchem, *Ricordati Pagan quando uccidesti* (Ariosto) (*Capriccio* [1561], bk. 1, no. 4)

Ri - cor-da-ti Pa-gan quan do uc-ci-de-sti D'An-ge - li-ca il fra-

tel che son quel i - o

Ex. 33.   Francesco Bifetto, *Ruggier qual sempre fui tal esser voglio*
(Ariosto) (*Il secondo libro a 4v di Francesco Bifetto* [1548], p. 2)

Ex. 34.   Jacquet Berchem, *Che debbo far perch'io son giunto tardi*
(Ariosto) (*Capriccio* [1561], bk. 1, no. 6)

Ex. 35. (*a*) Philippe Verdelot, *Ogn'hor per voi sospiro* (*Libro secondo a 4v* [1534], no. 14)

O - gn'hor per voi so - spi - ro   Don - na   poi ch'io non o - so a

di - sco - pri - re

(*b*) Costanzo Festa, *Dur'è'l partito dove m'astringete* (Verdelot, *Libro secondo a 4v* [1534], no. 12)

Dur' è'l par - ti - to do - ve m'a-strin-ge - te Ch'io deb-ba de sì o no

dar - vi ri - spo - sta

(*c*) Anselmo Reulx, *S'io credessi per mort'esser scarco* (Petrarch) (RISM 1542 [17], no. 15)

S'io cre-des - si per mort' es-ser scar - co Del pen-sier' a - mo - ro - so che

m'a-ter-ra

(*d*) Hubert Naich? Matteo Rampollini? Jacquet Berchem?, *Che giova saettar un che si muore* (Bembo) (RISM 1542 [17], no. 25)

Che gio - va sa - et - tar un che si mo - re

(e) *Sì vivo è lo splendore* (RISM 1549[30], no. 28)

Sì vi - vo̱ è lo splen-dor don-na de bei vostr'oc - chi ch'io m'a -

re - tro

Ex. 36. *(a)* Giovan Domenico da Nola, *Tosto ch'il sol si scopr'in ori-ente* (RISM 1555[27], p. 10)

Tos- to ch'il sol si scopr' in o - ri - en te La-gri-mo - sa tem-pest' a gl'oc-

chi sor - ge Nè per-che si ri-sco-pr'in oc-ci den te Trie-gu'al mio la-

gri- mar la do - glia por - ge

(b) Paolo Animuccia, *La fiamm'ove tutt'ardo* (RISM 1558[13], no. 13)

Il mio nuo - vo gran ma - le sì so - a - ve mi strugg' à po-co̱ a po - co

Che non è ben mor-ta - le Ch'ag-gua-gl'il gran pia-cer del mio do-lo - re Perch'

in fiam-ma gen-til m'ab-brug' a-mo - re, ij.

195

(*c*) Palestrina, *Perch'al viso d'amor portava insegna* (Petrarch) (RISM 1562⁷, no. 24)

Ex. 37.   (*a*) Cipriano de Rore, *Se ben il duol che per voi donna sento* (*Libro secondo a 4v* [1557], no. 19)

sto con la vo - ce

fe - sto con la vo - ce

fe - sto con la vo - ce

sto con la vo - ce

sto con la vo - ce

(*b*) Stefano Rossetti, *Soleano i miei pensier soavemente* (*Libro primo
a 4v* [1560], no. 4)

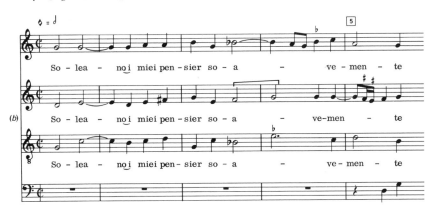

So - lea - no i miei pen - sier so - a - ve - men - te

So - lea - no i miei pen - sier so - a - ve-men - te

So - lea - no i miei pen - sier so - a - ve - men - te

(c) Giaches Wert, *Quando non più d'amor gl'aurati strali*, 2ª *parte*, mm. 18–27 (*Libro terzo a 5v* [1563], no. 12)

Ex. 38. Adrian Willaert, *L'aura mia sacra al mio stanco riposo*
(*Musica nova* [1559], p. 84)

quel sguar-do a - mo-ro - so Che fu prin-ci-pio a sì lun - go tor-men-

min - cio da quel sguar - do a - mo - ro - so Che fu prin-ci-pio a

cio da quel sguar-do a - mo-ro - so Che fu prin - ci-pio a sì lun - go tor-

cio da quel sguar-do a - mo-ro - so Che fu prin-ci-pio a sì lun -

Io in - co - min - cio da quel sguar-do a - mo-ro - so

to, che fu prin - ci - pio a sì lun - go tor-men - to

sì lun - go tor-men - to, che fu prin - ci-pio a sì lun - go tor-

men - to

go tor - men - to, che fu prin-ci-pio a sì lun - go tor - men -

Che fu prin-ci - pio a sì lun - go tor - men -

202

dì in dì,   di dì in dì   d'ho - ra in hor' A - mor m'ha ro -

so,   di dì in dì   d'ho - ra in hor' A-mor m'ha ro-so,   A-mor m'ha ro -

ro - so,   di dì in   dì   d'ho - ra in hor' A-mor m'ha ro - so.

so, di dì in dì   d'ho - ra in hor' A - mor m'ha ro-so,   d'ho-ra in hor' A-mor m'ha

dì in dì,   di   dì in dì   d'ho - ra in hor' A-mor m'ha ro -

Seconda parte

so.   El - la si ta - ce

so.   El - la si ta - ce   e di pie -

El - la si ta - ce

ro - so.   El - la si ta - ce   e di pie -

so.   El - la si ta - ce   e di pie -

204

e di pie – tà di – pin – ta Fi – so mi –

tà di – pin – ta Fi – so mi – ra pur me; par-

e di pie – tà di – pin – ta Fi –

tà di – pin – ta Fi – so mi – ra pur me;

tà di – pin – ta Fi – so mi – ra pur me;

ra pur me; par – te so – spi – ra, par – te so-spi-ra

te so-spi – ra, par – te so-spi-ra, par – te so – spi – ra

so mi – ra pur me; par-te so – spi – ra E

par – te so-spi – ra, par – te so-spi – ra E

par – te so-spi – ra, par – te so-spi – ra E

205

On - de l'a-ni-ma mia dal do-lor vin - ta

do - lor vin - ta, on - de l'a-ni-ma mia dal do-lor vin - ta

mia dal do - lor vin - ta, on - de l'a - ni-ma mia dal do-lor vin -

l'a-ni-ma mia dal do-lor vin - ta, on - de l'a - ni - ma mia dal do-lor

l'a - ni - ma mia dal do-lor vin - ta, dal do-lor vin -

Men - tre pian-gen-do al - hor se - co s'a - di -

Men - tre pian-gen - do al-hor se - co s'a-di -

ta Men - tre pian-gen-do al - hor se - co s'a - di -

vin - ta Men - tre pian-gen-do al - hor se - co s'a-di -

ta

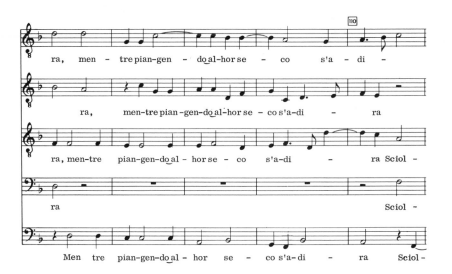

Ex. 39.   (a) Cipriano de Rore, *Tu piangi e quella per chi fai tal pianto* (*Libro primo a 5v* [1542], no. 9)

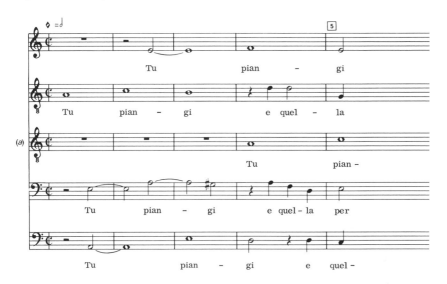

(*b*) Rore, *O sonno o della queta humida ombrosa* (*Libro secondo a 4v* [1557], no. 5)

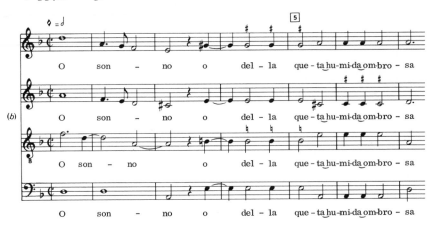

(*c*) Rore, *Mia benigna fortuna è'l viver lieto, 2ª parte*, opening (*Libro secondo a 4v* [1557], no. 9)

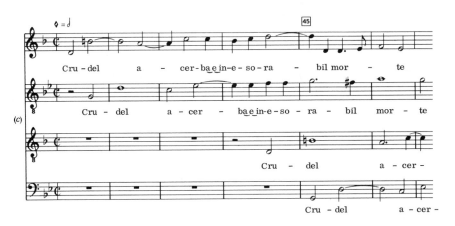

Ex. 40.   (*a*) Claudio Veggio, *Donna per acquetar vostro desio* (Doni?) (Doni, *Dialogo della Musica* [1544], no. 1, as printed in Alfred Einstein, *The Italian Madrigal* [Princeton, 1949], p. 532)

(*b*) Andrea Gabrieli, *Donna per acquetar vostro desio* (Doni?) (*Libro primo a 5v* [1566], no. 12, as printed in Alfred Einstein, *The Italian Madrigal* [Princeton, 1949], p. 532)

Ex. 41. Giaches Wert, *Giunto all tomba ove al suo spirito vivo* (Tasso) (*Libro settimo a 5v* [1581], no. 9, after Carol MacClintock, ed., *Giaches de Wert: Opera Omnia*, vol. 7 [American Institute of Musicology, 1967], no. 9)

di ca-lor di mo - to pri - vo Già mar-mo in vi-sta al mar-mo il vi-so af-fis - se

di ca-lor di mo - to pri - vo Già mar-mo in vi-sta al mar-mo il vi - so af-fis -

di ca-lor di mo - to pri - vo Gia mar-mo in vi-sta al mar-mo il vi - so af-fis -

mo - to pri - vo Gia mar-mo in vi-sta al mar-mo il vi-so af-fis - se

di ca-lor di mo - to pri - vo Gia mar-mo in vi-sta al mar-mo il vi - so af-fis -

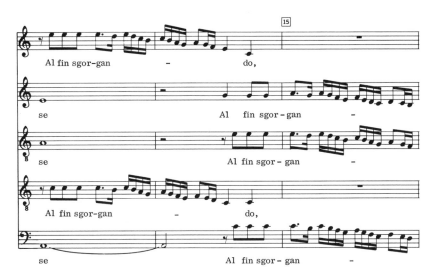

Al fin sgor-gan - do,

se Al fin sgor-gan -

se Al fin sgor - gan -

Al fin sgor-gan - do,

se Al fin sgor - gan -

213

Ex. 42.   Giaches Wert, *O primavera gioventù de l'anno* (Guarini)
(*L'undecimo libro a 5v* [1595], no. 2, after Carol MacClintock, ed.,
Giaches de Wert: Opera Omnia, vol. 12 [American Institute of Musicology, 1972], no. 2)

Ex. 43. (*a*) Jacques Arcadelt, *Il bianco e dolce cigno cantando more*
(*Primo libro a 4v* [1539], no. 1)

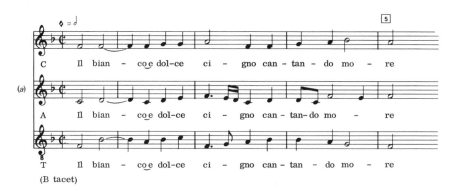

(*b*) Orazio Vecchi, *Il bianco e dolce cigno cantando more* (*Libro primo
a 5v* [1589], no. 1)

Ex. 44.   Giaches Wert, *Ah, dolente partita!* (Guarini) (*L'undecimo libro a 5v* [1595], no. 1, after Carol MacClintock, ed., *Giaches de Wert: Opera Omnia*, vol. 12 [American Institute of Musicology, 1972], no. 1)

re, Che dà vi - ta al do - lo - re

ri - re, Che dà vi - ta al do - lo - re, che dà

ri - re, Che dà vi - ta al do - lo - re,

re, Che dà vi - ta al do - lo - re

ri - re, Che

Per far che mo - ia im-mor-tal-men-te il co - re, Che

vi - ta al do - lo - re Per far che mo-ia im-mortal-

Che dà vi - ta al do-lo -

Per far che mo - ia im-mor-tal-men - te il co - re, il co -

da vi - ta al do - lo - re Per far che mo-ia im-mor-tal-

Ex. 45. Gesualdo, *Ecco, morirò dunque* (*Libro quarto a 5v* [1596], no. 12, after Wilhelm Weismann, ed., *Gesualdo di Venosa: Sämtliche Madrigale für fünf Stimmen*, vol. 4 [Hamburg, 1958], no. 16)

dun-que!   Nè fia   che pur ri-mi-re, Tu ch'an-ci - di mi-

dun-que! Nè fia che pur ri-mi - re,   che   pur ri-mi - re, Tu ch'an-ci - di mi-

dun-que! Nè fia   che pur ri-mi - re,   che   pur ri-mi - re, Tu ch'an-ci - di mi-

dun-que! Nè fia   che pur ri-mi - re,   che pur ri-mi-re, Tu ch'an-ci - di mi-

dun-que!   Nè fia che pur ri-mi - re,   Tu ch'an-ci - di mi-

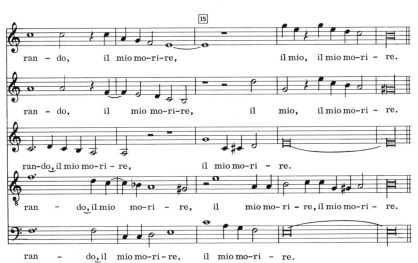

ran - do,   il mio mo-ri-re,   il mio, il mio mo-ri - re.

ran - do,   il   mio mo-ri-re,   il   mio,   il mio mo-ri - re.

ran-do, il mio mo-ri - re,   il mio mo-ri - re.

ran - do, il mio   mo-ri - re,   il   mio mo-ri - re, il mio mo-ri - re.

ran - do, il mio mo-ri-re,   il mio mo-ri - re.

Seconda parte

Ahi, già mi dis-co-lo - ro, ahi,

Ahi, già mi dis-co - lo - ro, ahi, già mi

Ahi, già mi dis-co - lo ro, ahi,

Ahi, ahi, già mi dis-co - lo -

Ahi, ahi, già mi dis-co - lo -

già mi dis-co - lo - ro; oi - mè,

dis - co - lo - ro, già mi dis - co - lo - ro;

già mi dis-co - lo - ro; oi - mè,

ro, già mi dis-co - lo - ro;

ro, già mi dis - co - lo - ro;

oi - mè,   vien me - no   a gli oc-chi miei,

oi - mè, vien me - no   La lu - ce a gli oc-chi miei,   la

oi - mè,   vien me-no   La lu - ce a gli oc-chi miei,

oi - mè,   vien me-no   La lu -

oi - mè,   vien me-no   La lu -

la lu - ce a gli oc-chi miei,   la   vo - ce al se - no,   la

vo - ce al se - no,   la lu - ce a gli oc-chi miei,   la lu-ce a gli oc-chi

la lu - ce a gli oc-chi miei, la vo - ce al   se - no,

ce a gli oc-chi miei,   la   vo - ce al se - no,

ce a gli oc-chi miei,   la   vo - ce al se - no, la lu -

225

lu – ce a gli oc-chi miei, la vo – ce al se – no! O che mor – te

miei, a gli oc-chi miei, la vo – ce, la vo – ce al se – no! O che mor-

la vo – ce al se no, la vo-ce, la vo-ce al se – no! O che mor-

la vo-ce al se – no, la vo – ce al se – no! O che mor-

ce a gli oc-chi miei, la vo – ce al se – no! O che mor –

gra-di – ta, "Mo – ro, mia vi – ta,"

te gra-di-ta, Se al-men po-tes-si dir: "Mo – ro, mia vi – ta,"

te gra-di-ta, Se al-men po-tes-si dir: "Mo-ro mia vi – ta,"

te gra-di-ta, Se al-men po-tes-si dir: "Mo – ro mia vi – ta,"

te gra-di-ta, Se al-men po-tes-si dir: "Mo – ro mia vi ta,"

226

se al-men po-tes-si dir: "Mo - ro, mia vi - ta, mo - ro, mia vi - ta!"

se al-men po-tes-si dir: "Mo-ro, mia vi - ta, mo-ro, mi vi - ta!"

se al-men po-tes-si dir: "Mo - ro, mia vi - ta!"

se al-men po-tes-si dir: "Mo - ro, mia vi - ta, mo - ro, mia vi-ta!"

se al-men po-tes-si dir: "Mo - ro, mia vi-ta!"

INDEX

INDEX

Designer:	Sandy Drooker
Compositor:	G & S Typesetters, Inc.
Text:	10/13 Baskerville
Display:	Baskerville
Printer:	Braun-Brumfield, Inc.
Binder:	Braun-Brumfield, Inc.